PROF

GOODHART

HIS

BOOK

Regulating International Financial Markets: Issues and Policies

Regulating International Financial Markets: Issues and Policies

edited by
Franklin R. Edwards
Arthur F. Burns Professor of Free and Competitive Enterprise, and Director,
Center for the Study of Futures Markets, Graduate School of Business,
Columbia University, New York

Hugh T. Patrick
R.D. Calkins Professor of International Business, and Director,
Center on Japanese Economy and Business, Graduate School of Business,
Columbia University, New York

Kluwer Academic Publishers
Boston / Dordrecht / London

Distributors for North America:
Kluwer Academic Publishers
101 Philip Drive
Assinippi Park
Norwell, Massachusetts 02061 USA

Distributors for all other countries:
Kluwer Academic Publishers Group
Distribution Centre
Post Office Box 322
3300 AH Dordrecht, THE NETHERLANDS

Library of Congress Cataloging-in-Publication Data

Regulating international financial markets: issues and policies/edited by
    Franklin R. Edwards, Hugh T. Patrick. p.   cm.
    Includes bibliographical references and index.
    ISBN 0−7923−9155−1
    1. International finance.   2. Financial institutions, International.
    I. Edwards, Franklin R., 1937−   . II. Patrick, Hugh T.
HG3881.R363   1991
332.6′73—dc20   91−12935
                                                                    CIP

Printed on acid-free paper.

Printed in the United States of America

Contents

Contributors

Wayne D. Angell
Member, Board of Governors of the Federal Reserve System, 20th and C St., N.W., Washington, D.C. 20551
Wayne D. Angell was sworn in as a member of the Federal Reserve Board in February 1986. He is Chairman of the Board's Committee on Federal Reserve Bank Activities and Chairman of the Group of Experts on Payment Systems. Prior to becoming a member of the Board, Angell was a professor of economics (1956–1985) and Dean of the College (1969–1972) at Ottawa University in Ottawa, Kansas. He served as an officer and director of several banks in Kansas and Missouri (1971–1985), and was State Representative in the Kansas House of Representatives (1961–1967).

George J. Benston
John H. Harland Professor of Finance, Accounting, and Economics, School of Business, Emory University, Atlanta, GA 30332
George J. Benston has been the John H. Harland Professor of Finance, Accounting, and Economics at Emory University since 1987. Prior to this, he taught at the William E. Simon Graduate School of Business Administration (1969–1987) and the College of Business Administration (1966–1969) at the University of Rochester, and at the Graduate School of Business at University of Chicago (1966–1972). He is the author of numerous articles and books.

Dennis M. Earle
Executive Director, U.S. Working Committee, Group of Thirty, 55 Water Street, 22nd Floor, New York, NY 10041
Dennis M. Earle is Executive Director of the U.S. Working Committee

of the Group of Thirty. He is also a member of the Regulatory Coordination Advisory Committee of the CFTC as well as the Clearing Organization and Banking Roundtable.

Prior to joining the Group of Thirty, Dennis M. Earle was the Vice President for Strategic Planning of the Global Operating and Information Services Group of Bankers Trust Company. He was also the manager for Bankers Trust's Study of "International Clearing and Settlement," performed under contract to the Office of Technology Assessment of the U.S. Congress.

Mr. Earle is also on the Board of Advisors of the *Journal of Business Strategy*.

Franklin R. Edwards
Arthur F. Burns Professor of Free and Competitive Enterprise, and Director, Center for the Study of Futures Markets, Graduate School of Business, Columbia University, New York, NY 10027

Franklin R. Edwards holds the Arthur F. Burns Chair in Free and Competitive Enterprise at Columbia University's Graduate School of Business and is Director of the Center for the Study of Futures Markets. He served the School as Vice Dean from 1979 to 1981. Prior to joining Columbia University, he held positions at the Federal Reserve Board and at the Office of the Comptroller of the Currency.

From 1982 to 1987 Edwards served as a public director of the Futures Industry Association Board of Directors. He has published numerous articles in his areas of expertise, including regulation of financial markets and institutions, banking, securities markets, and futures and options markets.

Edwards holds a Ph.D. degree from Harvard University and a J.D. degree from the New York University Law School.

Jane F. Fried
Vice President, Bankers Trust Company, 1 Bankers Trust Plaza, 130 Liberty St., 21st Floor, New York, NY 10015

Jane F. Fried is Vice President and product manager for the Global Settlement Group of Bankers Trust Company. She was also the Northeast Asia and Australia coordinator/specialist for "The Study of International Clearing and Settlement", a project undertaken at the request of the Office of Technology Assessment, a research arm of the U.S. Congress. Fried joined Bankers Trust after four years with Citicorp as an acquisitions manager in its consumer credit card business. She is the author of numerous articles on clearing and settlement.

Charles Goodhart
Norman Sosnow Professor of Banking and Finance, London School of Economics, Department of Economics, Houghton St., London WC2A 2AE, United Kingdom

Charles Goodhart is the Norman Sosnow Professor of Banking and Finance at the London School of Economics. Before joining the London School of Economics in 1985, he worked at the Bank of England for 17 years as a monetary advisor, becoming a chief advisor in 1980. Earlier he taught at Cambridge University and LSE. He has written several books on monetary policy and theory.

Wendy L. Gramm
Chairman, Commodity Futures Trading Commission, 2033 K St., N.W., Washington, D.C. 20518

Wendy L. Gramm was sworn in as the Commodity Futures Trading Commission's fifth chairman in 1988. Before joining the Commission, she was Administrator for Information and Regulatory Affairs at the White House Office of Management and Budget (1985–1988). She has served as Executive Director of the Presidential Task Force on Regulatory Relief and as Assistant Director and then Director of the Federal Trade Commission's Bureau of Economics. Gramm taught at Texas A&M University from 1970 to 1978, after which she joined the research staff of the Institute for Defense Analyses.

Joseph A. Grundfest
Professor of Law, Stanford University, Stanford Law School, Palo Alto, CA 94305

Joseph A. Grundfest is a professor at Stanford Law School. From 1985 to January 1990 he was Commissioner of the U.S. Securities and Exchange Commission. Prior to this he was Counsel and Senior Economist at the Presidents' Council of Economic Advisors. He has also practiced law and served as an economist with the Rand Corporation and the Brookings Institution.

Paul Guy
Secretary General, International Organization of Securities Commissions, 800, Square Victoria, 17 etage, Montreal, Quebec, H42 1G3, Canada

Paul Guy was appointed Secretary General of the International Organization of Securities Commissions in 1986. He has been very active in promoting the harmonization of securities regulation in Canada and on the international level. Prior to his appointment, Guy was Chairman of the

Quebec Securities Commission and Director of Operations at the Montreal Stock Exchange. Guy has served in the Quebec civil service in various positions.

Toyoo Gyohten
Special Advisor to the Ministry of Finance, Japan.
Woodrow Wilson School, Princeton University, Room 322, Bendheim Hall, Princeton, NJ 08544
    Toyoo Gyohten was recently appointed Special Advisor to the Ministry of Finance. From 1986 to 1989 he served as Vice Minister of Finance for International Affairs. Since he joined the Ministry of Finance in 1955, he has held a number of positions, including Director General, International Finance Bureau (1984–1986), Deputy Director General, Banking Bureau (1983–1984), and Assistant Vice Minister of Finance for International Affairs (1978–1980).

Michael E. Hewitt
Senior Advisor, Bank of England, and Chairman, OECD Group of Experts on Systemic Risks in Securities Markets, London EC2R 8AH, United Kingdom
    Michael E. Hewitt is Senior Advisor for Finance and Industry at the Bank of England, and Chairman of the OECD Group of Experts on Systemic Risks in Securities Markets. He joined the Bank in 1961 and has served in the areas of oil industry and finance (1974–1976), financial forecasting (1976–1978), and financial institutions (1978–1983). He was Head of Financial Supervision (1984–1987) and Head of Finance and Industry (1987–1988).

Philip McBride Johnson
Partner, Skadden Arps, Slate, Meagher & Flom, 919 Third Avenue, New York, NY 10022
    Philip McBride Johnson is the partner in charge of domestic and international futures, options and derivatives legal work at Skadden Arps, Slate, Meagher & Flom. He has practiced law for nearly 25 years, and was the founding chairman of the legal committees of both the American Bar Association and the International Bar Association in the field. During the first Reagan Administration, he served as Chairman of the Commodity Futures Trading Commission. Johnson has served repeatedly on the Futures Industry Association's board of directors and now serves on the FIA's International Committee. He is also a member of the New York Stock Exchange's Regulatory Advisory Committee.

Hideki Kanda
Associate Professor of Law, University of Tokyo, Faculty of Law, 7-3-1
Hongo, Bunkyo-ku, Tokyo 113, Japan
Hideki Kanda is Associate Professor of Law at the University of Tokyo.
Prior to this, he taught law at Gakushuin University (1982–1988), was
a visiting research scholar at the University of Virginia School of Law
(1982–1984), and was a visiting professor at University of Chicago Law
School (1989).

Edward J. Kane
Everett D. Reese Professor of Banking and Monetary Economics, Ohio
State University, Hagerty Hall–1775 College Road, Columbus, OH 43210
Edward J. Kane is the Everett D. Reese Professor of Banking and
Monetary Economics at Ohio State University. He has taught at Boston
College, Princeton University, and Iowa State University. Kane is a past
president of the American Finance Association and a former Guggenheim
fellow. In 1981 he won an Ohio State University Alumni Award for
Distinguished Teaching.

Takashi Kato
Director General, Yamaichi Research Institute of Securities and Economics,
Inc., and Chairman, Yamaichi Bank (U.K.) Plc., 1–14–8 Nihonbashi-
Ningyocho, Chuo-ku, Tokyo 103, Japan
Takashi Kato has been Director General of Yamaichi Research Insti-
tute of Securities and Economics since 1984 and Chairman of Yamaichi
Bank (U.K.) Plc. since 1988. He has worked in the Ministry of Finance
in different capacities since 1951, including as Director General of the
International Finance Bureau (1979–1983), Deputy Director General of
the Budget Bureau (1978–1979), and Councillor of the Minister's Secretariat (1977–1978).

George G. Kaufman
John J. Smith Jr. Professor of Finance and Economics, School of Business,
Loyola University of Chicago, Water Tower Campus, 820 N. Michigan
Ave., Chicago, IL 60611
George G. Kaufman has taught at Loyola University of Chicago since
1981. Prior to this he was the John B. Rogers Professor of Banking and
Finance, and Director of the Center for Capital Market Research in the
College of Business Administration at the University of Oregon. From
1959 to 1970 he was a research fellow, economist, and senior economist at
the Federal Reserve Bank of Chicago, and has been a consultant to the

Bank since 1981. Kaufman has published extensively in academic journals and is the author of numerous books on financial economics, institutions, markets, regulation, and monetary policy.

Iwao Kuroda
Advisor, Policy Planning Department and Institute for Monetary and Economic Studies, Bank of Japan, 2–1–1 Nihonbashi-Hongkucho, Chuo-ku, Tokyo 103, Japan
Iwao Kuroda is Adviser to the Policy Planning Department and the Institute for Monetary and Economic Studies at the Bank of Japan. He joined the Bank in 1966 after graduating from the University of Tokyo. From 1979 to 1981 he was an Associate Professor at the Institute of Socioeconomic Planning at the University of Tsukuba.

Leo Melamed
Chairman of the Executive Committee, Special Counsel to the Board of Directors, and Chairman of the GLOBEX Board of Directors, Chicago Mercantile Exchange.
Chairman, Dellsher Investment Co., Inc., 30 South Wacker Drive, 19th Floor, Chicago, IL 60606
Leo Melamed is Chairman of the Executive Committee and Special Counsel to the Board of Governors of the Chicago Mercantile Exchange. He is widely recognized as the founder of financial futures and is the principal architect of GLOBEX and Chairman of the GLOBEX Board of Directors. Melamed spearheaded the concept of international linkages between exchanges that led to the CME link with the Singapore International Monetary Exchange (SIMEX). Subsequently, in 1987, he pioneered the concept of electronic "after hours" trading which culminated in GLOBEX, the automated electronic transaction system that was developed in conjunction with Reuters Holdings PLC.

Yoshiteru Murakami
Deputy President, The Dai-Ichi Kangyo Bank, Ltd., 1–1–5, Uchi-Saiwaicho, Chiyoda-ku, Tokyo 100, Japan
Yoshiteru Murakami is Deputy President of the Dai-Ichi Kangyo Bank. He has worked in the Capital Markets Headquarters as Deputy President (1988) and Senior Managing Director (1987), and in the International Banking Headquarters as Senior Managing Director (1986) and Managing Director (1983).

Yuichiro Nagatomi
President, Institute of Fiscal and Monetary Policy, Ministry of Finance, Japan, 3–1–1, Kasumigaseki, Chiyoda-ku, Tokyo 101, Japan

Yuichiro Nagatomi has been President of the Institute of Fiscal and Monetary Policy since June 1989, prior to which he was Director General of the Ministry of Finance's Customs and Tariff Bureau. He has held a number of strategic positions both in the Ministry and in Japan's diplomatic service since 1958, including Counsellor in the Prime Minister's Cabinet (1978–1980), Director of the Public Relations Office (1975–1976), and First Secretary and Financial Attaché for the Embassy of Japan in the United States. He has published widely on the subject of Japan's budgetary policies.

Hugh T. Patrick
R.D. Calkins Professor of International Business, and Director, Center on Japanese Economy and Business, Graduate School of Business, Columbia University, New York, NY 10027

Hugh T. Patrick is R.D. Calkins Professor of International Business and the Director of the Center on Japanese Economy and Business at the Columbia University Graduate School of Business. He joined the Columbia faculty in 1984 after 24 years as Professor of Economics and Director of the Economic Growth Center at Yale University. He is recognized as a leading specialist on the Japanese economy and on Pacific Basin economic relations.

Patrick has received numerous grants including Guggenheim and Fulbright fellowships. His professional publications include 10 books and some 60 articles and essays. His major fields of published research on Japan include macroeconomic performance and policy, government–business relations, and Japan–U.S. economic relations, as well as economic development and comparative financial development. From 1979–1981 Patrick served as one of the four American members of the binational Japan–U.S. Economic Relations Group appointed by President Carter and Prime Minister Ohira.

Patrick received a B.A. from Yale, M.A. degrees in Japanese studies and economics from the University of Michigan, and a Ph.D. in economics from the University of Michigan.

Brian Quinn
Executive Director, Bank of England, Threadneedle St., London, EC2R 8AH, United Kingdom

Brian Quinn has been Executive Director of the Bank of England since

1988. Prior to this he held a number of positions in the bank, including Assistant Director and Head of Banking Supervision, Head of the Information Division, and Chief of the Cashier's Department. From 1964 to 1970 he worked as an economist in the African Department of the International Monetary Fund where he served for two years as the IMF Representative to Sierra Leone.

Shoichi Royama
Professor of Economics, Osaka University, Machikaneyama 1–1, Toyonaka, Osaka 560, Japan
   Shoichi Royama is Visiting Professor at the School of Oriental and African Studies, University of London for 1989–1990, on leave from his professorship at Osaka University. Before joining the Department of Economics at Osaka University in 1969 he was a research associate at Tokyo University. Royama is a member of the Forum for Policy Innovations and Chairman of the Fundamental Research Committee of the Securities and Exchange Council of the Ministry of Finance. He is the author and/or editor of 11 books in Japanese in the areas of money and banking, financial economics, and economic policy theory.

Phillip A. Thorpe
Chief Executive, Association of Futures Brokers and Dealers, Ltd., Plantation House, 5–8 Mincing Lane, London EC3M 3DX, United Kingdom
   Phillip A. Thorpe has been the Chief Executive of the Association of Futures Brokers and Dealers Ltd., the organization responsible for the regulatory oversight of futures and options business in the U.K., since 1989. He was previously Deputy Commissioner for Securities and Commodities Trading in Hong Kong, with responsibility for the regulatory oversight of the futures industry. In 1988 he was appointed an Executive Director of the Provisional Securities & Futures Commission Ltd., the body now regulating the Hong Kong securities and futures markets.

Robert K. Wilmouth
President and Chief Executive Officer, National Futures Association, 200 W. Madison Ave., 7th Floor, Chicago, IL 60606
   Robert K. Wilmouth has been President and CEO of the National Futures Association since its inception in 1982. Prior to this, he was President and Chief Executive Officer of the Chicago Board of Trade (1978–1982). Wilmouth worked with The First National Bank of Chicago for 25 years, holding positions in a number of departments. In 1972 he was appointed Executive Vice President in charge of international banking and

named to the Bank's Board of Directors in 1973. In 1975, he joined Crocker National Bank in San Francisco as President, CEO, and Director.

Shohei Yamada
Deputy President, The Mitsui Trust and Banking Company, Ltd., 2–1–1, Nihonbashi-Muromachi, Chuo-ku, Tokyo 103, Japan
   Shohei Yamada was appointed Deputy President of the Mitsui Trust and Banking Company in 1989. Since 1953 he has served as Senior Managing Director and Chief Executive, International Headquarters (1987–1989); General Manager, International Finance Department (1983–1986); and Director and General Manager, International Department (1981–1983).

Sponsors

CENTER ON JAPANESE ECONOMY AND BUSINESS
Graduate School of Business, Columbia University

The Center on Japanese Economy and Business was established in 1986 under the directorship of Hugh T. Patrick, R.D. Calkins Professor of Intenational Business at the Columbia Business School, and a specialist on Japan and the Pacific Basin.

The Center's mandate is to enhance American understanding of the Japanese economy and its business systems in a global, regional, and bilateral context. The current focus of its active program of research and training includes analysis of the Japanese financial system and comparative studies of Japan and other Pacific Basin economies.

Center on Japanese Economy and Business
521 Uris Hall, Graduate School of Business, Columbia University,
New York, NY 10027
Telephone: (212) 854-3976

CENTER FOR THE STUDY OF FUTURES MARKETS
Graduate School of Business, Columbia University

The Center for the Study of Futures Markets was established at the Columbia Business School in 1978. Its Director is Franklin R. Edwards, Arthur F. Burns Professor of Free and Competitive Enterprise.

The Center's purpose is to foster a better understanding of the economic, operational, and institutional aspects of futures and options markets. Its research and publications program focuses on the development and dissemination of new knowledge regarding these markets and their effect on greater economic welfare.

Center for the Study of Futures Markets
802 Uris Hall, Graduate School of Business, Columbia University, New York, NY 10027
Telephone: (212) 854–4202

INSTITUTE OF FISCAL AND MONETARY POLICY
Ministry of Finance, Japan

The Institute of Fiscal and Monetary Policy was founded in May 1985 as a research organization in the Ministry of Finance. Its President is Yuichiro Nagatomi.

The Institute's purpose is to study the implications for economic policy of structural changes in the Japanese economy and growing interdependence among nations. Goals include consolidating research efforts, developing an information system, and training personnel to deal with these issues. Sponsorship of conferences and a visiting scholar program reflects the Institute's emphasis on an exchange of views with scholars from abroad.

Institute of Fiscal and Monetary Policy, Ministry of Finance
3–1–1 Kasumigaseki, Chiyoda-ku, Tokyo 100, Japan
Telephone: (03) 3581–4111

FOUNDATION FOR ADVANCED INFORMATION AND RESEARCH, JAPAN

The Foundation for Advanced Information and Research, Japan was established in November 1985 as a private, nonprofit organization. FAIR's current President is Sadaaki Hirasawa.

FAIR's purpose is to promote international understanding and cooperation in the development of the Pacific Basin area. The Board of Governors and Partners of FAIR consists of representatives from major Japanese companies. Prominent figures from government, academia, and private organizations serve as advisors and councillors, while many leading scholars from abroad are associate members.

Foundation for Advanced Information and Research, Japan
Toranomon Central Building, 1–7–1 Nishi-Shimbashi, Minato-ku, Tokyo 105, Japan
Telephone: (03) 3503–0231

Acknowledgments

This project—the conference and now this book—would not have been possible without the support and assistance of many individuals and institutions in addition to the authors included herein.

The Institute of Fiscal and Monetary Policy of Japan's Ministry of Finance and the Foundation for Advanced Information and Research (FAIR), Japan, co-sponsored the project. They provided active organizational support and funding; otherwise the project would never have been initiated. We are particularly indebted to their respective Presidents, Yuichiro Nagatomi and Akira Nishigaki. Tatsuya Kanai at the Ministry of Finance Institute and Dan Suzuki and Yoshikazu Koike of FAIR efficiently handled many of the day-to-day administrative requirements for bringing the project to successful completion.

Funding for the American costs of this project were provided by generous grants from the New York Stock Exchange, the Dun & Bradstreet Corporation, and Sumitomo Corporation of America. As always, finance is an essential ingredient for any successful project, whether involving human or physical capital. We acknowledge our deep thanks to our supporters, both specifically for this project and more generally for our respective research organizations at Columbia University, the Center on Japanese Economy and Business, and the Center for the Study of Futures Markets.

The two-day conference held at the Waldorf–Astoria Hotel on May 14–15, 1990, was the focus for much of the intellectual ferment that infused this project. Much of the conference's success is due to the staff of the two centers—in particular, Sheri Ranis, Charles Curtis, Christopher Hoyt, Susan Thau, Karen Tonjes, and Robert Uriu of the Center on Japanese Economy and Business, and Mary Hennion of the Center for the Study of

Futures Markets, who in addition handled many of the other administrative chores. Catherine Davidson assiduously transcribed the discussion, and she and Larry Meissner skillfully copy-edited the chapters in this book.

Jennifer Duffy, Program Officer at the Center on Japanese Economy and Business, deserves special thanks, which we happily acknowledge. She worked closely with us both, and with her Japanese counterparts, from the inception of this project. She took care of the myriad of administrative details engendered by a project involving so many authors and a major conference involving so many internationally based participants. She has overseen and shepherded the publications process, deftly adding her own editorial touch. Without her inputs, we do not know what we would have done.

Our greatest debt is to those who provided the intellectual substance of this project. In addition to those who prepared papers for this book, John A. Bohn, President, Moody's Investors Inc.; James L. Cochrane, Senior Vice President and Chief Economist, New York Stock Exchange; Gilbert Durieux, Director General, MATIF, France; Koichi Hamada, Professor of Economics, Yale University; T.E. "Rick" Kilcollin, Executive Vice President and Chief Operating Officer, Chicago Mercantile Exchange; Yoshio Suzuki, Vice Chairman, Board of Councillors, Nomura Research Institute, Ltd., Japan; and Andrew Winckler, Deputy Chairman, The Securities Association, and Executive Director, Security Pacific Hoare Govett Ltd., U.K., contributed thought-provoking insights as conference moderators and panelists. Our deep thanks to you all.

INTRODUCTION

Franklin R. Edwards
Hugh T. Patrick

As the 1990s unfold, we stand on the threshold of a new age of global financial markets. The seemingly inevitable, market-driven dynamic of the international integration of banking, securities, and futures markets is bringing about a profound transformation of financial flows and the efficiency and effectiveness of the domestic and international markets serving them. Propelled in the 1980s by a variety of forces—technological, economic, political, and (de)regulatory—the implications of international financial market integration are pervasive.

This new era promises to raise a host of new public and business policy issues as well as opportunities. These include issues of financial market integrity, international competitiveness, and regulatory harmony. What will the rules of the game be? How will prudential concerns for the safety as well as the efficiency of international financial markets, and their national counterparts, be met? What are the appropriate new institutional arrangements? How and to what degree will international financial markets be supervised, harmonized, and regulated, and for what purposes? Who will be making these decisions and implementing them? These are the issues that confront—and bedevil—policymakers, practitioners, and scholars alike.

1

The Context

The 1980s were witness to major transformations of the international political, economic, and financial environment. Among the major developments was rapidly increasing international financial market integration across major nations and across financial product markets. The major sources of financial change were several, interrelated, and reinforcing.

Virtually revolutionary technological changes—in telecommunications, electronic trading, manipulation of data, and the like—linked financial markets more closely than ever before. We have entered the information age. The amount of financial information has expanded exponentially, and access to it has become instantaneous for major market players. In the 1990s 24-hour electronic trading is possible not only technologically but institutionally.

The major gaps between national saving and investment rates, with the United States becoming a huge debtor and Japan and, to a lesser extent, Germany becoming huge creditors, reinforced the already-strong drive for effective financial intermediation across countries. So, too, did the expanding global horizons of major financial institutions and other investors. Competition made foreign, Eurocurrency, and domestic securities increasingly perfect substitutes, and linked ever closer stock, bond, loan, and derivative markets, both domestically and internationally.

Domestic and international deregulation of major national financial markets—the United States in the early 1980s, Japan on its gradualist path throughout the 1980s, London in the mid-1980s, and the European Commission 1992 targets—reinforced the impetus given by the changes in technology, saving-investment imbalances, and financial behavior.

London, New York, and Tokyo became the physical and symbolic locations of the international markets. Almost all the major players in these markets—commercial banks, securities dealers, underwriters, merchant banks, insurance companies, pension funds, exchanges, other financial institutions—have headquarters either in Western Europe, the United States, or Japan. In essence, the global financial system has as its core the United States, Japan, and the United Kingdom. They are the dominant free markets for transnational and international financial transactions. In the 1990s, the major continental Western European countries will join the core as their process of financial liberalization—represented by the slogan of Europe-1992—proceeds apace. Other countries will enter this "global system" of international financial markets as they terminate exchange controls and other barriers that impede effective integration of their national financial markets with the international system.

Financial integration has also taken place within each of the major national markets as well. Market segmentation has been ended by deregulation or by increasingly competitive market forces. Domestic and international financial market integration are mutually reinforcing; competitive market pressures in one rapidly spill over into the other. However, the pace is uneven, more so across financial product markets than across nations. Western Europe, led by Germany, is based on universal banking—one institution engaged both in commercial banking (making loans to clients) and investment banking (underwriting and trading in securities). The Glass–Steagall Act in the United States and Article 65 of the Securities Act in Japan persist in 1990, so that the same financial institutions cannot engage in both commercial and investment banking. However, competitive pressures have already eroded these artificial distinctions, and in the 1990s they will almost certainly disappear.

Domestic financial deregulation and liberalization appropriately stop far short of complete laissez-faire. After all, traditional regulatory concerns persist: the public goods and externalities inherent in an effective financial system continue to be significant. How can the safety of the financial system be maintained? How can the system, and its participants, be protected from the dangers of fraud, excessive risk-taking, and other aspects of moral hazard? One of the major issues in the 1990s for regulatory authorities and participants alike is how to meet these needs effectively and efficiently, in what is a radically new financial environment. These issues will be addressed, as in the past, first at the level of the nation-state and its domestic financial markets and institutions.

But that will not be sufficient. By their very nature international financial markets transcend the regulatory reach and capability of any single nation-state.

Foreign exchange markets for major currencies and the Eurocurrency markets are outstanding examples of international markets not directly subject to regulation or supervision. However, their participants are subject to the national laws under which contracts are stipulated, and to the welter of regulations of their respective home countries. The success of these markets is founded on the knowledge of market participants, their mutual trust as they deal with each other in repeated transactions, and the discipline of the marketplace that continually reinforces these arrangements for players who want to maintain access to the markets.

But market discipline alone will not solve all the problems facing international financial markets. Self-regulating organizations are important features of national securities exchanges, and every country has its own regulatory rules and apparatus. But, as this book explores, there are as yet no international institutions or mechanisms for regulating international financial markets. Although the G-10 Supervisors' Committee is attempting to provide an oversight mechanism, it falls short of being an effective regulatory body. Perhaps the most significant step toward international harmonization of rules is the "capital-standards" agreement negotiated through the Bank of International Settlements (BIS). Banks engaged in international business must now maintain a minimum capital-assets ratio of 8 percent. Some specialists, however, as is evident in this book, regard these standards as not sufficiently well-articulated and, therefore, seriously flawed.

This Volume

To address these issues, we organized, under the aegis of the Center on Japanese Economy and Business and the Center for the Study of Futures Markets at Columbia University's Graduate School of Business, a project to bring together distinguished financial market experts from the full range of relevant institutions—regulators and other governmental and central bank officials, bankers, managers of securities and future exchanges, practitioners, and academics. They come from Japan, the United Kingdom, continental Europe, and the United States. Accordingly they represent a full panoply of institutional and national experiences and perspectives. The importance of both different and similar national, institutional, and individual perspectives on common issues cannot be overemphasized.

The chapters in this book emanated from a two-day conference titled "Regulating International Financial Markets: Issues and Policies," held in New York City on May 14–15, 1990, that brought together these authors with an audience of practitioners, academics, and other specialists. The major themes of the volume are identified in the seven section headings under which the chapters are presented. The individual essays present not only a great deal of information but, even more importantly, the insights, judgements, and perspectives of the authors. Nor surprisingly, at times their views differ, particularly when it comes to policy prescription for the future. That is as it should be. After all, we have only begun the process of considering and debating the important regulatory and other public policy issues posed by the international integration of financial markets.

The process of discussion at the conference raised issues which enabled the authors to sharpen their arguments. At the same time, it inevitably engendered discussion of some issues beyond the scope of the papers themselves. We have selected some points and issues emanating from that discussion to include here, more as an agenda of topics for future research than as a definitive resolution of issues. We make no attempt to summarize the rich and provocative papers of what, after all, is a distinguished group of authors who ably articulate their own definitive views in their respective areas of expertise.

A central theme in Section I, The Evolving International Environment, is the interplay among technological innovations, market forces, and the concerns of regulators. Leo Melamed, the progenitor of GLOBEX (for 24-hour, global trading of futures and options), stressed the inevitable force on financial markets of the technology-driven information revolution. Toyoo Gyohten, former Vice-Minister of International Finance of Japan's Ministry of Finance, expressed concern over conflicts between the perceived short-term evaluation of financial market participants and the longer-run perspective of the regulatory authorities. One issue raised, though not satisfactorily answered, is how to deal with short-term instability (crises) in a domestic financial market (such as a stock market crash), and its international ramifications. Not surprisingly, Japan's future role as a gross and net capital exporter, and the future role of the yen as an international currency, were put on the research agenda. Gyohten's view is that the yen will increase in importance but that the dollar will continue as the major international currency; however, that does not imply the United States will continue to be the hegemonic manager of the international currency system. That came to an end with the termination of the Bretton Woods system of fixed exchange rates in 1973.

The internationalization of banking—banking and loan markets—is one of the central components of the international integration of financial markets. In Section II, Banking and Financial Intermediary Markets, the authors address the issues from the respective national experiences of Japan, the United Kingdom and continental Europe, and the United States. It is not clear to what extent the decline in the position of American relative to other world banks has been due to U.S. balance of payments deficits, decline in the value of the dollar, losses on Third World loans, or slower productivity growth. George Kaufman and other American academics urged higher capital requirements, more consonant with market-determined levels of safety, through the issuance of subordinated debt to raise bank capital without the penalty of the adverse tax treatment to which income on equity is subject. Shoichi Royama noted the importance of a bank's managerial and technological as well as capital resources in determining its efficiency and ability to compete. Hugh Patrick noted that deregulation in Japan has not yet proceeded to the elimination of interest rate ceilings on small time deposits at banks, and the postal savings system, and accordingly some 47 percent of bank time deposits (and all postal savings) remain regulated. Shohei Yamada opined that remaining ceilings on small time deposit interest rates will be fully liberalized by the end of 1993, and that indeed is the desire of many bankers, including members of the trust bank association. Charles Goodhart noted that one should be concerned about the possibility that differing national regulatory or other public policy measures have a distortionary effect upon the competitiveness of financial institutions headquartered in different countries. He saw the regulatory issue, in Europe at least, of less immediate concern in banking than in the securities industry, since the BIS capital requirements establish a basis for the international regulation in banking. There is no comparable mechanism for the establishment of overall international minimum standards in the securities industry. At the same time, he expressed concern that, when a financial institution's capital is impaired, regulators tend to forgive or soft-pedal so as not to create informational problems with serious and excessive adverse effects; it is in practice not as easy to handle mark-to-market valuations of assets in bank portfolios as some academics would have it.

While underwriting, trading, and investing in securities and futures instruments have become increasingly transnational, transactions still occur within the framework of national markets and exchanges, and their quite distinct institutions and regulatory environments. Each has its own rules and systems. In Section III, Securities Markets, and Section IV, Futures Markets, the authors treat major issues related to the internationalization of these markets. In Japan regulation is centralized in the Ministry of Finance. In the United States, there are multiple regulators, governmental as well as self-regulating exchanges; and there are jurisdictional disputes among the regulators, notably the Securities and Exchange Commission (SEC) and Commodity Futures Trading Commission (CFTC). The regulatory system in the U.K. is similar, though with perhaps greater reliance on self-regulation, fewer formal mechanisms of compliance, and less clear-cut lines of jurisdiction and responsibility.

In spite of the multiplicity of jurisdictions, Philip Johnson and Brian Quinn noted that the most common locus of a financial crisis is the banking system: defaults in financial markets create problems of clearance and settlement which quickly involve banks, and the central bank may therefore have *de facto* jurisdiction in the sense that it must be prepared to consider the case for acting as lender of last resort either directly or indirectly.

The mechanisms for international cooperation in the event of a crisis are informal. They evidently were effective between the U.S. and the U.K.

regulatory authorities in the handling of the Drexel Burnham bankruptcy. Robert Wilmouth foresees the possibility of international cooperation and coordination among self-regulating associations based on the experiences of the U.S. National Futures Association, while stressing that its activities were limited to customer protection; the functioning of markets on the trading floors are left to the supervision of the exchanges making those markets. Yoshiteru Murakami stated that despite initial concerns and claims, index arbitrage (program) trading was not to blame for the sharp fall in the Tokyo Stock Exchange prices in early 1990; rather, such arbitrage is a normal, indeed necessary, function of the market. He agreed that an electronic trading network linking all the major markets is not only technologically feasible but is likely to develop as a tool for international trading, something like a generic GLOBEX.

The chapters in Section V address issues of clearing, settlement, payments procedures, and trading systems, particularly in light of new technologies. Settlement and clearance frequently are taken for granted; yet it is precisely there that default and systemic risks manifest themselves in a crisis. How are these systemic risks managed? Who bears the risks? How can they be reduced, while maintaining the social benefits of these systems? As Wayne Angell stresses, coordination of central bank policy so as to achieve greater macroeconomic stability of the global economy reduces systemic risk. In terms of settlement, clearance, and payments, in the United States the Federal Reserve System bears the intraday risk without charge; Angell argues that such risk should be privatized (as happens in Japan) through the development of an active, intraday federal funds market. Will electronic, screen-based trading replace open outcry? Wendy Gramm and others were uncertain, suggesting that both systems are likely to exist for some time to meet the differing needs of both traders and customers.

Section VI asks a rhetorical question: Is There a Systemic Risk Problem in International Financial Markets? Following Michael Hewitt's definition of systemic risk as those factors which have the potential to cause or aggravate a disturbance in the system so as to bring on a system crisis, Koichi Hamada noted that such disturbances are likely to be nonlinear, and external or global shocks can upset a local equilibrium situation. Yoshio Suzuki stressed that systemic risk in settlement, the determining factors of which were identified by Hideki Kanda—the amount of unsettled balances and interdependence—can be reduced by shortening the time lag between trade and settlement through the efficient functioning of the central bank gross settlement systems, such as the Fedwire (USA) or BOJ-Net (Japan).

Edward Kane emphasized the potential long-run, hidden costs (contingent liabilities) of such central bank guarantees of finality. More generally, he criticized safety nets as altering behavior so as to increase moral hazard, and the short-term time horizons of American regulators who thereby underestimate the longer-run costs of such guarantees. He sees regulators' lack of accountability for the long-run harm they cause as a significant source of systemic risk (at least in the United States). He is skeptical about a negotiated system of international regulation since concessions are likely to retard needed adaptations. Michael Hewitt noted that, unlike the U.S. where regulators move on to more lucrative careers in the industry (a point made by Kane), in the U.K. (and the argument would apply to Japan, too) he and other central bank regulators have long-term careers as central bankers, and hence take a longer-term view. The ways to reduce system risk are to improve market settlement mechanisms, to have capital adequacy rules, and other approaches as discussed in his essay. In the end, the central bank must be the last resort; the trick is to make "last" very far down the road, not to make commitments in advance, and to deal with each crisis as seems best under the circumstances.

In a very real sense Section VII is the culmination, not just the final section, of this book. There the central issue of international regulation is directly addressed by the authors. George Benston argued that a highly competitive banking system is the most efficient and the most beneficial to its customers, and that the instabilities in the United States have frequently been engendered by lack of competition (nationwide segmentation of financial product markets and institutions). Easy entry prohibits predatory pricing from being a problem in the long run. Moreover, while international harmonization may be desirable in abstract principle, in practice it is likely to be counterproductive. He argued that the BIS capital-adequacy requirements are defined too crudely and inaccurately to be meaningful; for instance, they do not take into account differences in country risk, interest rate risk, foreign exchange risk, or covariance of risk. The danger is that the public will be lulled into thinking these standards are meaningful. Rather, Benston pushed for higher national capital adequacy ratios as suggested by the Shadow Financial Regulatory Committee.

Paul Guy saw international harmonization as desirable, but in terms of common, minimum standards rather than identical regulation throughout the world. He proposed international capital adequacy standards for securities companies as well as banks. He emphasized how long it took to negotiate the harmonized BIS bank rule, and noted that the International Organization of Securities Commissions (IOSCO) is a quite recently created institution.

Other practitioners/policymakers took a similar view, while viewing harmonization as a long-run process that has only barely begun. As Johnson put it:

Regulatory harmonization is obviously desirable. It is, however, a long way off. Regulators are operating pursuant to laws which are adopted by the political bodies of their country; they tend to set the priorities and values that are to be maintained. Although in general terms those values are probably common across many different regulatory structures, the business of how to implement them and what to emphasize, what priorities to give, can differ from one nation or one state or one province to the next. So when it comes to harmonization, each regulator somehow has to justify each compromise from the existing local standards which he or she is prepared to agree to. That is one reason for the reticence to adopt in any substantial measure a different system being proposed by someone else. But I don't think it is private interests of regulators nearly so much as it is the different philosophies and policies that are driving different regulatory programs.

Gyohten expressed a similar view:

I think under the given reality, it certainly is premature to aim at very extensive and quick harmonization of the regulatory regimes among different markets. There are three elements which are relevant to this issue. One is, to what extent in reality are different markets really globalized. Second, to what extent is each market receptive to this globalization and prepared to be harmonized. Third, because competition between different national markets is also being intensified, to what extent each national market can afford not to be harmonized without risking some loss of influence in the global market environment.

Quinn added:

There are differences between the views expressed by the academics and the practitioners. But they seem to me to be differences of emphasis rather than differences of principle. I do not think anyone argues the market should be allowed to let rip in any absolute sense. The complaints one has about the BIS regulatory regime are complaints about the precise nature of capital harmonization that has been taking place rather than the fact that a measure has been agreed to. The criticisms of the BIS capital accord are that it is not sufficiently well-articulated, and not accurate enough, rather than that there is no case for having it. Similarly, the academic view seems to be that harmonization is being sought on the wrong things rather than to get some minimum capital standards, for which I think there is broad agreement. The regulator will always, and I think understandably, have a greater concern about contagion, about the spread of the problems, and about the resource and the political costs of dealing with particular events than academics have. I also observe that there have been massive amounts of equity raised by banks in a number of countries in order to comply with the BIS minimum standard, and that there is now a greater association between the nature of the risk and the capital required to support that risk than there was beforehand. In that important sense more level playing fields are being fashioned and are welcomed.

Frank Edwards provocatively suggested that the United States often seeks international regulatory imperialism rather than harmonization—the imposition on others of its own regulations. Johnson, as a former U.S. regulator, suggested that this characteristic may not be unique to U.S. regulators; more importantly, in order to defend themselves from accusations from the public, or Congress, of weakening the regulatory system, regulators are reluctant to take any unnecessary risks, including compromising with foreigners or others on regulatory issues.

Quinn, as a U.K. central banker, judiciously responded:

It is largely a domestic issue for you; I don't have the feeling that it is a huge problem for others. It is an irritant, from time to time, for other countries, but I don't think it is confined to the financial regulators. If one sees the provisions of the legislation to control drugs and drug money laundering which emanate from the U.S. Congress, they have exactly the same characteristics as those which people sometimes attribute to the banking and financial regulations, which is that they reach beyond the United States national boundaries. So I think it is a national characteristic if it's anything. It also seems to me to have something to do with your political process. Your political process is very, very lively. The politicians are very close to the grassroots, and they pass on the pressures that come from the grassroots to the regulators. If you have an election every other year, it is actually surprising you don't have more of that kind of thing. But I think regulators are kept much more under scrutiny in the U.S.; and they therefore feel that there can be no suggestion that they have failed to cover any loophole; and if that takes them overseas then that is where the political process drives them.

I THE EVOLVING INTERNATIONAL FINANCIAL ENVIRONMENT

1 GLOBAL FINANCIAL MARKETS: THE PAST, THE FUTURE, AND PUBLIC POLICY QUESTIONS

Toyoo Gyohten

Dramatic changes have taken place in the structure and function of financial markets and in the financial services industry during the last two decades. The key features have been the rapid globalization of the markets and the enhanced role of the financial services industry. This chapter discusses the main dynamics behind these historic changes and speculates on what lies in the future. While I intend to examine the subject from a global perspective, it will be inevitable that I make more frequent references to the Japanese situation.

There seem to have been three major factors behind the change in global financial markets. The first is the major shift that has taken place in the stock and the flow of financial resources. Financial deregulation is the second, and the third is innovation in information technology. Although I am fully aware of the danger of trying to understand history with simplified analysis, I think these three factors explain a good deal of what has happened, and thus they are the topics considered in this chapter.

Shifts in Resource Flows

The two oil price crises that occurred in the 1970s marked the first major shift in global financial flows in the postwar period. These events demonstrated clearly that industrialized countries by themselves could no longer dictate the destiny of the world economy. Substantial financial assets were accumulated in the hands of the oil producers. The money was invested in securities with high credit standing or was deposited with major money center banks in the United States, Europe, and Japan. These banks recycled the money (petrodollars) to the rest of the world, notably to borrowers in Latin America.

The new pattern of money flow brought about important change in the global financial scene. First, the sudden absorption of financial resources by oil producers exerted a strong stagflationary impact on the economies of oil importers, and this slower economic growth drove their governments into deficits that had to be financed. The increased issue of government obligations, in turn, facilitated the development of a secondary market and thereby contributed to the securitization of financial markets in these countries. Second, weaker domestic demand in oil-importing countries compelled their financial institutions to explore overseas markets, thereby accelerating the globalization of the business. While the accumulation of financial wealth in oil-producing countries quickly decelerated with the decline of oil prices in the 1980s, the structural change brought about in the financial markets has remained.

Indeed, the decade of the 1980s brought even greater change in the international financial scene. In the United States, stimulative fiscal policy and the countervailing high interest rate policy succeeded in controlling inflation and accelerating growth in the domestic economy—including surging imports. However, this success came at the cost of intractable budget deficits and external disequilibrium. On the other side of the Pacific there was an amassing of large external surpluses. In Japan, slower growth of domestic demand was offset by strong overseas demand, so that exports soared. During the five-year period from 1985 to 1989, Japan's current account surplus amounted to $350 billion. Other East Asian countries, notably Korea and Taiwan, also succeeded in building strong export industries.

In Europe, the Federal Republic of Germany offset sluggish domestic demand with exports by its highly competitive capital goods industry, enlarging its trade surplus with other European countries, which were experiencing higher inflation. In Latin America, the heavy external borrowing of the 1970s failed to achieve the desired strengthening of export competitiveness and domestic savings because of ill-conceived or poorly executed development strategies. The decline of oil prices and high interest rates on dollar-denominated debt dealt an additional blow. As a result, the debt problem was aggravated ominously in the 1980s and, indeed, there was a reversal of trade and financial flows.

Probably the most outstanding phenomenon in financial markets in the 1980s was the emergence of Japan as a leading capital exporter on a global scale. The ascendance of Japan to its present status was so rapid that its impact on the international stage has been quite sensational. Indeed, supported by the large current account surplus, the appreciated yen, and the accumulation of domestic liquidity from the booming domestic stock and real estate markets since 1987, Japan has become the world's largest capital exporter.

The situation has sometimes aroused alarmist concerns about the undesirable domination of the world financial market by a single country. However, in my view, one should not overlook an important feature of Japanese capital exports. In 1987, Japan's current account surplus hit a historic high of $87 billion. That year Japan's capital exports amounted to $131 billion. In 1988 the surplus was reduced to $80 billion but capital exports rose to $150 billion. In 1989 the surplus declined further, to $57 billion, but capital exports increased further, to $192 billion. In other words, Japan's capital exports expanded while the current account surplus was shrinking steadily.

Obviously the widening gap was financed by foreign investment in Japan, Japanese nonfinancial corporations borrowing abroad, increased external liabilities of the Japanese banking system, and the drawing down of official reserves. The numbers quoted seem to indicate the increasing role played by Japan as an intermediary in the international flow of financial resources. The Tokyo market is now functioning as a huge turntable in global capital circulation.

I should not forget to mention that a similar role of intermediation is now being played, of course to a much smaller extent, by other East Asian countries, notably the NICs (newly industrialized countries), which are significantly expanding overseas investments and credit activities.

Financial Deregulation

It goes without saying that each market has developed in a different environment and with a different historical background, and these differences have created varying rules and practices. In London, where the emergence of financial markets in the nineteenth century was more or less a spontaneous process accompanying the country's economic growth, explicit control by the authorities was not something familiar. Activities in the market were guided more by a type of gentlemen's agreement between the authorities and the market players, and among market players themselves. In New York, after the Civil War, aggressive capitalists began to create the most dynamic and efficient market in the world. The role of the authorities in that environment was to moderate the uncontrolled play of the law of the jungle. Antitrust laws, the Glass-Steagall Act, and the like, have their roots in such a philosophy. In Tokyo, where the market was developed as a conscious effort by enlightened authoritarianism, beginning in the late nineteenth century, it was subject from the start to a general framework of supervision and protection by regulatory authorities. The financial services industry was viewed as a kind of public utility, expected to play a key role in national economic development.

In spite of all such differences, one development that occurred in all markets in the 1970s and '80s was a change in the vendor–customer relationship. Customers became more demanding and selective, seeking more convenient and favorable service from vendors. Securitization, for instance, clearly was prompted by such demands by customers. Vendors, faced with these customer demands and the pressure of competition, came to favor deregulation so they could provide a wider range of products and services to attract more customers, even at the risk of giving up some of their existing turf. Thus, as the global economy grew, the way of doing business, investment, and consumption all became diversified and sophisticated.

Globalization intensified the pressure for deregulation as competition between markets became a real issue for national players and national authorities alike. The maintenance of international compatibility is a crucial test for the survival of any market. Development of the Euromarket in the 1960s has provided a lesson for national authorities, if not a strong argument for deregulation: introduction of capital controls in New York simply moved activities elsewhere.

Movement toward financial deregulation gained momentum in the 1970s. In every major market a series of measures was implemented, covering areas such as interest rate regulation, exchange and investment control, the introduction of new products, foreign entry, and so on. The wall that once separated different types of financial services is also being removed or lowered. Both the Glass-Steagall regime in the United States and the Article 65 framework in Japan are undergoing erosion.

There is no doubt that the progress of deregulation in major markets has significantly contributed to enhanced efficiency in the world market. It is also true, however, that there is a growing cognizance of the critical importance of preserving the credibility of financial markets. This conviction was fortified by the fact that national economies and national markets are now so closely interdependent that a disruption occurring in one market can hardly be prevented from spreading to others. Hard lessons learned from Latin American debt problems, stock market crashes, the S&L (savings and loan) crisis, and illicit market practices have all been perceived as warning signals of possible danger.

Under the circumstances, the process of financial deregulation seems to have entered a new phase in the 1990s. This is not because a suspension or even a reversal of deregulation is needed, but because certain minimum ground rules are called for so the deregulated market will continue to function without jeopardizing its credibility and viability. Efforts at a multinational level concerning capital adequacy, liquidity standards, and the like, indicate the positive direction toward which financial markets can be expected to develop in coming years.

Technological Innovation

The progress made in computer technology and communication satellites during the 1980s was truly breathtaking. An enormous amount of information can be collected, sorted, analyzed, and transmitted almost instantaneously to practically any corner of the world. Because financial services is an industry that uses numbers as a major part of its operations, it is advantageous to make use of these innovations.

The same financial products are traded in different markets in the world in real time and around the clock. The massive use of computers enables highly sophisticated financial engineering to create new financial products and transactions. A good example is the birth and development of the swap market in the 1970s. It was quickly followed by other new markets, such as options and futures. The rapid growth of mergers and acquisitions activity and program trading would not have been possible without the quantum leap made in computer capability.

It is quite obvious that these innovations in information technology enhanced the efficiency of the financial market and strengthened the power of the financial services industry. Information today is no longer a subsidiary element in economic activity, it is a major market force. The financial services industry is nothing but an information industry based on the computer industry.

However, we should always be reminded that the extensive use of, and the heavy dependence on, information made available by technological innovation can also have destabilizing effects on financial markets. False but sensational news can have a greater impact on the market than accurate but more prosaic news.

Excessive computerization has also tended to deform the financial services industry into a game driven by sheer lust for financial gain, without a broader sense of self-discipline or concern for the overall welfare of the economy or society. The worldwide prevalence of greed among players of the money game poses a serious threat to the healthy development of manufacturing. Promising engineering graduates are lured into financial services while manufacturing firms are more excited about playing money games than creating something tangible. This is certainly not a desirable situation for the solid and balanced growth of the world economy.

Looking to the Future

So far, I have outlined my view on three major dynamic forces that led the development of international financial markets in the 1980s. Now, with the 1980s behind us, we need to look ahead and seek what might be in store. I talked about changes in the global financial balance and the shift in the stock and flow of financial resources. Will there be further changes in the 1990s? Yes. There are various signs indicating new developments.

In the United States there is increased recognition of the need to improve the domestic savings-investment balance and to strengthen the international competitiveness of industry. The world is anxiously watching the President's lips to hear them deliver new words.

In Japan, there is a sign of stabilization; the momentum of the explosive expansion of financial power is subsiding. The external surplus is declining, and domestic liquidity creation will be moderated. However, it is likely that some current account surplus will continue for at least a few more years, and the stock of financial resources will continue to grow. In mid-1990 Japanese investors possessed some $540 billion in foreign port-folio assets and $150 billion in direct investment abroad (at cost). Any significant reallocation within this collection of assets will have an inevit-able impact on interest rates and exchange rates.

East Asian countries seem to sustain the strong dynamism they need to continue higher than average growth. However, many of them still face political uncertainty. In Korea and Taiwan, the struggle toward the solid foundation of social and political democracy will continue. Hong Kong has to pass the test of 1997 when it reverts to China.

In China, suspension of economic reform seems to be accentuating internal disequilibrium. The agricultural reform carried out in the early 1980s precipitated the need for fundamental reform in nonagricultural industries. The crucial task for China in the 1990s is to secure a political environment congenial to such reform.

In the new Europe, Frankfurt may join or even replace London as financial center. For successful performance, it seems to me that London needs the revitalization of economic strength of the domestic economy, while Frankfurt needs the further globalization of financial markets and further internationalization of the D-Mark. The implication of a single European market in 1992 was amplified but at the same time complicated by German unification and the collapse of the centrally planned economies of the Soviet Union and Eastern Europe. The economic and social reform that the USSR and Eastern Europe must go through is enormously difficult, and it is not prudent to speculate on the eventual outcome of this process.

In Latin America, a decade of muddling through, which culminated in the new debt strategy, taught us a valuable lesson. No financial arrangement, be it a debt cancellation or new money, can provide a viable solution unless the debtor country succeeds in calling forth the national will to make a genuine effort to mobilize domestic savings and increase exports. The biggest achievement of the new debt strategy was that it delivered a clear message to all parties concerned that the ball is now in the debtors' court. It is indeed encouraging to note that in Mexico, Brazil, and elsewhere, the governments, in response to this message, seem to have launched serious self-help efforts.

For West Asia and Africa, however, the situation is still far from promising. Many of the countries in these regions are still simply unable to prepare for a take-off. It is obvious that they will need very large flows of resources on concessionary terms from the developed countries for many years to come.

The foregoing view of the macroeconomic situation of various regions of the world may imply further changes in the global financial scene. In any event, the most important issue before us is whether we can secure the smooth and adequate flow of financial resources to where they are truly needed, and whether the global financial market and the financial services industry can carry out their important tasks satisfactorily.

I have tried to outline possibilities and risks inherent in each dynamic force that has been driving international financial development. Based on this analysis, I conclude that what is most needed in the 1990s is better coordination between public policy and private strategy. This is by no means to recommend introduction of a new regulatory regime. It is rather a recommendation for both the public sector and the private sector to understand and respect each other's power and responsibility.

For the public policy maker, it is indispensable to recognize that the private financial market has grown so powerful that public policy cannot be effective unless it is based on an understanding of the basic currents moving the market. The role of policy makers is somewhat similar to that of a credible advisor; instead of trying to dictate to the market, they must provide necessary incentives or disincentives through macro- and microeconomic policies. For the financial services industry, it should be fully understood that in this globalized and interdependent economy there is no deal that is totally private or without public implication. As was the case in the Mexican debt reduction package and the S&L salvage operation, more often than not the last entry in the ledger is a charge to taxpayers.

Both public policy makers and the financial services industry must provide the other with a place in their own frame of reference. Through enlightened cooperation we may be able to establish a new framework of market mechanisms with which to navigate the uncharted ocean of global financial development.

2 THE TELECOMMUNICATIONS AND INFORMATION REVOLUTION: IMPLICATIONS FOR FINANCIAL MARKETS, TRADING SYSTEMS, AND REGULATION[1]

Leo Melamed

It seemed like just another traditional May Day celebration in Moscow's Red Square. As usual, all the government top brass were present. As usual, there were banners and marches and songs. As usual, there was all the expected pomp and circumstance.

But something was drastically different. The banner! The colors were right—yellow letters on a red background—but the words were all wrong. "Communists: have no illusions—you are bankrupt," it blatantly proclaimed! Right there, in the middle of Red Square, on May Day, 1990!

That this incredible event occurred—and that it occurred without fear of retribution—is first and foremost vivid and commanding testimony of the failure of communism. Or, to state it in the affirmative, it represents a magnificent triumph of capitalism, of democracy, of market-driven economic order, of Adam Smith, Ayn Rand, and Milton Friedman.

As Alan Greenspan reflected earlier this year, it is almost as if a great economic experiment had been undertaken some 50 years ago. "The world was divided into two," the chairman of the U.S. Federal Reserve said. "On one side, there would be market-driven capitalism and, on the other, a centrally planned economic order. Today we can compare the results."

The results are stunning. Soviet President Mikhail Gorbachev himself

21

admits the Soviet Union is suffering from "economic deadlock and stagna-
tion." Or, as Irwin M. Stelzer, political columnist for the London *Sunday
Times*, succinctly summed up the situation in the USSR by quoting Nikolai
Shmelev and Vladimir Popov, two prominent Soviet economic experts,
"There is not enough of anything, anywhere, at any time."

The inexorable result: a plan to dismantle central economic controls and
move to free markets.

Tangentially, of course, the experiment was equally a triumph for
futures and options markets. These markets are integral and indispensable
to the economic order that demonstrated its supremacy over an inferior
economic system whose structure and function depended on the edicts of
government. Indeed, what markets better epitomize price determination
by virtue of the free forces of supply and demand than do the futures and
options markets?

But the Red Square banner is testimony to still another truth, one that
has even greater implications for the world of tomorrow. Let's face it, the
failure of communism is not news; it failed long before the autumn of 1989.

What is news is that the people who were hostage to this economic and
political order suddenly had the temerity and courage to publicly denounce
the system that had enslaved them. What is news is that the truth, officially
kept secret within a world isolated by an iron curtain, was out.

Unquestionably, a substantial measure of the credit belongs to Andrei
Sakharov, Mikhail Gorbachev, Lech Walesa, and, no doubt, many others
whose names historians will ultimately determine. These giants of human
history forged a political environment that made the events of last autumn
possible. However, with all due respect, their monumental achievement
was not conceivable without the parallel consequence of yet another
human endeavor: the inexorable march of technology.

The Telecommunications Revolution

More than any other single factor, the telecommunications revolution, or
what Walter Wriston dubbed the "information revolution," made it impossible to continue the charade and hide the unmitigated bankruptcy of
the communist order. Modern communication techniques between people,
coupled with massive media penetration in disregard of national boundaries, offered everyone a stark, uncompromising comparison of economic
systems.

As journalist Mike O'Neil predicted years before the historic events
of 1989, the consequences of new telecommunications technology "is

hurrying the collapse of the old order, accelerating the velocity of social and political change, creating informed and politically active publics, and inciting conflict by publicizing the differences between people and nations."

To put it another way, the technological revolution of the last decade made *perestroika* inevitable.

Therefore, as it has throughout the history of mankind, technology again is dictating fundamental change in our social structure and is reshaping both the political and economic landscape of our planet. Its immediate impact on the populations of Eastern Europe is now a historical reality.

However, effects of the information revolution reach far beyond social and political change. As Carver Mead of the California Institute of Technology points out, "The entire Industrial Revolution enhanced productivity by a factor of about a hundred, but the micro-electronic revolution has already enhanced productivity in information-based technology by a factor of more than a million—and the end isn't in sight yet."

Clearly, consequences of the telecommunications revolution will be felt in every facet and niche of civilized life, and will dramatically change the nature and structure of financial markets. Already, what were once dozens of scattered national economies are inexorably becoming linked into one interrelated, interdependent world economy.

It is, by now, a cliche to explain that sophisticated satellites, microchips, and fiber optics have changed the world from a confederation of autonomous financial markets into one continuous marketplace. There is no longer a distinct division of the three major time zones. Today's financial markets are worldwide in scope, ignoring geographic boundaries and time of day.

Today, as Wriston stated, by virtue of the information revolution, "we are witnessing a galloping new system of international finance—one that differs radically from its precursors" in that it "was not built by politicians, economists, central bankers or finance ministers...it was built by technology...by men and women who interconnected the planet with telecommunications and computers...."

The consequences are global as well as regional and affect public as well as private financial policy objectives. That is good news for futures and options markets.

Indeed, futures and options markets were the first to read the handwriting on the wall and discern the meaning, as well as the potential, of the new information standard. The financial futures revolution, launched in Chicago in 1972, blazed the trail for much of what has followed since in world capital markets.

It established that there was a need for a new genre of risk management tools responsive to institutional money management and modern telecommunication technology. It led to the acceptance and integration of futures and options within the infrastructure of the financial establishment. It acted as the crucible of ideas for new off-exchange products. It became the catalyst for the development of the futures markets worldwide. And it induced the introduction of risk management as a regime.

It is the latter consequence which, perhaps, will have the greatest impact on the use and expansion of futures and options markets in the coming years. Because greater interdependence, more globalization, instant informational flows, immediate access to markets of choice, more sophisticated techniques, and intensified competition seem to be the trends of the future, the management of risk is bound to be at the core of every prudent long-range financial strategy.

Two decades ago, financial risk was apt to be defined by most in fairly simple terms as the possibility of suffering financial loss. At that time, it was doubtful that many thought of risk management as a discipline. Nor is it likely that many outside of academia or the actuarial business spent much time tinkering with mathematical models for weighing different strains of strategic exposure—that is, a firm's sensitivity to changes in tax rates, interest rates, exchange rates, the price of oil, and so forth.

Two decades ago, the identifiable risks were the rough equivalent of what Claude Rains told his lackeys in the final scenes of *Casablanca*: "Round up the usual suspects." Farmers, for example, have always been at the mercy of the weather. Beyond that were all the usual insurable risks: fire, theft, natural disasters, and so on. Oh, recessions came and went all right. But, at the end of the day, it was an era in which Treasury instruments yielded about 5 percent and foreign exchange rates were fixed.

Defined in the context of the world of commerce as we know it in the 1990s, risk is not merely a potential drought, an earthquake, a gas leak, or even an oil spill or other environmental disaster. Today's interdependent world is a place where:

1. Two contaminated grapes are found in Philadelphia and, a hemisphere away, Chilean farmers suffer $100 million in losses as a result.

2. Europeans worry about growth hormones fed to cattle and American beef growers suffer the consequences.

3. Bundesbank monetary policy must be weighed right along with that of the U.S. Fed.

4. A head tax imposed in London can affect the corporate bottom line every bit as readily as a value-added tax levied by Washington.

5. A drop in the Nikkei average can trigger a decline in every other stock market in the world.

6. U.S. budget and trade deficits impact not just the U.S. economy but the economies of all nations and all those who are business participants.

7. The Third World debt is everyone's burden.

8. Every action in any part of the world is immediately known by everyone else, its impact swift and sometimes—as in the case of Iraq's invasion of Kuwait—of critical significance.

Futures and Options Markets

In such a world, risk is radically more complicated, intensely more concentrated and devastatingly swift. Risk today is any one of a myriad of contingencies that could negatively impact an enterprise, thereby altering its value, its cash flow, or its future.

And, because the implicit counterpart to risk is opportunity, the complexity of the world of tomorrow is—as has previously been noted—good news for the futures and options markets. Moreover, as Mead said, the end isn't in sight yet.

Futures and options markets are ideally suited for a world where innovation and competition will intensify, where demand for tailored risk-management strategies will increase, and where opportunities will rapidly appear and disappear on a constantly changing financial horizon. Indeed, while the lines between exchange-traded and off-exchange products may become somewhat blurred in the coming years, no markets other than futures and options offer a blend of so many credible instruments to safeguard or enhance one's assets.

Consider for a moment the salient properties of futures and options markets:

1. The widest array of agricultural and financial instruments—from beans to bonds, from cattle to crude, from stocks to silver, from Euros to yen, from coffee to the Consumer Price Index.

2. A measure of liquidity (on balance) not available anywhere else.

3. A cost-efficiency through incomparably narrow bid/ask spreads.

4. An ability to institute swiftly a variety of strategies, programs, or fine-tuning techniques.

5. The ability to adjust portfolio exposure cost-effectively by moving back and forth between securities and cash.

6. A flexibility to choose between the most fairly priced alternative instrument at any time.

7. A facility to preserve credit lines within a market system offering the highest degree of creditworthiness.

8. A fluency to access all markets globally.

9. A speed and certainty of execution difficult to duplicate.

10. And, soon, market coverage on a 24-hour basis.

I dare say that the foregoing represent a uniquely impressive array of components in the arsenal of tools imperative for the financial manager to possess.

The Rise of Financial Engineering

At least two more profound consequences brought about by the technological revolution have a material impact on futures and options markets as well as significant financial implications for this decade.

First is the growth of institutional investment funds. Scientific and technological advancement have forced the world to become highly specialized, expertise-oriented, and professional—a trend that will not abate but, rather, will accelerate and is nowhere more obvious than in the world of finance.

In the United States, investment managers now represent more than 23 million mutual fund shareholders and control a trillion dollars in assets for them.

U.S. pension funds now total 60 million plan participants plus beneficiaries and hold $2 trillion for them, compared to only $400 billion a decade ago.

Whether we like it or not, whether it is good or bad, is not the relevant issue. Investment and pension funds managed by professionals who apply complex strategies increasingly will dominate the markets.

These managers will continue to invent investment techniques and demand instruments of trade (principally found in futures and options) that serve their needs.

In this context, it is (parenthetically) important to note that many trading activities will not be conducted relative to strict fundamental evaluations. With respect to equity investments in particular, portfolio management is likely to continue with the current trend of following index enhancement strategies. (Bear in mind, this nation's 200 largest pension funds now have 30 percent of their assets committed to some form of indexation.)

These investment strategies may require adjustments to portfolios that sometimes cause price movements in individual stocks that bear little relationship to their fundamental values. Thus, the debate between fundamental and technical investment philosophies will continue for the foreseeable future.

Moreover, financial management will continue to become increasingly more disciplined, professional, and pre-programmed. To meet the demands of competition, financial engineering will become an exacting art form, and money managers will need to refine and upgrade the process by which they make investment decisions continuously. There will be no time simply to react during a moment of panic or pressure.

To succeed in the coming decade, managers will have to employ precise blueprints and models for all eventualities. Investment strategies, protective hedging techniques, or decisions with respect to asset allocation will need to be in place far in advance of the time they are necessary.

It goes without saying that professional management will need the most efficient tools, the know-how to use them, and the technology to apply them.

The Erosion of American Market Dominance

Second, the loss of dominance by American financial markets is striking and will continue to have a pivotal influence on money management.

In the fixed-income markets, the Japanese have become major participants. For instance, Tokyo's trading of Japanese government bond futures, which did not exist five years ago, is currently nearly twice as great in dollar value as Chicago's trading of U.S. T-bond futures. In 1988, Japanese investors accounted for 44 percent of the nearly $50 billion net foreign purchases of U.S. government notes and bonds.

Similarly, the U.S. equity market is no longer the dominant force that it was years ago. In 1975, the United States accounted for 57 percent of the capitalization of the world's equity markets: today the figure is only 31 percent. Japanese investors alone represented nearly 30 percent of the $360 billion in U.S. stock transactions made by foreigners in 1988; in 1983, Japanese investors accounted for less than 3 percent of the $135 billion in foreign transactions.

And, bear in mind, the foregoing erosion of American market dominance occurred prior to the effects of "Europe 1992" (or is it Fortress

1992?) and the revitalization of the emerging nations of the Pacific Rim, Eastern/Central Europe and the Soviet Union.

Many significant national sovereignty consequences will flow from this altered financial panorama, but one of the most profound effects on the United States will be that American businesses and their markets (no differently from foreign businesses and their markets) must adopt a global posture if they are to survive in the business world in the coming decade.

"The multinational of the 1970s is obsolete," *Business Week* says (May 14, 1990, issue). "Global companies must be more than just a bunch of overseas subsidiaries that execute decisions made at headquarters."

Enter in its place instead "the stateless corporation"—a modern company that "does research wherever necessary, develops products in several countries, promotes key executives regardless of nationality, and even has shareholders on three continents."

And, *Business Week* might have added, enter also the risk management discipline. Because the international marketplace no longer will be dominated by a single nation as it was during the last century, no international entity will continue to exist for very long unless it has mastered the ability to manage risk on a global scale. Market coverage will have to be worldwide as well as around-the-clock.

As the *Business Week* article concluded, "In this world of transparent borders, governments and nations that fail to create the right climate will find their living standards and well-being short-changed. But those that can extract the benefits that stateless corporations can offer will emerge clear winners."

Once again, this is highly constructive for futures and options markets. President Gorbachev knew this when he recently called for the establishment of both securities and commodity exchanges in the USSR.

Predictions

Finally, one sobering caveat and one fascinating prospect: obviously, crystal ball gazing is both difficult and dangerous. It is interesting to note that nobody predicted the cataclysmic European events of autumn 1989 even days before they occurred, although they represented a happening that will totally reshape the world of the coming decades.

Consider that we ignored all warnings about Iraq's invasion of Kuwait until hours before it occurred, although the event portends financial upheavals reminiscent of the early 1970s with threatening consequences for all financial markets.

One must make predictions only with a carefully defined set of qualifications and caveats. Indeed, in the volatile and rapidly changing world in which we live, few prognostications are easy to make. Every prediction is subject to unforeseen events or forces over which we have no control.

Clearly, the international economic repercussions stemming from the recent upheavals in the Soviet Union and in Eastern Europe cannot be underestimated.

As Joseph A. Grundfest, Stanford Law School professor who formerly served on the Securities and Exchange Commission, wrote recently, "It is difficult to overstate the severity of the problems faced by the Soviet Union and its temporarily constituent republics, on either the political or economic front... As a practical matter, the economic condition of the USSR is indistinguishable from that which would exist had the USSR lost a conventional hot war—its economy has to be rebuilt from the bottom up and top down."

The financial reverberations undoubtedly will be serious and undoubtedly will be global.

Even when focusing on only one segment of the revolution which swept over Europe—the reunification of Germany that took place on October 3—we must conclude, as did Grundfest, that it "may well turn out to be the most significant single economic development over the short-term economic horizon. From a macroeconomic perspective, it can, indeed, be compared to West Germany conducting a leveraged buyout of East Germany, its physical plant and its 16.6 million people."

Can there be any doubt that such an LBO, when coupled with the attempted emergence of neighboring economies, will have profound ramifications for the financial future of all of Europe and beyond? Its economic consequences for the world at large cannot be estimated and must be viewed with extreme caution.

Aside from the foregoing, there are heavy clouds in the sky above us.

"(The United States) enters the decade of the 1990s," to quote Charles R. Hulten's writing in the May 1990 issue of *The American Enterprise*, "riding one of the longest economic expansions in our history. But far from being the source of great optimism, other economic trends are the cause of much gloom: America is no longer competitive, we save too little and are burying the future under a mountain of debt, the standard of living of many workers has not risen in a decade."

Indeed, the decade of the 1980s is often described as one of excesses. The world accumulated debt as if it were on an unlimited credit card. But, as Milton Friedman taught us, there is no such thing as a free lunch. Ultimately, debt must be paid, and that process can be long and painful.

When you add to the fragile and problem-ridden state of the U.S. economy the oil crisis that exploded recently in the Middle East with its grave financial implications for the economies of the entire world, one cannot help but believe that a recession in the United States is certain, perhaps of a severity we fear to spell out.

Even if the Iraq-Kuwait oil crisis turns out to cause but temporary dislocations, more "fundamental financial forces are now inexorably pushing their way to the surface," financial columnist John Liscio says (*Barron's*, August 13, 1990)—fundamentals that are of a much more permanent and serious nature and a consequence of a decade-long "unprecedented reliance on debt to fuel economic growth."

Editor Alan Abelson strikes an even more ominous tone in the same issue of *Barron's* by suggesting that the coming recession will be "a credit-contraction recession" and quite different from the inventory recessions with which U.S. consumers are so familiar.

"A credit recession," Abelson says, "is something there's no modern memory of and, hence, one can only conjecture at its workings and its consequences. At worst, it would seem to encompass an unraveling of 30 years of debt abuse and entail, among other unpleasant things, an epidemic of bankruptcies. At least, it would be attended by more financial dislocation than we've experienced since the end of World War II."

Of course, not everyone subscribes to an America-in-decline thesis or even to the gloomy picture portrayed by the global debt structure.

Herbert Stein, senior fellow at the American Enterprise Institute, states, "The most important thing to know about the American economy is that it is very rich...in real terms, after allowing for inflation, the GNP (gross national product) now is six times as high as in 1929 and three times as high per capita...the GNP of the United States is probably 2½ times that of Japan and five times that of Germany...Some people think that the United States is becoming poorer because Americans and their government borrow a good deal abroad. But actually Americans are becoming richer. The productive assets owned by Americans—at home and abroad—are rising much faster than their liabilities to foreigners."

On the Global Horizon

Thus, the discussion continues—one that is of great relevance to us. The fortunes of futures markets, no differently than any other market sector, are highly dependent upon the state of national as well as global economic conditions. Should the United States (and, thus, the world) fall into a state of severe depressed economic activity, futures and options markets could very well suffer with the rest of the financial community.

Of course, in the past the world always seemed to muddle through somehow, and, even if there are some rough years ahead, beyond them is certainly a brighter tomorrow. Moreover, as in the case of Saddam Hussein's oil grab of Kuwait, world upheavals are often fuel for the fortunes of our markets and spell a continued and even greater demand for the features of futures and options.

Allow me, therefore, to finish this review on a positive note and move to a rather alluring expectation.

The tomorrow we foresee—as an unyielding consequence of the telecommunications revolution—will unquestionably include automated electronic systems for the execution of futures and options—as well as, by virtue of recent announcements, for every other form of financial medium, be they stocks, securities, options, or cash market instruments. In this respect, true to their tradition, futures markets once again blazed the trail.

Indeed, back in 1984, recognizing that the financial world was at the threshold of increased international competition as a consequence of Wriston's information revolution, the Chicago Mercantile Exchange (CME) became the first futures exchange to respond by establishing a mutual-offset arrangement with the Singapore International Monetary Exchange (SIMEX). And, not much later, the Chicago Board of Trade (CBOT), with the same purpose in mind, instituted an evening session to trade its U.S. T-bond futures contracts.

Ultimately, however, both Chicago exchanges, as well as most of the others in the world, concluded that futures and options markets must make the giant leap toward automated technology if they are to respond to the demands of globalization. The breakthrough occurred in 1986, when the CME initiated its development of GLOBEX with Reuters Holdings PLC as a joint-venture partner; this revolutionary direction for our industry was confirmed irrevocably when the CBOT subsequently also set about to develop an electronic after-hours system.

With the recent agreement between the CME and CBOT to unify their separate after-hours electronic trading systems and with the Paris-based Marche a Terme International de France already a member of the same system, GLOBEX will become the premier international futures and options trading mechanism. Indeed, when GLOBEX becomes operational early next year, it will automatically include more than 50 percent of the world's financial futures and options business. Ultimately, GLOBEX envisions linking with a number of other world markets, affording these markets the capability to present their unique product lines on an international system.

Thus, in our view, GLOBEX represents the logical extension of the financial futures revolution that began in the early 1970s. It is the only realistic response to the demands for an efficient and cost-effective capability for managing risk on a global basis.

GLOBEX will integrate the open-outcry sessions of the regular business day with the state-of-the-art, computer-generated screen technology. It will offer the world a 24-hour risk management regime that includes all the vital features of futures and options markets—their products, liquidity, trade-clearing capability, and creditworthiness. It will facilitate competitive prices, a centralized marketplace, access to markets, and a continuous flow of price information to the public.

It represents the avant garde of the financial services arena and the precursor of market systems that will serve every segment of the financial world. In a word, GLOBEX will offer the world a transaction capability that is as advanced as the imagination will allow and as far-reaching as the future itself.

Clearly then, as the old Chinese curse admonishes, we live in interesting times. That is particularly true for those of us who participate in the markets, be they securities, options, or futures.

Indeed, markets developed in the United States over this century are at the epicenter of the cause that toppled the communist order. They are at the heart of the reason why the American standard of living, its social structure, and its potential for the future are the envy of almost everyone else around the world.

It is these markets that are the quintessential element of any successful global economic system for the coming era.

Note

1. Reprinted from *Futures* magazine (November 1990), 219 Parkade, Cedar Falls, Iowa 50613.

3 THE FINANCIAL SYSTEM AND GLOBAL SOCIOECONOMIC STRUCTURAL CHANGES

Yuichiro Nagatomi

In premodern times people lived with nature's cycle—what can be called the "path of nature" or the "soft path." Then Great Britain, the United States, other parts of Europe, and Japan attained modernization and industrialization by pursuing the "path of mechanization and automation" or "the hard path" in the century and a half or so after the Industrial Revolution. That path has brought them to great material affluence, but also created environmental problems worldwide, as well as deterioration in the vitality and quality of society.

In recent years, the advanced countries' socioeconomic structure has been changing in a way that can be termed "softnomization." This means a seeking of harmony between the hard path of modern times and the soft path of premodern times—in short, a softening of the hard path. We see this process in such things as the questioning of the meaning of affluence, including the observation that the "gross national product" is just that— gross—and in the shift of emphasis from "quantitative enlargement" to "qualitative enhancement."

Softnomization

Whether one questions affluence or not, the "quantitative expansion" era, in which uniform commodities were mass produced, is being replaced with a new era in which personalities and sensibilities are given serious consideration. Emphasis is now put on producing diversified products in limited quantities and supplying various services to meet diversified and high-quality needs. There is a shift from heavier and larger industries to smaller and lighter ones. Thus, the economy is undergoing softnomization, along with science and technology.

Amidst the softnomization and service orientation of the economy, the concepts and statistics of the age of industrialization, which were geared to measuring mere goods production, should be reviewed. For example, improvements in quality and in service productivity are not adequately taken into account in the System of National Accounts of the United Nations (SNA). With limited adjustment, usually much-delayed, a price increase is assumed to be the result of inflation rather than a reflection of any improvement in the product or service. Measurement problems are particularly true for services, where output is often measured simply as the time input. If one makes the assumption that productivity in service activities was equal to that of manufacturing, annual GNP growth in the United States and Japan in the 1980s was 2 percent higher. For these sorts of reasons, GNP figures for advanced countries are less than their "real" GNP, and the gap has widened with time.

The Emergence of "Excess Money"

When the now-industrialized countries were still in the process of rapid industrialization, their business corporations required great amounts of capital for their production activities, for which they depended on banks. In short, financing and production were closely linked in this period. Now, however, after the accomplishment of industrialization in developed countries, we see the generation of "structural excess money"—massive funds exceeding those required for normal manufacturing activities. Such excess money moves freely and quickly across country borders and time zones, flitting among spot and futures markets in currency, stocks, gold, crude oil, and other commodities. This is a reflection of socioeconomic change, including softnomization, emphasis on information, service orientation, and internationalization. This socioeconomic change has caused a fundamental change in the financial structure of advanced countries.

The relevance of recent Japanese experience casts light on the phenomenon of excess money. There are three elements.

The shift from heavier, larger industry to lighter, smaller industry has meant a reduction in corporate funds required for capital equipment and inventory per production unit. Just-in-time inventories and flexible assembly lines are aspects of this softnomization; growth of the service sector is another, and is accelerating the trend.

On a more aggregate level, as industrialization progressed, the retained earnings and cash flow of corporations grew. Large corporations have increasingly come to finance production and capital investment internally, and have diversified their sources of external financing beyond banks. Many corporations have had funds in surplus to their near-term needs, and have aggressively engaged in portfolio investment activities to achieve financial gains.

Third, individual investors also have accelerated their profit-generating behavior by investing in equities and high-yield financial instruments, based both on the increases in their financial assets from saving (and borrowing) and shifts in their asset composition.

Changes in the Effects of Monetary Policy

As changes have come about in monetary policy and its effects, as well as in the financial system, banks have had to develop new fields of financing, resulting in aggressive lending for mergers and acquisitions and commercial real estate. This might trigger a market crash from overleveraging the sustainable cash flow. In any case, it has increased the risks of financial institutions, as is seen in the bankruptcies of Campeau and Drexel Burnham.

Currently such psychological factors as *omowaku*—speculation or emotional expectations and political expectations—are more influential in determining prices in financial markets than supply and demand for funds. This has brought about large fluctuations in stock prices and foreign exchange rates.

The linkage between the flow of funds through banks to businesses to finance normal production and economic activities has been weakened. Interest rates are directly affected by both international capital movements and fluctuations in foreign exchange rates. These factors have caused great changes in the effects of monetary policy on the business cycle, prices, and other economic activities. Since the flow of excess money is not strongly linked with the usual production activities, its rapid shifts have little impact on production. The greatest difference between Black Monday in 1987 and 1929 is that the former had hardly any effect on the real economy.

The linkage between money flows and inflation rates also seems to be weakened. In addition, although it requires further examination, it seems to me that the linkage between monetary indicators and the real economy has been weakened, except for the close tie to sales of real estate, where excess money is heavily invested. In order to study this issue, the Institute of Fiscal and Monetary Policy (IFMP) of Japan's Ministry of Finance has established the Research Committee on Financial Structure and Policy Effectiveness chaired by Professor Ryuichiro Tachi, former president of IFMP and a professor emeritus at Tokyo University.

Structural Measures To Reduce Excess Money

Although excess money is not strongly linked with the real economy, massive and drastic shifts of excess money can make the world economic system unstable. In light of the changes in the financial environment, policy coordination and cooperation among the monetary authorities of the major industrialized nations have been well established and have shown great success.

At the same time, in each major country and region, policy makers must respond to the factors causing these structural changes, in addition to seeking remedies to lessen the instability of the world economic system. Structural measures are needed to reduce the total quantity of excess money through the private recycling of funds. The money game in developed countries must be reshaped in more constructive ways.

In the United States, a famous professor advocates imposing on each financial market so-called circuit breakers to prevent sudden and drastic movement of funds. However, I do not think we can expect sufficient benefits from such a scheme, and it may well disturb the smooth flow of funds.

In the global society there are some regions—such as the Asia-Pacific and Eastern Europe—that need massive funds for economic development, employment expansion, and improvement of the standard of living. This is where the excess money can be used usefully.

Asia-Pacific Money and Capital Markets

The ASEAN countries (Indonesia, Brunei, Malaysia, Singapore, the Philippines, and Thailand) intend to promote export-oriented industries and actively seek to attract direct investment by foreign firms. In response, massive amounts of capital have flown in from corporations based in the industrialized countries. This has enabled the economies in the region to achieve remarkable progress. However, their domestic industries have not yet fully developed; nor, except in Singapore, have their money and capital markets, although industrial development and finance are inseparable.

The major characteristics of the financial markets in this region can be summarized as follows. First, ASEAN markets do not have long-term financial instruments, such as long-term loans, straight bonds, or convertible bonds. This is possibly due to the important role in both finance and industry played throughout the region by overseas Chinese and thus the prevalence of their concepts on financing, namely that most loans have rather short maturities.

Foreign corporations typically meet their initial (long-term) investment needs with funds from their home countries. They have difficulty raising local funds for operational activities (working capital). The second characteristic is thus the need by foreign corporations to renew local short-term borrowings again and again, or raise and bring in dollar funds from Singapore. Domestic markets have not developed enough to justify reinvesting profits or portfolio investments in these countries.

Responding to these problems, the financial authorities of these countries have made extensive efforts toward the rapid reform of their financial markets, especially since 1989. Japan would like to cooperate in the development of their financial markets. For this purpose, I have been exchanging views on financial markets with finance ministers, central bank governors, and others in the region.

Long-term capital for industrial growth is indispensable, and there is a strong demand for it to promote the growth of domestic industries in ASEAN. In order to bring about economic development in the Asia-Pacific region, and partly to provide greater stability for financial markets in the advanced countries in light of their excess money, it is important to foster ASEAN money and capital markets so they can play an intermediary role for the excess money and other private funds from advanced nations.

IFMP and FAIR (the Foundation for Advanced Information and Research) have jointly established the Committee for the Development of Money and Capital Markets, chaired by Tomomitsu Oba, former vice minister for international affairs in the Ministry of Finance (MOF), in cooperation with financial authorities in each country in the region.

Investment in human resources is essential for the development of financial markets. In 1990 IFMP, in cooperation with ADB (the Asian

Development Bank), launched a training program for high-ranking officials of Asian governments and financial institutions. It is designed to bring trainees to Japan and to send instructors from industrialized countries. Funds for the program have been appropriated in the Japanese government budget.

Conclusion

When accepting an honorary doctorate from Columbia University in 1986, former prime minister, then finance minister, Noboru Takeshita noted he had been called the "stronger yen minister." This is because during his first term at MOF the yen appreciated from 242 to 219 against the U.S. dollar. When he was appointed finance minister the second time, the yen was 250 and it subsequently strengthened to 200. Of course he played a central role in the 1985 Plaza Accord. After a later meeting with President Ronald Reagan, he told the press the yen was in the hands of market forces, at which point it started to appreciate to less than 200, peaking around 120 in 1988.

In May 1990 the yen was hovering at the 155–160 level, after almost a year and a half of steady weakening. A G-7 meeting warned that the relatively weak yen level would have adverse effects on the world economic adjustment process. We must pay careful attention to the consequences of the depreciation of the yen. These include slowing the improvement in the balance of trade and potential shortages of international liquidity.

In the United States there are views that the German emphasis on saving and resulting German investable funds, which have maintained a major part of world liquidity, will dramatically diminish because West Germany is expected to devote large amounts to reconstruct East Germany. Hence, in order to deal with such matters as the environment and Latin American problems, more attention needs to be paid to the availability and movement of Japanese funds.

I sincerely hope a world system with full freedom and vitality will be constructed through the cooperation of the United States, Japan, and Europe, and that global society will make further progress.

II BANKING AND FINANCIAL INTERMEDIARY MARKETS

4 JAPANESE BANKING, FINANCIAL MARKETS, AND COMPETITIVE EQUALITY

Shohei Yamada

Focusing on the equality of competitive conditions in Japan's financial markets, this chapter provides a perspective on the financial reform process in Japan. Over the past ten years or so, reforms to make these markets a more competitive arena have achieved steady progress.

"Financial reform" means the efforts by both the market and its regulators to restructure the financial system and the monetary authority. It is referred to as "liberalization" in Japan and "deregulation" in the United States. But liberalization is an inaccurate description for the overall process that has taken place in Japan, since there should be no implication that financial markets and institutions will be left unregulated. Regulation will continue, although in different forms, to protect depositors, secure public confidence in the financial system, and ensure stable and sound financial markets. What is unfolding today, therefore, is an evolution, not a discarding, of the regulatory system. Thus, the word *liberalization* is used to emphasize relaxation or removal of constraints that have limited competition or isolated markets from general economic forces.

The Difference Between Liberalization and Deregulation

The financial reform processes in Japan and the United States share many similarities. However, there are also many differences. This section considers the differences between liberalization (in Japan) and deregulation (in the United States) that have produced changes in the process of improving competitive conditions, and reviews the catalysts for and characteristics of the reform processes in the two countries.

In the United States, the main catalyst for financial reform was the high inflation and high interest rates that developed under deposit interest rate regulations. In Japan, by contrast, a fundamental change in the economy—an end to high growth—and the associated changes in money flows were the main factors in financial reform. This difference explains why the reform process was very rapid (for a short time at least) in the United States, whereas it proceeded at a slower, steadier pace in Japan. This is the most conspicuous difference between the reforms in the two countries.

Moreover, the United States resorted to regulatory codification in promoting reforms in response to a crisis situation in financial markets. In Japan there was no situation requiring crisis management, so the liberalization process was pursued gradually on the initiative of the regulatory authorities. At the meetings of the Working Group of the Joint Japan-United States Ad Hoc Group on Yen-Dollar Exchange Rate Issues, Ministry of Finance Vice Minister Tomomitsu Oba, who led the Japanese delegation, often emphasized a step-by-step approach. This emphasis obviously stemmed from the historical background in Japan.

The Regulatory Authorities' Liberalization Initiatives

In Japan, "liberalization" is a broad concept covering the development of the bond and short-term money markets, the removal of constraints on interest rates and foreign exchange transactions, the expansion of cross-border financial transactions, the development of new financial products, and review of segmentation in the financial system.

The progress of liberalization has changed the basic orientation of Japan's banking industry from one of cooperation to one characterized by competition. It has also brought about diversification of banking services and, as a result, diversification in the tools of competition. It should be noted in this context that Japanese regulators have often taken a strong initiative in promoting liberalization. This initiative was driven by the progress of internationalization and the rapid expansion of Japanese-financial-institution presence in offshore markets. Therefore, it is generally thought, liberalization measures have in many instances been the product of a strong intention among regulators to create a more competitive market and to even out the playing field.

Factors Behind Liberalization

Advances in information and communications technology, which have lowered the costs of financial transactions and encouraged the development of new financial products, have spurred liberalization, as is discussed by other authors.

Liberalization has also been influenced by increased yield sensitivity in the household sector, the ultimate source of funds in the economy. This subject is returned to later.

Changes in the fundamentals of the economy have been a major influence on liberalization. Accompanying the shift from the high-growth era to one of slower growth, the central government budget deficit expanded rapidly to colossal proportions. Starting from 1975, government bonds with maturities of ten years were floated in enormous sums. In mid-1990, the balance of outstanding government bonds stands at approximately 160 trillion yen.

Before 1975, a bond market where interest rates were determined by market forces was virtually nonexistent. The need to expedite placement of government bonds issued in large volume, however, led to expansion and systemic improvement in the securities market as well as phenomenal growth and development. Long-term government debt gradually reached maturity, beginning from 1985. These near-maturity government bonds, which were freely traded in large volume on the unregulated secondary market, had a great impact on the liberalization of short-term interest rates.

In addition, liberalization has been affected by the rapid internationalization of finance. This process was fueled by the complete revision in 1980 of the Foreign Exchange and Foreign Trade Control Law, which removed in principle all restraints on foreign transactions, and by the strong expansion of the Japanese economy. Accompanying the increasingly closer linkages between domestic and overseas markets, systemic and transaction practices were gradually made to conform to international standards, while the expansion of operations in open markets overseas contributed to the growth of "open market financing" or financial liberalization as explained below.

Spurred by these four factors, the liberalization process has been steady but gradual, spanning a period of over ten years. Its specific aspects in the late 1980s are described in the next section.

Characteristics of Liberalization

The Decline in the Share of Indirect Financing

Japanese banks traditionally have played a far more important role in financial intermediation than their counterparts in the United States. One of the principal reasons is that the securities market was considerably underdeveloped. Until the first half of the 1970s, there was no keenly felt need for a large, developed securities market to absorb government bonds, nor did businesses actively use the securities market as a major channel for their funding operations. In fact, bond financing was a privilege granted only to a small number of large capital-intensive corporations (such as electrical power utilities and railroads) with various restraints imposed on the primary market. In the short-term money market, interbank and *gensaki* (repurchase) transactions constituted the main components.

The predominance of indirect financing, characteristic of Japan's financial markets, has gradually declined in tandem with the progress of liberalization. And the most important contributing factors to this trend are the powerful development of the securities market and the start of new short-term money markets. This is evident from the evolution in corporate funding sources shown in Table 4–1. Among the market developments since the late 1970s the following phenomena are worthy of special note.

Decline in Market Share of Private Financial Intermediaries

In this era of decline in the share of indirect corporate financing, the market share of private financial intermediaries, commercial banks in particular, has shown the most pronounced decrease. In this context, the shift in corporate financing implies new market entries by other categories of financial institutions. It is not difficult to imagine that this evolution has transformed the banking industry into a more competitive arena. Another point of note is the major change in bank behavior patterns in the lending market, which was evident during this period and is discussed later.

Table 4–1. External Funding by Enterprises.

Overall (in 100 million ¥, %)

Category	Fiscal Year	1975	1983	1984	1985	1986	1987	1988
External funding		183,183(100.0)	193,180(100.0)	251,225(100.0)	269,446(100.0)	319,074(100.0)	484,664(100.0)	475,767(100.0)
Capital increases	(I)	13,152(7.2)	21,682(11.2)	25,464(10.1)	26,048(9.7)	29,744(9.3)	48,772(10.1)	73,541(15.4)
Bond issuance	(II)	15,486(8.5)	13,528(7.0)	18,932(7.5)	20,623(7.7)	35,425(11.1)	42,655(8.8)	31,297(6.6)
(I) + (II)		28,638(15.6)	35,210(18.2)	44,396(17.7)	46,671(17.3)	65,169(20.4)	91,427(18.9)	104,838(22.0)
Long-term loans	(III)	76,176(41.6)	61,067(31.6)	62,211(24.7)	92,883(34.5)	128,467(40.3)	207,629(42.8)	192,924(40.6)
Short-term loans	(IV)	78,369(42.8)	96,903(50.2)	144,618(57.5)	129,892(48.2)	125,438(39.3)	185,607(38.3)	178,005(37.4)
(III) + (IV)		154,545(84.4)	157,970(81.8)	206,829(82.2)	222,775(82.7)	353,905(79.6)	393,236(81.1)	370,929(78.0)

Companies capitalized at 1 billion ¥ or more

Category	Fiscal Year	1975	1983	1984	1985	1986	1987	1988
External funding		98,358(100.0)	45,503(100.0)	66,022(100.0)	71,298(100.0)	83,662(100.0)	139,999(100.0)	194,001(100.0)
Capital increases	(I)	9,655(9.8)	20,315(44.7)	24,800(37.6)	24,773(34.7)	28,088(33.6)	47,962(34.2)	73,144(37.7)
Bond issuance	(II)	15,380(15.6)	13,134(28.9)	18,420(27.9)	20,118(28.2)	34,763(41.5)	41,136(29.4)	29,826(15.4)
(I) + (II)		25,035(25.5)	33,449(73.5)	43,220(65.5)	44,891(63.0)	62,851(75.1)	89,098(63.6)	102,970(53.1)
Long-term loans	(III)	43,163(43.9)	△ 3,704(△ 8.1)	△ 4,897(△ 7.4)	4,570(6.4)	14,873(17.8)	26,458(18.9)	27,453(14.1)
Short-term loans	(IV)	30,160(30.7)	15,758(34.6)	27,699(42.0)	21,837(30.6)	5,938(7.1)	24,443(17.5)	63,578(32.8)
(III) + (IV)		73,323(74.6)	12,054(26.5)	22,802(34.5)	26,407(37.0)	20,811(24.9)	50,901(36.4)	91,031(46.9)

Notes:
1. Figures indicate increases during the fiscal year.
2. Figures inside ( ) indicate component percentages.
3. △ denotes a negative number.
Source: Ministry of Finance, Annual Statistics on Corporate Businesses 1975, 1983–1988.

Shift to Open-Market Financing

Seen from another perspective, this trend means increased reliance on open markets, such as the securities market, by the financial system as a whole. It is also referred to as "securitization" and has brought about a significant change in the flow of money during this period.

It should be mentioned in this connection that seeing such securitization merely as a change in the form of funds transfer is not the whole picture. Why is this so? The securities market, as a segment of the financial system, supplies liquidity to the real economy. An economic unit can obtain liquidity by disposing of its assets. If such assets are nonstandardized financial products—as in the case of bill discounts, for example—a long-term bank–client relationship should exist as a prerequisite. If, by contrast, the assets in question are standardized financial products such as marketable securities, they can be easily cashed in the open market. The resulting liquidity can be called market-oriented liquidity. As a result of the growing weight of "open market financing" within the financial system, the traditional bank–client relationship has been undergoing significant change. Furthermore, the shift to open-market financing has encouraged the introduction of new financial products and has thus stimulated competition within the financial system.

Growing Yield Sensitivity of Individuals and Businesses

During the 1970s and '80s, financial assets held by the household sector increased at a rapid pace, and, from 1975 onward, the rate of growth in the balance of financial assets outpaced the rate of growth in nominal GNP by a large margin (occasionally by more than double the rate). This rapid accumulation of financial assets brought about higher interest rate elasticity in asset selection and a wider variety of asset forms. These are some of the factors behind the decline of bank funding in the corporate sector and concomitant growth in open market financing, and the liberalization of interest rates.

The shift in financial behavior toward greater emphasis on yield performance also became highly visible as a matter of course in the corporate business sector. As the means of financing diversified, funding operations in the form of bank borrowings were gradually curtailed, while equity financing, often in foreign currency, increased its share of the total financing. In funds management, the share of ordinary bank deposits and other financial products under interest rate controls was reduced in favor of investment in market interest rate assets, taking advantage of the diversification of funds management vehicles.

The Recent Progress of Liberalization

The "Report of the Working Group of the Joint Japan-United States Ad Hoc Group on Yen-Dollar Exchange Rates Issues" (May 30, 1984) and "The Current Situation and Outlook for Financial Liberalization and the Internationalization of the Yen" released in May 1985, the "Action Program" of July 1984, and the "Current Outlook on Financial and Capital Market Liberalization and Internationalization" published in June 1987, provided important guidelines for the progress of financial liberalization. However, since much is already known about these reports, they are not discussed here. Instead, this section briefly explains recent liberalization measures based on the reports, namely, the liberalization of deposit interest rates and expansion and systemic improvements in the short-term money market and various other financial markets.

Liberalization of Deposit Interest Rates

In examining liberalization of deposit interest rates, it is necessary to go back to the introduction of negotiable certificates of deposits (CDs) in May 1979. With the interest rates freely determined by the offering bank dependent on maturity, this new instrument marked the first step in the liberalization of interest rates. It should be noted, however, that the introduction of CDs had more significance as a measure for the expansion and systemic improvement of the short-term money market. Recommendation 1979 of the Council for Financial Systems Research stated its rationale as:

> The short-term money market has not been well developed in Japan as yet. Under such circumstances, the introduction of CDs as a new financial product, backed by the credibility of financial institutions, and the creation of the CD market provides organic linkages between the existing call and bill markets and the gensaki (repurchase) market through extensive participation by financial and non-financial organizations. This is expected to contribute to the further expansion and systemic improvement of the short-term money market.

When CDs were introduced, quotas on offerings were established, based on issuer net worth, with a view toward averting the drastic impact CDs might have on the entire short-term money market. Initially, this quota was set at 10 percent of the issuing company's net worth. The standard was gradually relaxed, and in October 1987 it was abolished altogether. (For foreign banks, the quota was abolished in April 1987.)

The minimum transaction unit for CDs was also progressively lowered from the initial 500 million yen to 50 million yen in April 1988, which remains in effect today. Moreover, maturities, initially from three months to six months, were extended to periods of two weeks to two years starting from April 1988.

Now let us turn to interest rate liberalization for large time deposits. In this respect, the Action Program mentioned earlier laid down a timetable specifying that "interest rate controls on large unit time deposits be gradually relaxed and abolished by the spring of 1987." As the first step, interest rates on time deposits of 1 billion yen or more were liberalized from October 1985. The minimum for deregulated time deposits has been lowered in stages, at 10 million yen since October 1989. This amount will be lowered to 3 million yen in the fall of 1991. The maturity range was initially set between three months and two years, the same range applicable to regulated time deposits. But in October 1987, it was changed to between one month and two years. These developments show that the substance of the Action Program has already been implemented.

Measures also have been taken to liberalize interest rates for small deposits. The first step was the introduction of deposits offering market rate-linked interest rates or money market certificates (MMCs). This move stemmed from the consideration that in any attempts for interest rate liberalization, including small time deposits, market disturbances from abrupt changes in the financial order should be avoided. In this context, MMCs were adopted as a strategic financial product. They display a middle-of-the-road orientation between a completely freed interest product and those still subject to controls. It is expected at the time that, if MMCs were introduced as quasi-large-unit time deposits (beween large-unit and small-lot time deposits in size) and offering interest rates determined by a formula subject to reviews and gradual modifications, MMCs would serve as a catalyst for smooth expansion in the area of deposits offering flexibly changing interest rates.

MMCs were introduced in March 1985 with maturities ranging from one to six months and offering interest rates set at levels 0.75 percentage points lower than the average annual rate offered on CDs. The minimum acceptable deposit amount was initially set at 50 million yen while a ceiling for their total outstanding was set at 75 percent of the issuing bank's net worth. These limits were relaxed step by step: maturities were changed in April 1987 to range from one month to two years, and the ceiling on outstanding

MMCs was removed in October 1987. (For foreign banks, the total balance ceiling was abolished in April 1987.) Similarly, the minimum acceptable amount was lowered in stages; since October 1987 it has stood at 10 million yen. In October 1989, MMCs became a category of large-unit time deposits and fulfilled their expected function in the process of interest rate liberalization.

Another item on the timetable laid down in the report "Current Outlook for Financial and Capital Market Liberalization and Internationalization," released in June 1987, was the introduction of small-lot MMCs. The report stated:

> In the liberalization of interest rates, the minimum acceptable deposit amount will continue to be lowered in stages, together with measures for the relaxation of remaining limits. In the process, efforts will be made to establish a clear perspective on the time frame for the introduction of small lot money market certificates as soon as possible.

Based on this recommendation, the small-lot MMC was put on the market in June 1989. This instrument can be bought for a minimum of 3 million yen in five maturities: 3, 6, 12, 24, or 36 months. It started with two different maturities (6 and 12). In October 1989, the three other maturities were added. The small MMCs are fast taking root as a popular vehicle of individual savings. The reduction in April 1990 of the minimum acceptable deposit amount to 1 million yen is expected to further enhance its MMC's role as the front runner in the game of interest rate liberalization for small deposits.

Pending issues are the liberalization of interest rates on time deposits in amounts less than 10 million yen and on liquid deposits. The Ministry of Finance has commissioned the Financial Issues Research Group (a private advisory body to the Director General of Banking Bureau, Ministry of Finance) to research these issues and is studying the necessary procedures in concrete terms for pursuing work with the group in early 1991.

Liberalization of interest rates in Japan, which started in 1979 with the introduction of CDs, has been a slow and gradual process. It was particularly so at the early stage. By the late 1980s, however, the pace of growth in the share of "free interest" deposits including small MMCs has accelerated considerably. As of October 1989, that share accounted for 52 percent of the total balance of deposits. (Free interest deposits here are made up of the total of large-unit time deposits, small-lot MMCs, MMCs, nonresident yen deposits, foreign currency deposits, and CDs.) By comparing this figure with 38 percent in the same month a year earlier, one can see how rapidly these accounts have increased their share in total savings.

Deposit interest rates in Japan have not yet been fully liberalized, and interest rate liberalization for liquid deposits is awaiting the outcome of further study. On the other hand, steady progress has been achieved in the liberalization of time deposit interest rates. In this area, further lowering of the minimum acceptable deposit amounts for large-unit time deposits and small-lot MMCs is expected to continue. Thus, in May 1990, the Financial Issues Research Group published a report on interest rate liberalization for time deposits of less than 10 million yen. The report urged that remaining regulations be dismantled and liberalization be completed at the earliest possible date. While the report gave no specific date, the chairman of the group, Professor Keimei Kaizuka, reportedly responded to a press inquiry with his personal view that the most desirable time span would be approximately three years. In the fall of 1990, new MMCs were introduced as transition vehicles in the process of liberalization.

Expansion and Improvement in the Short-Term Money Market

Development of the Domestic CP Market. Commercial paper (CP) is issued by corporations with superior credit standing to produce short-term funds on an unsecured basis. First developed (in somewhat different form than today's CP) in the United States, this instrument has come to play an important role in short-term funding in the Euromarket in the United Kingdom and in France. In Japan, controversy persisted as to the legal status of CP, which prevented its issuance until November 1987, when both banks and securities firms were approved to handle sales and secondary market dealing. In addition, call money brokers are also allowed to participate in the secondary market transactions.

In the beginning, the CP market in Japan provided businesses with a flexible means of short-term funding and offered investors an attractive short-term investment vehicle. As such, CP was expected to play an important role in fueling the expansion of Japan's short-term money market. The CP market has lived up to this expectation with rapid growth and a scale that exceeded 10 trillion yen in mid-1990.

Since the CP market began operations, rules for issuance have been reviewed at regular intervals, and, at the review in January 1990, the number of companies qualified for CP issuance was increased from 410 to 530. More significantly, securities firms were put on the list.

Direct Dealing in the Call and Bill Markets. In Japan, the call and bill markets have long held an important position in the operation of monetary policy by the central bank. For this reason, there has been a de facto obligation to use call money brokers as intermediaries for dealings in these markets. The rationale is that such intermediation enables the central bank to monitor market developments easily. Call money broker intermediation surely expedites procurement and management of short-term funds by financial institutions. On the other hand, commission payments are involved. Against this background, Japanese banks and foreign banks together sought permission for direct dealing, and obtained it in December 1989.

The Emergence of New Financial Markets

Growth and Diversification of the Futures Markets.   In May 1987 residents in Japan were allowed to participate in overseas financial futures transactions. The permission to deal with nonresidents was limited to institutions having strong needs and sufficiently equipped with professional know-how in risk management, such as banks, securities companies, life insurance companies, casualty insurance companies, and investment trust management companies.

Within Japan, bond futures trading started in October 1985 on the Tokyo Stock Exchange, and stock futures trading was introduced in June 1987 on the Osaka Stock Exchange. These developments were followed by the enactment of the Financial Futures Trading Law in May 1988 to regulate and foster the development of the financial futures markets. Stock price index futures trading made its debut in September 1988. In 1989 the Tokyo Financial Futures Exchange was established and transactions began that June.

With construction of the legal and other infrastructure mentioned above, the futures markets are expected to achieve steady growth, with many parties participating from various sectors.

The Euroyen Market.   Euroyen loans have been liberalized in stages since 1983 and, as a result, the loan balance has shown a marked increase. The liberalization process started with permission granted to nonresidents to engage in short-term lending transactions in June 1983, followed by liberalization regarding short-term lending to residents in June 1984, and medium-term and long-term loans to nonresidents in April 1985. With permission to engage in medium-term and long-term lending, granted to residents in May 1989, the liberalization process was complete.

As recommended in the 1984 Report of the Working Group of the Joint

Japan-United States Ad Hoc Committee on Yen-Dollar Exchange Rate Issues, the guidelines for the issuance of Euroyen bonds by nonresidents were gradually relaxed to push the internationalization of the Japanese currency through the expansion of the Euroyen market. In the process, the qualification standards for bond issuance were relaxed in stages. In April 1986, standards for private corporate bonds were completely suppressed by the credit rating system, combined with the removal of all remaining restrictions on bond issuance by those with A or higher ratings, in the same way as with public bonds. This measure has produced significant growth in the number and amounts of bonds issued in the market. In June 1986, foreign banks were added to the list of Euroyen bond issuers.

Issuance of Euroyen bonds by residents began in 1980 under a special measure that only allowed private placements in Middle East markets to encourage inflows of oil money. Later, in April 1984, guidelines were relaxed to support the internationalization of the yen. The market infrastructure was completed in April 1985 with the exemption from income tax of interest and discounts payable to nonresident investors. The number of qualified issuers has risen markedly following the introduction of the credit rating system in July 1987.

Increased Market Access by Foreign Banks

In the context of the recent liberalization process, the preceding discussions mainly concerned the liberalization of deposit interest rates, the diversification of financial markets, the improvement in the market infrastructures, and the relaxation of various constraints. These measures foster competition on an equal footing among all financial institutions, including foreign banks in Japan. We now look specifically at the expansion of market access by foreign banks.

In April 1984 foreign banks were allowed to participate in the government bond underwriting syndicate and, since then, their underwriting shares have gradually increased. On the other hand, as demand became increasingly vocal for a shift from syndicate underwriting to a full tender formula, 40 percent of the amount issued was put to competitive tender, beginning from April 1989. This percentage rose to 60 percent by October 1990. Moreover, a complete shift to the tender formula by the end of 1991 is under study. This development suggests that foreign banks and securities companies will be able to secure larger underwriting shares and participate even more actively in the determination of offering prices.

In 1985 nine foreign banks were allowed to enter the trust business market. This followed the Report of the Working Group of the Joint Japan-United States Ad Hoc Committee on Yen-Dollar Exchange Rate Issues and included a consensus that foreign banks should be given access to trust business to the same extent as given to Japanese trust banks. (There are eight Japanese trust banks, including Daiwa Bank.) All the new entries have posted satisfactory results by staging aggressive operations, each in its own way. As of March 1989, combined trust properties held by these nine foreign banks stood at 3 trillion yen, almost 86 percent above the level of one year earlier. In the field of specified money in trust (*tokkin*) and fund trusts particularly, these banks now have a combined share of 5.3 percent and 8.5 percent, respectively, in just a little over four years since their market entry.

Competitive Equality Within the Banking System

The main theme here and in the next section is the competitive relations between foreign banks and their Japanese counterparts, but the scope of this examination is not confined to just that. Rather, it considers the degree of competition among all of Japan's financial markets.

This section examines competitive conditions or the degree of competitiveness using a method of analysis based on the theory of industrial organization. At one time the Japanese banking system had an extensive regulatory framework that limited competition. Some believe, nonetheless, that even in those days the Japanese system was more competitive than generally thought. They even assert the Japanese banking system was more competitive than that of the United States (Sakakibara and Feldman, 1983). Although the first argument is now generally accepted, there are strong counterarguments to the second assertion. As Cargill (1985) points out, there are many critics of the "structure-performance" framework approach, drawing on both econometrics and economic theory, who have serious doubts about the framework's credibility as a tool for analysis of any significance.

As noted by Royama and Tsutsui, it is not clear whether the traditional thesis in industrial organization theory (a correlation between market structure and market performance) has been valid in Japanese banking (Tsutsui and Royama, 1986). Generally following the work of Tsutsui and Royama, the paragraphs below examine several important issues taken up in the theory of industrial organization.

Table 4–2.   Cumulative Concentration Among All Member Banks (Loan Balance: Fiscal Year-End, in Percentages).

Top banks	1960	1965	1970	1975	1980	1984
Top bank	7.1	6.7	6.1	7.3	7.1	7.0
3 banks	20.6	19.6	17.9	19.2	18.8	19.1
5 banks	32.0	31.4	28.0	30.8	30.2	30.8
10 banks	51.8	54.2	45.4	48.9	48.2	48.5
No. of banks	87	86	86	86	86	86

Notes:
1. Member banks (87) consist of city banks (13), long-term credit banks (3), trust banks (7), and regional banks (64). All are members of the Federation of Bankers Associations of Japan (see text).
2. The years 1970 and 1975 lack continuity due to mergers of banks (Daiichi–Kangyo in 1971 and Taiyo–Kobe in 1973).
Source: Royama, Shoichi and Tachi, Ryuichiro, *Japanese Finance (I) A New Perspective* (Tokyo: Tokyo University Press, November, 1986), p. 211.

Industrial Concentration

Industrial concentration is regarded as the most important factor giving shape to market structure. In the case of banking, however, there is no clear consensus on the concept of industrial concentration. City banks, regional banks, credit associations (*shinkin*), credit unions, and agricultural cooperatives all compete with commercial banks by offering clearing functions through their checking accounts. If they are to be grouped together as "banks," there would be a very low industrial concentration among the Japanese banks. Of these various institutions, 87 are members of the Federation of Bankers Associations of Japan. Industrial concentration, examined on the assumption that Japan's banking industry comprises all 87 members, is no higher than in other industries, using loan balances as the "output" measure. The cumulative concentration of the top ten banks has been around 50 percent (see Table 4–2). Of the approximately 200 sectors in Japanese industry, there are only 10 or so sectors in which the cumulative concentration comes to less than 50 percent (*The Fair Trade Commission Report*, 1969).

If the assumption is that the banking industry forms regional markets rather than a national market, the degree of concentration becomes higher. Assuming that the banking market is segmented into prefectural markets, the market concentration is higher still. Among regional banks and credit unions, the cumulative concentration ratios of the top three banks (CR3) in each prefecture range from 0.967 (Kochi) to 0.251 (Tokyo). In almost all prefectures, however, the figure is higher than 80 percent, much higher than the figure (approximately 20 percent) calculated on the assumption all these banks form a single nationwide market. Because this chapter primarily concerns the competitive relations between foreign banks and their Japanese counterparts, institutions in the prefectural markets are of little significance.

In the past, empirical analyses have focused mainly on whether positive correlations exist between the degree of industrial concentration and the rate of profit. But the results are not at all conclusive. The analyses certainly indicate positive correlations. Still, the overall conclusion is that they are of minimal significance.

New Entry

A bank licensing or approval system exists in every country. In Japan, a bank must obtain approval from the Minister of Finance before it begins operations (Article 4 of the Banking Law). Except during a short period after World War II, it seems the Ministry of Finance has had no intention of approving new banks. It appears rather that the Ministry has sought to enhance efficiency in the management of banks through mergers. The rationale for this policy orientation can be found in the two basic principles of banking administration: (1) depositor protection and stabilization of the banking system, which has always been a major priority since the enactment of the banking Law in 1927 (after the banks' failure in the common confusion arising from the Great Earthquake of 1923 and the global Depression), and (2) efficiency in bank management, which came to be emphasized somewhat later. It can probably be said that in terms of these principles, restriction of new entrants into banking has had positive implications for both city and regional banks. It should not be forgotten in this regard, however, that insofar as these banks are concerned, market concentration has never been high. On the other hand, the number of credit unions serving small local markets increased from 232 in 1954 to 540 in 1968. (After that, the number of credit unions gradually declined to 419 by 1988.) This means the policy of limiting new entry was managed quite flexibly as far as credit unions are concerned. Although new domestic banks were a rarity, the number of foreign banks rose from 53 in 1977 to 83 in 1988. Moreover, foreign banks established trust bank subsidiaries in 1985.

Nonprice Competition

The number and location of branch offices, gifts, advertising, business days, business hours, and service installations such as CDs and ATMs (automated teller machines) are seen as means of nonprice competition. Opening branches and business days are regulated by law, while other means are subject to administrative guidance or autonomous regulations among the members of the Federation of Bankers' Associations of Japan. That is, there have been practically no unregulated means of competition. Of these means of nonprice competition, the number and location of branches are the most important.

The opening and relocation of branches requires approval by the Minister of Finance (Article 8 of the Banking Law). Japan is not exceptional in this regard. However, it is necessary to examine whether control of the branch network has been effective in actually curtailing the number of branches. There are observations that, although control of the branch network is supposed to have been effective for a fairly long period of time after the war, its effectiveness has declined in recent years. Opening and maintaining branches is costly and regional competition is excessive. Given such considerations, it is widely recognized that even complete liberalization of branch opening regulations would not result in a rapid spread of new branches in many parts of the country.

Simply put, control of the branch network is no longer as effective as before. Tsutsui and Royama conducted an analysis on the premise that if control of the branch network is effective, the number of branches becomes a given exogenous variable for a bank and thus appears in the bank's cost function (Tsutsui and Royama, 1986, p. 206). This suggests that the effectiveness of control of the branch network began to weaken from 1979.

At present, foreign bank applications to open new branches are granted as long as standard legal requirements are met. Therefore, assuming that the start of banking operations by a newly formed company and the commencement of banking services through a new branch should not be differentiated in practical terms, it is safe to say that there are no impediments to new entries by foreign banks into the Japanese banking market.

Economies of Scale

There are several empirical studies that offer evidence for the existence of economies of scale in the banking industry. Tsutsui and Royama (1986, p. 207) for example, conducted an estimation based on the Cobb-Douglas function and the trans-log expense function, using 145 city and regional banks as samples. They also conducted two additional estimations after dividing the banks into two groups based on size (in 1982). The results showed economies of scale exist, and larger banks exhibit larger economies of scale in proportion to their size.

The existence of economies of scale is believed to form a barrier to entry. However, there is not much point in emphasizing this fact since, as far as banks of national scale are concerned, no new entries were permitted for many years. Rather, the existence of economies of scale was quoted as a rationale by those who advocate the policy of encouraging banks to merge to enhance management efficiency. Those in academic circles generally responded to this policy stance unfavorably. As one of the reasons for their objections, they contended that economies of scale in the banking industry, if they exist at all, are insignificant.

In this connection, there is a growing popularity for the view that real advantages can be achieved when a bank provides a variety of services under the same roof. Resulting higher productivity of information is cited as a reason. This view emphasizes the importance of joint production or economies of scope rather than economies of scale. Equally appealing is the view that larger banks have a greater ability to pool risks, and that this ability is the source of any economies of scale.

Increased Competition from Liberalization Since 1975

There is no doubt that financial liberalization and internationalization have caused the basic orientation of the banking industry to shift from cooperation to competition. Although such changes in circumstances appeared within both financial institutions themselves and the regulatory regime, the development of the bond market and participation in open markets abroad had a major impact. The shift to open-market financing has meant new entry in a broader sense of the term. There is little doubt that these changes have had a substantial impact on industrial organization and increased competition within the banking industry. Closer analyses of these developments, using the methods developed by the theory of industrial organization, must be undertaken in the future.

Foreign Bank Performance and Competitive Conditions

The 1981 amendment to the Banking Law established the principle of equal national treatment for foreign banks operating in Japan, meaning foreign banks are to be treated on the same basis as their Japanese counterparts in the domestic financial system. If the main objective of liberalization is to build an infrastructure for fair and equitable competition, then, as many argue, this objective has already been achieved as far as the banks themselves are concerned. That is, at the very least, equal competitive conditions now exist in the regulatory framework and regulations, and there is little evidence that foreign banks are discriminated against in favor of their Japanese counterparts in Japan's financial markets. Moreover, in light of the main factors of the market structure analyzed in the previous section, there seems to be little evidence to substantiate the contention that competitive conditions are not equal for these two groups.

Decline in Foreign Bank Market Share

Now let us consider foreign bank performance and competitive conditions based on common-sense business observations. Bank performance can be shown by various indicators such as profit, rate of profit, profit from fund management, and the expense ratio. However, this section uses lending share as a performance indicator because data are readily available and easy to compare with those for Japanese banks (mainly, for the purpose of discussion here, comprising members of the Federation of Bankers' Associations of Japan). At the end of 1979, the share of foreign bank loans outstanding as a percentage of the total loan market was 3.41 percent. Nine years later, by the end of 1988, this share had declined to 1.95 percent. (Different figures are often cited, depending on the statistical bases.) During this period, the number of foreign banks operating in Japan increased from 71 to 83. Moreover, the liberalization process made great progress during those years and competitive conditions were made more equal in the financial markets. These developments notwithstanding, the market share held by foreign banks declined substantially. At a glance, this fact raises strong doubts about the credibility of the contention that liberalization has made competitive conditions more equal or even that competitive equality has almost been realized in Japanese financial markets. The first half of this section is devoted to an assessment of this development.

In considering this subject, let us assume a market where structure, functions, and behavior patterns, combined with official regulations, ensure competitive equality for all participants. Even in such a market, certain groups may diminish their shares. As time passes, the market and its environment are subject to constant and dynamic changes. Even if competitive conditions remain equal, a negative bias can develop in a company's performance if its management has failed, for one reason or another or due to inherent impediments, to respond effectively to such changes with a precise demand analysis, investment priorities, manpower strategy, and expense allocation.

The Decline in City Bank Market Share

Exposed to the harsh wind of liberalization, Japanese bank operations have undergone radical changes during the period from about 1975 to 1989. This evolution, which has resulted in a significant decline in the role banks play in corporate funding, has similarly taken place in the United States. In Japan, however, it occurred with far greater magnitude. This difference resulted mainly from the existence of a highly underdeveloped bond market and the predominance of indirect financing in Japan up to 1975 (the year symbolically marked, by the consensus view, as the starting point of liberalization).

The decline in the share of banks in financial markets has been most pronounced in the intense turf war between banks and securities companies. It flared up in 1975 when securities companies started drastically increasing *gensaki* (repurchase) transactions. This type of transaction was introduced during the 1950s but came into importance in 1975 when a large quantity of government bonds was offered for trading, thereby making available a highly liquid free interest rate instrument for corporate customers. It was followed during the 1980s by the medium-term government bond fund developed by securities companies, which targeted individual investors.

The decline in bank borrowings was far more conspicuous in corporate funding, which developed at a particularly rapid pace in the case of large corporations. Table 4–1 shows this transition from 1975 through 1988. During this period, businesses with capitalization of 1 billion yen or more cut their reliance on bank borrowings from three-fourths to less than half of their total funding.

Responses to the Declines

There have been many changes in interest rates and other economic factors in the last 16 years. Underlying these changes, the decline in the share of banks in the financial markets can be observed as a long-term trend. How have banks responded? Major changes in their behavior patterns can be summarized as follows: (1) middle and retail markets have been cultivated; (2) manpower has been cut and other cost reduction measures have been taken in tandem with greater investment in automation; (3) international and securities operations have been strengthened; and (4) new products have been developed and services diversified.

Of these items, discussion here focuses only on the first two. As illustrated in Table 4–3, customer composition has shifted from big businesses (until the 1970s) to middle-market companies to individual customers, reflecting business defection in both fund raising and fund management. Consequently, as is well known, banks have been engaged in intense competition in their efforts to acquire new customers. In this context, foreign banks were placed in a different position. To begin with, the operations of most foreign banks were based on a philosophy of entirely excluding retail banking from their lines of business, and in terms of the scale of their operations and the number of branches, they were severely handicapped in responding to changes in the market environment. In other words, foreign banks suffered from internal constraints blocking their active participation in the race for new market development. (Foreign bank behavior patterns have also changed along with the evolution in the market environment. Despite differences in their outlook for the Tokyo market and the basic philosophy held by each foreign bank, they have generally displayed (1) an emphasis on dealing operations, (2) cultivation of fee-earning business, (3) new product development, and (4) pursuit of higher return on assets. For this reason, they even curtailed lending to certain customers during a period of time. It should be added, however, that there are still foreign banks that place emphasis on long-term bank-customer relationships.)

Let us reconfirm here that, as mentioned earlier, the decline in the share of banks in the financial markets represents new entry opportunities in a broader sense of the term. It has sparked more intensive competition and, as a result, gradually squeezed spreads on loans. To offset the thinning margins, banks have aggressively pursued manpower cuts, rationalization, and automation in office operations. As evidence of the success of such efforts, the amount of funds per employee increased from 301 million yen in March 1975 to 1.6 billion yen in March 1989. It is understandable that the drive for cost reduction was easier for Japanese banks with large-scale operations and considerably more difficult for foreign banks far smaller in size.

Table 4–3. Shares of Loans to Middle and Small Businesses and Individuals (in Percentages).

	1978	1979	1980	1981	1982	1983	1984	1985	1986	1987	1988
A bank	45(9)	45(9)	46(9)	45(9)	47(10)	49(9)	52(10)	54(11)	59(12)	63(15)	66(18)
B bank	58(9)	50(9)	50(9)	51(10)	50(9)	52(9)	54(8)	56(8)	61(10)	67(13)	69(15)
C bank	57(11)	48(10)	48(10)	48(10)	48(10)	49(10)	51(9)	54(9)	59(10)	64(15)	69(16)
D bank	46(9)	48(10)	48(10)	48(10)	48(8)	49(9)	51(9)	53(10)	61(12)	67(15)	73(18)
E bank	60(9)	51(10)	51(10)	52(10)	52(10)	52(9)	54(8)	56(9)	61(10)	68(14)	73(19)

Notes:

1. Figures indicate shares of loans to middle- and small-sized companies and individuals in total loan balances at five city banks. Figures in ( ) show percentages of loans to individuals.

2. Percentages are based on loan balances at each fiscal year-end (March 30).

3. Middle- and small-sized companies are those with a capitalization of less than ¥ 100 million (¥ 30 million for wholesale business and ¥ 10 million for retail, restaurant industry, and other services), or with regular employees numbering fewer than 300 (100 for wholesale business and 50 for retail, restaurant industry, and other services).

Source: Japan Company Handbook, (Tokyo: Toyo Keizai Shinposha, 1978–1988).

Liberalization of Impact Loans

A certain aspect of the actual development of liberalization itself has proved disadvantageous to the operations of foreign banks. More specifically, foreign banks have lost their privileges in the course of liberalization. The first of such instances was the liberalization of impact loans. These are foreign currency-denominated loans tied to no specific purpose or project, which differentiates them from tied loans. These consist of several categories; however, the category that bears discussion here is out-in impact loans in which residents (Japanese enterprises) were the borrowers and foreign banks generally were the lenders. Before the Foreign Exchange and Trade Control Law was amended in December 1980, impact loans were subject to government approval. This approval system was liberally applied to foreign banks, which had wide access to foreign currency funds, but was very strictly applied in the case of Japanese banks, which had significantly less access. This brought about virtual domination by foreign banks of the impact loan market until the amendment to the law. As the amendment removed this approval system, the impact loan business opened up to Japanese banks as well. Table 4–4 shows the development in this market.

Second, the change in yen conversion quotas adversely affected foreign banks. Before the law's amendment, yen conversion quotas were liberally allocated to foreign banks. Using these quotas, they could take dollar funds from their main offices, convert their funds into yen, and lend the yen to their customers in Japan. After the amendment, the market opened up for Japanese banks as well.

F.M.P. Riding, principal manager of Lloyds Bank, describes this process of foreign banks losing privileges in the course of liberalization.

> Until the latter half of the 1970s, foreign banks could gain very handsome profits. The liberalization of the impact loan business, which included Japanese banks in 1979, quickly squeezed interest margins. The greater liberalization brought on by the 1980 amendment to the Foreign Exchange and Trade Control Law made competition even more fierce and pushed up funding costs. In Tokyo, higher wages and other expenses led by room rents exacerbated this situation ("Financial Issue Supplement" 1986, p. 214).

During this period, big businesses (which are thought to have formed the core of the foreign bank client base) activated their funding operations in capital markets both within and outside Japan, lessening their reliance on bank borrowings. It is comprehensible that under such circumstances, financial liberalization, including the amendment to the Foreign Exchange

Table 4–4. Impact Loans (in $ Million).

	Japanese Bank			Foreign Banks			Total		
	Short-term	Medium/long-term	Sub total	Short-term	Medium/long-term	Sub total	Short-term	Medium/long-term	Total
1977					1,484	1,484		1,484	1,484 (100)
1978					2,692	2,692		2,692	2,692 (100)
1979					4,468	4,468		4,468	4,468 (100)
1980	378	1,471	1,849 (24)	80	5,880	5,960 (76)	458	7,351	7,809 (100)
1981	6,077	2,621	8,698 (56)	1,158	5,792	6,950 (44)	7,235	8,413	15,648 (100)
1982	10,498	4,601	15,099 (64)	2,639	6,011	8,650 (36)	13,137	10,612	23,749 (100)
1983	16,332	6,511	22,843 (71)	3,143	6,159	9,302 (29)	19,475	12,670	32,145 (100)
1984	25,430	8,327	33,757 (79)	3,816	5,393	9,209 (21)	29,246	13,720	42,966 (100)
1985	31,948	13,103	45,051 (83)	4,467	5,063	9,530 (17)	36,415	18,166	54,581 (100)
1986	49,797	24,578	74,375 (89)	4,491	4,604	9,095 (11)	54,288	29,182	83,470 (100)
1987	122,310	42,892	165,202 (95)	4,299	4,924	9,223 (5)	126,609	47,816	174,425 (100)
1988	168,602	57,689	226,291 (95)	5,064	6,109	11,173 (5)	173,666	63,798	237,464 (100)

Notes:

1. Figures in ( ) show share percentages.

2. The original data consist of figures of impact loans approved or reported. The terms vary considerably from a week, a month, three months, six months, or a year, three years, or more. The average outstanding amounts of loans for each year were estimated based on these data.

3. Data are available from 1977 onward. The lack of data before 1977 means that the estimated figures for 1977, 1978, or 1979 in the table are almost certainly a great deal (in particular for 1977) smaller than the figures which would have been calculated, if data before 1977 were available.

Source: Annual Reports, International Finance Bureau (1977–1988), Ministry of Finance.

and Trade Control Law and the liberalization of the capital market transactions, dismantled the foreign bank client base and resulted in the diminution of their market share.

Interest Rate Control

The process of interest rate liberalization was discussed earlier. It should be noted here that deposit interest rates have been strictly controlled while controls on loan rates have been relatively lenient. As a matter of fact, however, when a company keeps deposits with a bank, in many cases, it is a borrower from that bank. A view persists, therefore, that "effective interests rates," which take actual balances into account, have been effective in the adjustment of supply and demand in the loan market. This focus on "effective interest rates" can be developed in such a way that, at a bank with a client base consisting mainly of corporations, interest rate movements have not been as rigid as is generally believed.

It may be argued, therefore, that liberalization of interest rates on small deposits has had no immediately significant impact on banks serving mainly corporate accounts (virtually all foreign banks fall under this category) and nonbank banks (leasing companies, for example) with no involvement in retail banking. From the viewpoint of competitive conditions for foreign banks and Japanese banks, however, the relative advantage or disadvantage in funding costs can have certain implications. The trend of relative shares between deposits offering regulated interest rates and deposits as well as CDs paying interest at unregulated rates is shown in Table 4–5. As liberalization has progressed, the share of deposits offering regulated interest rates has steadily declined. If the comparison of competitive conditions is confined to this issue, foreign banks were definitely at a disadvantage since regulated interest rates were always lower than the levels of free interest rates. Whether this trend has caused the decline in foreign bank market share since 1975 is open to question. As Table 4–5 clearly shows, for foreign banks, this disadvantage in funding costs was greater as we trace back to 1975.

At any rate, interest rate liberalization is accepted as an inevitable result of historical evolution and is, therefore, not an issue for debate. Further, as is widely recognized, the regulatory authorities have energetically promoted it. Although the liberalization process has been gradual, it continues a steady progress.

Table 4–5. Share of Free Interest Rate Deposits in City Bank Total Deposits (in 100 Million Yen, Percents).

	(A) Total Deposits	(B) Market Rate-Linked Deposits	(C) Negotiable CDs	(B + C) Free Interest Deposits	(B + C/A + C) Free Interest Deposit Share
1979	800,736	47,249	8,832	56,081	6.93
1980	876,377	73,188	7,751	80,939	9.24
1981	971,680	93,467	15,652	109,119	11.05
1982	1,022,932	93,088	22,294	115,382	11.04
1983	1,105,671	101,986	38,640	140,626	12.29
1984	1,188,188	116,409	48,378	164,787	13.33
1985	1,306,429	192,201	55,827	248,028	18.21
1986	1,441,904	295,515	65,936	361,451	23.97
1987	1,630,457	525,539	90,577	616,116	35.80
1988	1,763,003	716,400	108,675	825,075	44.08
1989	1,799,630	920,788	104,976	1,025,764	53.86

Note: 1. Figures at each fiscal year-end (March 30) with the exception of 1989, which shows figures at the end of September.
Source: Bank of Japan, "Monthly Bulletin of Economic Statistics. (1979–1989)

The Short-Term Money Market

In November 1988, reform was implemented in the short-term money market to advance liberalization in the interbank market (where banks mutually withdraw and place short funds). As a result, interest rate formation became more flexible and linkages increased with open market rates such as CD rates.

The unsecured call market began operations in July 1985. As is often pointed out, this was in consideration of the weak collateral base of foreign banks. Unsecured call rates were liberalized in stages in November 1988 and January 1989 and, as a result, converged with open market interest rates through the function of intermarket arbitrage. This liberalization came at a time when interest rates were on a firm upward trend and put a damper on the profitability of foreign banks heavily reliant on the short-term money market as their funding base. On the other hand, there is a large body of opinion that appreciates the enhanced ability of the unsecured call market to expedite bank liquidity management, resulting from the reform in the short-term money market. City banks, one of the chief supporters of this development, have said: "Today, we can raise enough money at any time by offering higher interest rates." In this way, although liberalization intensified competition and hurt foreign bank profitability, active participation by Japanese banks significantly increased the depth of the unsecured call market (with the average balance reaching approximately 10 trillion yen in January 1990) and stimulated its functions.

In the secured call market, which posts quotations, efforts are being made to implement a more flexible system for rate setting. As for unconditional call transactions, a new system was introduced to allow changes in quotations during business hours and to set quotations after seeing actual trades in the unsecured call market. These efforts toward more flexibility have narrowed the interest rate differential between the secured and unsecured call markets. In May 1989 the interest rate differential between unsecured overnight call and secured unconditional call was 10 to 20 points (1 point is 1/32 percent). In May 1990 it was 4 to 6 points.

Interested parties are not in complete agreement as to the role of call money brokers in the call market and the setting of quotations in the secured call market. For example, some of them argue that if the quotation system is replaced by case-by-case rate setting, work pressure on clerical staff will become unbearable because transactions must be processed in a very short time. Moreover, they continue, there is a risk that wild rate fluctuations will occur on the final days of reserve deposit accumulation under the reserve requirement system. These are technical matters, however, and need not be further discussed here. The Group for Short-Term Money Market Research and the Committee on Short-Term Money Market Transactions, whose members include foreign banks, have been reviewing and recommending improvements in market practices. The Group for Short-Term Money Market Research published its report on June 8, 1990. Recommendations include:

1. The quotation system for secured call rates should desirably be reviewed as soon as possible in order that it might in principle be replaced by an offer-bid system in which offered rates and bid rates are matched on an individual basis.

2. It is quite natural that direct dealing transactions in the interbank market increase together with transactions made through the intermediation of call money brokers. As the market enlarges, the expansion of direct dealings would be desirable in order to meet the growing needs of the market.

3. Interbank market intermediation (including new entry into call money brokerage) is open to all financial institutions. Applications for new entry by Japanese or foreign institutions should be processed if they meet the standard requirements for business performance, management capability, and so on.

Main Banks and Financial Affiliation

This section considers bank–client relationships with a focus on their relations in the loan market. These relations are generally referred to as the "main bank system" and "financial affiliation," references that appear to indicate the closed nature of, or the existence of barriers to new entry in, Japan's financial market. The following discussion aims to answer such questions as, "Are foreign banks competing with Japanese banks for the same customers?" and "Is competitive equality realistic?"

Banks that operate by Gurley-Shaw's "intermediative technique" presuppose a world in which information is incomplete or skewed.[1] As this theory is widely known, it is not discussed here in detail except for the following two observations.

First, the formation and maintenance of a business relationship requires the input of resources such as information gathering, transmission, and analysis. These activities are similar to an investment in that today's information activities not only are useful for current operations but also can remain effective for future operations or at least reduce costs for future information activities. Because of this characteristic of information activities, business relationships, more often than not, are maintained over a long period of time. In general, this may imply the existence of a barrier to new entry equal to the cumulative value of such investment.

Second, financial intermediation (in particular, intermediative technique) exhibits economies of scale. This stems from the fact that information activities require sizable fixed expenditures and the safety of lendings per unit of amount increases in proportion to the growth in the number of borrowers. In addition, banks, as producers of information, have a kind of benefit of joint production through their financial deals with borrowers or, in other words, banks can benefit from economies of scope.

The main bank system in Japan is often cited as a typical example of long-term lender (bank)–borrower (businesses) relationship. A great majority of Japanese enterprises borrow large amounts of money from many banks and, in this borrowing structure, consistently owe the largest sum to a specific bank.

It is generally thought that this top lender bank rarely changes its position of predominance which is called the main bank for the corporation. The main bank often maintains especially close business relations with the company, not only in financing but in other ways such as stockholding and appointment of bank personnel as executive directors in the company. However, a survey by Horiuchi (1986) shows that a main bank relationship can change over time. Of all the companies listed in the First Section of the Tokyo Stock Exchange, one in four changed main banks during the years from 1962 through 1972 (this includes cases where main banks changed twice during this period). Another survey, for the period 1973–1983, revealed that one in five changed main bank.

A corporation that enjoys this kind of relationship with a bank is called an enterprise in "financial affiliation" from the bank's standpoint. This is an informal relationship which cannot be called a system. As mentioned above, long-maintained business relations mainly reflect the characteristic of investment in information gathering and analysis. Different from dealings in other goods and services, moreover, financial transactions require postdeal monitoring activities for the preservation of claims. The above-mentioned theory dwelling on banks as producers of information has been gaining popularity in recent years. Inasmuch as this theory can explain long-term business relationships, this phenomenon is not at all unique to relations between banks and borrowers in Japan. In fact, West Germany has its own version of this phenomenon, known as *housbanken*. In somewhat different degrees, long-term bank–client relationships can be found in the United States as well.

Table 4-6. City Bank Financial Affiliations (1962–1983) (in Percentages).

Bank	1962	1967	1972	1977	1983
Daiichi-Kangyo	36.5	44.7	29.9	27.1	26.1
Mitsui	28.4	25.6	24.2	21.9	19.7
Mitsubishi	41.4	32.0	31.0	29.4	28.0
Sanwa	40.0	31.7	32.0	31.9	28.1
Sumitomo	40.8	35.1	30.3	28.3	26.5
Fuji	36.8	34.8	32.9	27.4	24.5
I B J	39.7	42.9	38.2	40.3	37.5
Tokai	41.5	40.7	37.4	40.5	31.8
Daiwa	55.5	56.9	40.4	40.2	34.4
Kyowa	39.4	55.7	62.3	49.6	33.6
Takugin	47.4	53.7	40.2	18.3	22.6

Note: Shares of main bank loans to companies (listed on the First Section of the Tokyo Stock Exchange) in each financial affiliation in their total bank borrowing.

Source: Royama, Shoichi and Tachi, Ryuichiro, *Japanese Finance (I) A New Perspective* (Tokyo; Tokyo University Press, November, 1988), p. 211.

In Japan, due to historical background, special emphasis has been placed on the main bank system and financial affiliation. It is worth noting in this connection, however, as shown in Table 4–6, among Japan's big businesses (those listed on the First Section of the Tokyo Stock Exchange) in 1983, loans from main banks account for 20 to 38 percent of total bank borrowings, with the remainder coming from other banks. This extensive financial participation by nonmain banks can probably be explained by the following considerations. These banks can save information production costs by lending smaller amounts to many companies for which other major banks act as main banks. Furthermore, main banks can avoid the risk of overcommitment to businesses in their own financial affiliation. The main bank function performed in this context can be viewed as a form of loan syndication arranged by a lead manager, as is observed in international loan markets.

Table 4–6 also indicates a gradual decline in major businesses' reliance on main bank borrowings over time. Liberalization and internationalization have been fueling a decline in the share of banks in corporate financing. Many large corporations have emerged in the financial markets within and outside Japan as borrowers of very high credit standing. As far as these big businesses are concerned, incompleteness of information has been losing its significance. In other words, with regard to the financial services demanded by these corporations, the focal point is shifting from Gurley-

Shaw's intermediative technique to the distribution technique, indicating the growing advantage of providing comprehensive services.

In reality, however, not all borrowers are the top corporations as mentioned above. The vast majority of borrowers, which constitute the so-called middle and small markets, lack name recognition in the marketplace. In relationships with these firms, therefore, incomplete or skewed information is still significant.

Finally, it is notable that, in recent years, financial services have been emerging that can be seen as transcending or even destroying the framework of financial affiliations backed by old *zaibatsu* traditions. Interestingly, these services are related to new financial products that have resulted from financial liberalization.

The Stability of the Financial System

There is an abundant literature regarding bank functions and accompanying responsibilities. Four points are summarized here as a basis for the following discussions.

First, bank deposits consist of countless numbers of individuals' savings and possess the attributes of currency or quasi-currency. It is therefore the first and foremost responsibility of banks to avoid defaulting on their obligations by maintaining soundness in their assets. Maintaining the infrastructure for sound currency and efficient clearing systems is the most important prerequisite for smooth production and trading activities in a nation's economy. In this sense, securing a stable financial system is of crucial importance for the management of the economy as a whole. In this context, banks bear the heaviest responsibility in protecting the soundness of their assets at all times.

Second, banks supply funds to the economy through loans and securities investments. It is desirable that these funds be efficiently allocated to ensure the best distribution of material resources available in the economy. Efficient allocation requires smooth functioning of the price mechanism. It must be conceded in this connection, however, that sometimes the price mechanism alone cannot ensure fund allocation in the way desired by guardians of the collective public interest. The supply of funds for speculative purposes is an example:—an example calling for public intervention.

Third, banks are expected to perform their social functions as efficiently as possible. To this end, they are obligated to streamline their management and contribute to the reduction of costs. Encouraging competition facilitates an effective response to changes in social needs and helps to reduce overall social costs.

Finally, banks are obligated to cooperate with the government in the management of monetary and economic policies to help stabilize business cycles. This logically follows from the fact that banks are suppliers of currency and quasi-currency, which account for a very high percentage of the monetary aggregate, and thus they have a significant impact on overall economic activities.

Toward a Stable Financial System

Of the foregoing four points, the requirement for maintaining stability and public confidence in the financial system is of primary importance. As is widely agreed, public intervention is necessary for banks to fulfill this important responsibility. Cited as the grounds for the need for regulations are, for example, the danger that, if left entirely unchecked, competition among banks could lead to excessive expansion of credit and risk-taking. This would not only destabilize business cycles but would result in the deterioration of bank asset quality and ultimately the collapse of bank management. Excessive expansion of credit, and investment in risky assets in particular, this argument holds, must be limited by an adequate system of regulations. There are counterarguments and rebuttals which are well known and need not be discussed here in detail. Such theoretical assessments aside, each country has a regulatory regime to maintain order in its credit system and stability in the financial markets.

For a period of about 45 years after the war, no bank failure occurred in Japan. Given this historical background, Japan's financial system enjoys very high public confidence. In this context, one single case of bank failure would have an adverse impact of immeasurable proportions on the confidence in the financial system. Such unfortunate events have not occurred in Japan's liberalization process. This can be seen as a manifestation of Japanese banks' adaptability. It can also be read as evidence of regulator capability, the dedication with which they have drawn up a timetable for the liberalization process consistent with the adaptability of Japanese banks, and their prudent exercise of gradualism in coordinating the process of liberalization.

Points To Be Emphasized

Financial reform was earlier defined as the efforts of both the market and the regulator to restructure the financial system and monetary authority. This is probably a generally accepted definition of the term (Cargill, 1985,

p. 115). The financial reform under way since 1975 represents efforts to restructure the financial markets to make them better suited to responding to the needs of the new age and adapting to the changing conditions of the new environments explained in previous sections. In this connection, I would like to emphasize the following six points.

First, as the term *liberalization* reveals, the past financial reform process in Japan has consisted in a large measure of the relaxing and removal of regulatory elements that limit competition and isolate markets from general economic forces.

Second, in the process of restructuring toward a better financial system, it goes without saying that all four of the responsibilities assumed by banks or embodied in the behavior patterns of the financial system as summarized above must be realized to the fullest extent possible. In other words, liberalization is just a part of the financial reform process.

Third, of the four responsibilities, which should have a top priority? The answer varies depending on the circumstances at a given point in time. Furthermore, an answer requires a value judgment, so a consensus seems impossible. All this having been said, stability in the financial system emerges in my mind as the most important. Certainly this is the one responsibility that most observers would agree must always be taken into consideration.

Fourth, it is reasonable to expect that regulations intended to restrain competition that could result in bank failures would probably receive wide support in any country. Since this point directly relates to the question raised earlier—"What are the actual or potential problems confronted in establishing competitive equality?"—it is discussed below in some detail.

When direct controls are appropriately exercised on credit expansion in the market, those measures will no doubt check excessive credit expansion and reckless risk-taking. In the long term, however, direct controls pose the problem of encouraging the development of substitute means of finance as seen in the growth of intertrade credit and the expansion of substitute financial institutions which, in turn, weaken the effectiveness of monetary policy and distort reasonable allocation of funds. Except when direct controls are used as a short-term measure, therefore, it would seem preferable to scale them down as much as possible.

In the same vein, although restrictions on new entry based on a set of standard requirements is entirely acceptable, direct controls through interest rate regulations or nonprice means of competition should be refrained from as much as possible. Instead, capital adequacy standards, liquidity ratio control, and such regulations on portfolio as limits on large lending amounts and restrictions on investment in excessively risky assets are more desirable as a preventive safety net for the stability of the financial system and its institutions. Competition should be encouraged on an equal footing under such ground rules. Furthermore, in view of the vital importance of the stability of the financial system, both the central bank's role as the lender of last and deposit insurance are thought to have great significance as a safety net.

Fifth, the financial reform process has developed in stages, each closely linked with the other but with a period for readjustment. This resembles the brewing process, which requires an appropriate period for completion of each stage from initial preparation to final maturation. Hasty manipulations only produce a poor brew. Likewise, liberalization pushed through hastily will cause needless friction and high social costs and, at times, even necessitate re-regulation.

Finally, I would like to touch on the relations between liberalization and internationalization, supplementing the earlier discussion. Relaxation of financial regulations in many individual countries has stimulated internationalization. Conversely, the progress of internationalization has fueled the financial reform process in each country. The increasing need for matching investments and savings on a global scale has spurred the growth of cross-border financial transactions while phenomenal advances in communications and data-processing technology have rendered round-the-clock dealing possible. Furthermore, pursuit of income through the fund circulation process itself in the financial and capital markets has expanded the scale of transactions to an extraordinary level. Integration has rapidly progressed among many national markets, incorporating them into a closely knit global system. A disturbance or crash in any market can in no time cause similar problems in other markets, with the possibility of amplified confusion. Thus, as London, New York, and Tokyo have come to share new responsibilities as anchors, these three markets are expected to develop effective mechanisms for the mitigation or isolation of fear and confusion that may develop in any part of the world.

Harmonization of Capital Adequacy Standards

The basic framework for international harmonization of bank capital adequacy ratios adopted in June 1988 in Basel is understood to have two objectives.

First, it aims to safeguard the soundness of bank management and particularly seeks to secure the stability of financial systems in major world financial centers. Second, it strives to promote competitive equality among banks engaged in international operations. The first objective has special relevance in financial and capital markets that have already undergone considerable integration. The second objective is to provide a set of conditions for fair and equitable competition while securing the stability of the global financial system. In other words, the framework seeks to eliminate excessive competition by establishing guidelines for lending or securities investment based on capital that has been raised or accumulated under different conditions. This certainly requires a consensus among the parties concerned as to capital adequacy standards, capital components, and risk weights applicable to each asset category. The basic Basel framework is based precisely on such a consensus (representing the parties' perceptions) under which a minimum standard ratio of 8 percent is to be applied at the end of 1992, the last year of the transition period. At present, banks in the participating countries are taking various steps to meet this standard by raising additional capital through the securities markets within and outside their home countries. To the extent that this financing is conducted in unregulated primary markets, there seems to be no issue as to the climate of equal competition among banks.

Note

1. This section draws extensively on the works of Horiuchi (1986) and Ikeo (1986).

References

Annual Report of the Fair Trade Commission 1969, September 1970.

Cargill, Thomas E. 1985. A U.S. Perspective on Japanese Financial Liberalization. *Monetary and Economic Studies* 3(2), Bank of Japan.

Financial Issue Supplement. 1986. *Chuo Koron* (July), 214.

Horiuchi, Akiyoshi. 1986. The Functions of Financial Institutions—Theory and Reality. *Japanese Finance (I) New Perspective*, 23–56.

Ikeo, Kazuto. 1986. Applied Microanalysis of Bank Behaviors. *Japanese Finance (I) New Perspective*, 57–92.

Sakakibara, Eisuke, and Feldman, Robert. 1983. The Japanese Financial System in Comparative Perspective. *Journal of Comparative Economics* 7 (March), 1–24.

Tsutsui, Yoshiro, and Royama, Shoichi. 1986. The Industrial Organization of the Financial Business. *Japanese Finance (I) A New Perspective* (Ryuichiro Tachi and Shoichi Royama, eds.) (November), 177–220.

5 BANKING IN THE UNITED KINGDOM AND CONTINENTAL EUROPE

Charles Goodhart

Political Background

On April 19, 1990, French President Mitterrand and German Chancellor Kohl issued a joint message, declaring that: "In view of the profound transformations in Europe, of the establishment of the internal market and of the achievement of economic and monetary union, we think it necessary to accelerate the political construction of the 12-member Europe."

Whereas to British eyes at least, it is somewhat premature to claim that economic and monetary union has already been achieved, since steps in that direction have yet to be agreed (in the course of the intergovernmental meeting to be held in December 1990), there is no question but that the establishment of the single internal market by the close of 1992 and the current transformation of the map in Central and Eastern Europe are accelerating the process of change in Europe so much that some of us occasionally wish for a pause to catch our breath and collect our thoughts.

It is against this background of upheaval in Central and Eastern Europe that Mitterrand and Kohl see the need to construct even closer political and economic ties between France and Germany in order to prevent a reversion to the balancing of powers between the Central European states of Germany, Austro-Hungary, and its allies on the one hand and the West European states (France, Belgium, and the U.K. on the other), a division that tore Europe apart in the first half of this century. This puts Mrs. Thatcher in a difficult spot, since she shares Mitterrand's concern about possible domination by a reunified Germany within Europe, but detests the means whereby he intends to meet this threat, by a move toward a more federal and centrally coordinated European system, with more economic and political power passing to Brussels.

Be that as it may, the profound nature and rapid pace of change on both the political and economic fronts has made Europe once again the most interesting, and potentially the most dynamic, area in the world at present. To revert, however, to the more mundane subject at hand, how is all this going to affect banking?

Eastern Europe

In a command, or planned, society such as the Eastern European states have been, loanable funds are primarily decided by the central planners with the single, monolithic state bank acting as conduit, accountant, and plan monitor. There usually are, in addition, some specialist banks, for export/import, agriculture, construction, and so on, and some cooperative savings banks, which take in savings deposits but do not take independent lending decisions. But there was virtually no true financial intermediation, no market-determined interest rates, no private sector credit allocation, and no real commercial banking in those systems.

With the shift to a market economy, there will have to be a market allocation of loanable funds, and that implies the establishment of financial markets and associated financial intermediaries, especially and notably commercial banks. This will need to be done quite fast. Initial steps in this direction have already been taken. Each of the East European countries (apart from Romania, but including the U.S.S.R.) has, during the last four or so years, split the "monobank" into a smaller national bank—intended to become a Western-style central bank—and four or five other banks. In some of these countries (notably Hungary but also Bulgaria, to some extent), these other banks are beginning to resemble Western commercial banks. They are no longer agents of the planners, and are competing in varying degrees with each other. Some countries (e.g., Hungary again) have also admitted a few foreign banks, and this is helping to stimulate competition and introduce Western banking practices. Dozens of new banks have recently been created in Bulgaria by selling off branches of the national bank. In the Soviet Union, some 250 commercial and cooperative banks have been set up by groups of entrepreneurs (or sometimes ministries), and these are attracting business away from the state banks by using their freedom to set interest rates and reduce bureaucracy and delays.

Although East Germany was one of the laggards in making such changes in previous years, the events of 1989–1990 have now given a tremendous push to the process of financial reform there, too. We can by now discern the outline of such changes there also. The original monolithic Staatsbank has been divided into a pure central bank part, and a commercial bank segment, taking the branches, with the new name of Kreditbank. Now, in spring 1990 (on April 18–19) a link between Kreditbank and Deutsche Bank was announced; meanwhile closer relationships—for training, exchange of staff, and so on—have been developed among the savings and cooperative banks in West and East Germany. All this leaves a lot of problems and loose ends: for example, how will East Germany prevent the Kreditbank/Deutsche combine from obtaining undue monopoly power? What will be the strategies of the other universal German banks? But at least developments are somewhat clearer in East Germany than elsewhere in Eastern Europe.

The problems of adaptation to a more competitive market-oriented financial system will, however, be as much ones of skills and manpower as of institutional forms. Credit assessment has not been practiced there and is, indeed, virtually impossible in a planned society with an administered price and production system. Against that background, outside of East Germany, it would be politically difficult to envisage a Western commercial bank establishing a complete retail banking system, *de novo*, in Eastern European countries, but various forms of participation, especially in personnel training, and the establishment of limited-branching wholesale banking outlets by Western banks might be much more welcome. After all, the likely success of the transition to a market economy will depend on the establishment of banks which can, and do, assess credit risks, and on a legal and institutional structure that enables them to foreclose on bad debts.

Western Europe

Even without the excitement of the revolutions in Eastern Europe, there were already major structural economic changes under way in Western Europe. The single European market (1992) will remove all barriers to the free movement of capital, such as exchange controls—apart from a short derogation for Spain and Ireland, and a somewhat longer one for Greece and Portugal—as well as national barriers to the establishment of businesses and the provision of financial services throughout Europe. Beyond that, the Delors Committee Report in April 1989 recommended, and an intergovernmental meeting later in 1990 will discuss, a three-stage plan for the achievement first of irrevocably fixed national currencies, to be followed shortly by a single European currency, with all this to be accompanied by the establishment of a European System of Central Banks (ESCB), rather loosely modeled on the Fed, indeed now generally called "EuroFed." Of course, as we have seen with earlier attempts at European monetary union, such as the Werner Report at the end of the '60s, there is many a slip 'twixt cup and lip; but it is arguable that the achievement of the single European market will in any case have the greater impact on microlevel, structural developments, and certainly so within the next few years at any rate.

The Implications of 1992[1]

Besides exchange controls, certain Western European countries had maintained extensive national controls over the establishment, branching (e.g. Italy), capital endowment and other features of banking, and other financial intermediaries. The principle of the European Economic Community (EEC) is that the member states should mutually recognize the authority and capacity of each other state to authorize and supervise their (financial) institutions (i.e., home country regulation), subject only to those minimal areas of oversight, such as capital adequacy requirements, for which the harmonization of minimum standards over the whole EEC was regarded as necessary, and achieved in the form of community directives, such as the Second Banking Directive of February 1989.

So, in theory, the establishment of a single European market in financial services should knock down a lot of barriers to competition, and thereby reduce costs and spreads, and increase welfare. An attempt was made to measure this in the Cecchini Report, in part based on a survey of comparative national financial costs, organized by Price Waterhouse; in this latter exercise a somewhat inadequate survey was taken of the costs of various financial services in the various countries; then, using heroic assumptions about the effects of competition on the subsequent distribution of costs, and the elasticities of demand and supply, a rough ball-park estimate of the value of the gain was attempted. The amount turned out to be rather large. As Joseph Bisignano of the Bank for International Settlements (BIS) notes in his recent paper on this topic:

The expected gains are considerable; in aggregate terms an expected reduction of 10 percent is expected in the cost of financial services in the EEC, amounting to approximately ECU 21 billion or 0.7 percent of GDP. The largest decline in financial services prices are expected in Spain, which some target as a prime candidate for entry based on assumed relative banking profits.

It is, however, possible to be skeptical about the extent of additional competition, or of structural change, which 1992 will actually bring. The argument for such doubts goes much as follows. The wholesale banking and financial markets, centered in London, are already internationally fully competitive and highly efficient, so that will not change. But at the same time the retail banking markets of the various European nations are ultimately protected by the continuing need to establish and run a branch network, and also by the necessity for local knowledge and links. It will be perfectly simple to open a branch, or subsidiary, to do wholesale business in Madrid, Milan, or Paris, but is that in any case necessary, given that such business can already be done in London? On the other hand, the cost of building a new chain of branches, *de novo*, would be massive, and the profitability of buying out and taking over an existing national or regional retail establishment somewhat dubious, particularly if there was a clash of cultures, or if the foreign takeover led to some local customer opposition. The overinvestment in the provision of market-making services as well as the checkered history and low profits of foreign financial institutions taking over British Stock Exchange broking and jobbing firms around the time of the Big Bang in London (October 1986) stand as a warning.

There is, however, no apparent rush by the major commercial banks to establish a pan-European retail network in all the major countries. Indeed it is Citibank that remains physically involved in retail banking in most European countries. It is possible that Deutsche Bank may have aspirations to develop a network throughout Europe, but it is worth noting that its recent U.K. purchase, Morgan Grenfell, was involved in wholesale/investment banking, and not in retail banking, and that Deutsche Bank has no foothold in France.

So, for the time being, it is perhaps dubious how much the structure of the national retail banking systems will be altered by the regime change inherent in 1992.

There have been, and may well be more, defensive mergers between regionally centered banks, especially in Spain and Italy, countries where various (regulatory) barriers have prevented the establishment of dominant (oligopolistic) national branch banks, and there have been some attempts (sometimes unsuccessful) at transnational associations and linkages between retail banks centered in different EEC countries. But that is about as far as such change has gone for the time being.

There are, however, a number of qualifications to be made in this respect. First, the main barrier to entry (preventing retail banking from becoming a contestable industry) is the technological need for a branch network and specialized local knowledge. It is possible that technological change—e.g., in the shape of electronic home banking, ATMs, and simplified, standardized lending arrangements (allowing for securitization) —could greatly cut the cost of entry for at least certain elements of retail banking.

Second, and perhaps more immediately probable, is that a widening range of customers will shop around internationally, in effect transferring themselves and their financing requirements from the retail to the whole-sale markets. In particular, the various national retail banking markets are currently subjected to a wide variety of burdens and levies, in the form of withholding taxes on interest income, cash and liquid asset reserve ratio requirements, and so on. These impose a wedge between the net of tax interest earnings of the depositor and the cost to the borrower in each country, distorting the differentials between countries. The complete removal of exchange control will allow a bank sited in one country in the European Monetary System (EMS) to intermediate in the currency of another country without being subject to the burdens imposed on the banking system of that second country. Moreover, the ease and flexibility of such transnational shopping around will be further advanced if and when irrevocably fixed parities, *pro tanto* a single currency, are achieved.

Thus the main thrust of competitive pressure may be indirect, through the threat of customers moving their business to the least burdened areas, rather than direct, in the shape of entry by new competitors into national retail banking markets. In this latter case we may expect continuing argument and concern about the harmonization of the relevant taxes and reserve ratios. The countries with high taxes, reserve ratios, or both will want these leveled up; those with low ones will point to potential disinter-mediation outside the Community, and press for leveling down.

Public Policy Issues

The latter discussion has already brought us into the center of one area of public policy: the effect, and future treatment of, differing national tax, and reserve ratio regimes as they impinge on banking.

There is, of course, an analogous concern in the field of regulation, though the urgency and force of this issue is, perhaps, not as acute as in the United States, perhaps because European countries made less of a mess of deposit insurance. Indeed, one key feature of U.K. deposit insurance is that it makes it easier for the authorities to let (small) banks go bust, since the political rumpus over "widows and orphans" losing their money is muted. With the recent U.S. S & L debacle in mind, it is unlikely that anyone in Europe would now propose either 100 percent insurance (at least not beyond some strictly limited ceiling) or that deposit insurance be made the central pillar of the regulatory system. Indeed the concern is, perhaps, rather the reverse, that capital adequacy requirements (related to some, often inadequate, measure of risk) will be seen as the sovereign remedy for all potential regulatory concerns, even when this is patently not the case, as in the example of the fraudulent handling of client monies by investment management companies.

Anyhow, the tripartite formula of EEC banking directives for matters of key transnational concern (directives that are in turn much influenced by the deliberations of the relevant world-level BIS Committee), home country control over authorization and establishment, and host country control over the local conduct of business seem broadly accepted and acceptable, though some rough edges remain. Nevertheless, the rough edges and concern over the ultimate "competitive regulatory equilibrium" seem, perhaps, less acute and more manageable in banking than in the field of securities markets. Given that risk-weighted capital adequacy requirements are now being put in place, one major remaining concern must be whether regulators will move fast and decisively enough to constrain the operations of those banks whose capital becomes impaired.

Another likely continuing concern will be the overlap, and potential "turf wars," between the regulations and regulators of banks on the one hand and of securities houses, investment firms, on the other; and also between national and community responsibilities. With the breakdown of compartmentalized barriers between the provision of financial services by a single institution (e.g., by a universal bank), there is bound to be some knock-on effect, contagion, between problems occurring in one part of the firm and the reputation and standing of other parts. Insofar as the regulation and supervision of the financial market activities of such an integrated financial firm is undertaken separately from the regulation and supervision of the banking activities of that same firm, there are likely to be recurring opportunities for the differing sets of regulators to get at cross-purposes. It has been suggested in the press that this, indeed, happened in the recent case of the closure of British and Commonwealth (B&C) financial group.

Against that, it may be argued that, even if all financial regulation were centralized within a single body, whether part of the central bank or not, the regulations, approach, and personnel involved in dealing with capital market operations would still differ from those involved with banking operations. The possibility for acting at cross-purposes would remain, even if it were entirely in-house. The conclusion may be that it is crucial for separate regulators to interact, share information, and cooperate and coordinate closely. The institutional form(s), wherein such regulators work (e.g., in a separate or a single institution, in a central bank or not), is of less central importance, except insofar as it bears on the question of such cooperation between regulators.

In regard to the relationship between Community-level institutions— i.e., Euro-Fed and national central banks in this area—there has been little discussion, as yet, of the division of responsibility between them for lender of last resort (LOLR) decisions and actions, or for banking supervision more widely. It is, however, widely expected, I believe, that following both the general Community principle of "subsidiarity" (i.e., that responsibility should be delegated as far down to the grassroots as possible) and the precedents from the United States, the responsibility for LOLR and supervision will primarily remain with national central banks rather than be assumed by Euro-Fed.

Two other public policy issues that rumble on are, first, the appropriate limitations, if any, on who might own a bank (e.g., a nonbank financial company, an industrial company, a nonresident company); and, second, reciprocity with non-EEC countries. I have expressed my doubts as to whether 1992 will bring about a spurt of mergers and takeovers in banking, but the normal course of events will no doubt resurrect such questions from time to time. There is, however, little or nothing specifically European about such issues, except that EEC regulations will prevent national governments from refusing takeovers by, or mergers with, banks head-quartered in other Community countries, on nationality grounds.

Up until now, the main retail branch banks in each major European country have, almost without exception, been headquartered in that same country—in France, Germany, Italy, Spain, England, and so on. It might still be psychologically difficult for some members of a country to accept that one of the cornerstones of their banking and economic systems was passing into foreign hands. Concern about such issues was raised some years ago in the U.K. at the time of the attempt by the Hong Kong and Shanghai Banking Corp (HSBC) to take over the Royal Bank of Scotland. But the move toward European Monetary Union (EMU) is already eroding such sentiments. The achievement of a single currency, with monetary policy managed by the Euro-Fed, rather than by national central banks, is also likely to reduce concerns about the national control of major commercial banking institutions. And, as noted above, it would not now be acceptable under EEC regulations for the authorities in one country to object to a takeover of one of its own banks by a bank headquartered in another EEC country purely on grounds of national origin.

The reciprocity issue has, I hope, largely been put to bed. Banks that already have a European subsidiary will be grandfathered; for the rest, reciprocity will, I understand, be assessed on an equivalent national treatment basis, though there may remain room for disputes over the detailed definition of this assessment in certain cases.

We have now had a number of years, since the mid-1980s, to prepare for the introduction of the single European market, in the process of which some of these public policy issues, such as reciprocity, have been specifically addressed in the structural, microeconomic field. It is probably going to be in the *macroeconomic* areas (e.g., of the split between federal and national control, and the appropriate handling of fiscal and monetary policies) that the recent moves toward European economic and monetary union (EMU) will throw up public policy issues that will be both complex and highly important for future discussion and resolution.

Acknowledgments

My thanks are due to J. Bisignano, L. Price, C. Taylor, and N. Walter for helpful comments and suggestions, but any remaining errors are strictly my own.

Note

1. Those seeking further reading and additional references are advised to consult the paper by J.R. Bisignano (of the BIS) whose excellent study on "Banking in the EEC: Structure, Competition and Public Policy" is being published in George G. Kaufman, ed., *Bank Structures in Major Countries* (Kluwer Academic Publishers).

6 BANKING AND FINANCIAL INTERMEDIARY MARKETS IN THE UNITED STATES: WHERE FROM, WHERE TO?

George G. Kaufman

As in every developed country in the world, financial intermediary institutions and markets in the United States have undergone dramatic changes in recent years. Indeed, the changes in the United States may even be more dramatic than elsewhere for two reasons. One, both by tradition and by regulation, financial institutions and markets have tended to be more specialized and segmented in the United States than elsewhere. Two, Americans have had a historical, deep-rooted distrust of banking, particularly of large institutions. As a result, public policy until recently was directed at keeping the industry fragmented in terms of both geographical location and product powers. Indeed, U.S. public policy toward financial institutions cannot be properly understood without an awareness of this historical fear.

When financial markets and institutions started to develop in the United States in the early 1800s, supervision and regulation were under the jurisdiction of the various state governments. Thus, banks and other financial institutions developed under different regulations and at different speeds. Two attempts to impose national banking—the First Bank of the United States (1791–1811) and the Second Bank of the United States (1816–1836)—did not succeed. All commercial banks were state chartered and could not operate branch offices in other states. Indeed, in many states, banks could not operate any branch offices whatsoever (unit banking), and a few states even banned banks altogether for a few years. What better way to prevent banks from increasing in size and power than to prevent geographic expansion!

Because of the limitations of technology and transportation, however, branching was not a major issue in those days. But the lack of branching did hinder the efficient flow of funds from surplus to deficit areas in the geographically large country and helped create periodic financial crises characterized by abrupt tightening of credit and increases in short-term interest rates in deficit areas. The resulting volatility and geographical disparities in interest rates contributed to a perception of the United States as an unstable financial system.

Moreover, until the Civil War, there was no national currency. Circulating notes were issued by each of a large number of relatively small banks scattered throughout the landscape. These notes traded at varying values to each other, depending on the perceived financial soundness of the issuing bank and the distance from the issuing bank at which the currency was being traded (Gorton, 1985).

Because of their state charters, the powers of banks differed from state to state, but were generally limited to shorter-term financial activities in the British tradition. These restrictions were accepted by the banks in exchange for the license to issue notes. Partially as a result of the restrictions, investment and merchant banking, which focused on longer-term credits, were started by wealthy individuals, who in time also accepted deposits but did not issue notes and therefore did not require charters. Likewise, specialized consumer saving and mortgage lending institutions, such as savings and loan associations and mutual savings banks as well as insurance companies, developed separately. Although commercial banks had to obtain charters (which in the early days required political connections in some states), were restricted geographically and in their product powers, and subject to examination, reporting, and minimum capital requirements, regulation was not overly onerous relative to modern experience.

The federal government increased its involvement in the financial markets greatly during the Civil War in the early 1860s by chartering national banks, restricting note issue entirely to these banks, and requiring the banks to collateralize the notes with government debt, much of which was issued to finance the war. Although national charters were freely available if minimum capital standards were met, the national banks were restricted in geographic and product powers more than state banks were. Thus, national charters did not lead to national (nationwide) banking.

At the turn of the twentieth century, the U.S. banking structure was highly fragmented both geographically—more than 12,000 commercial banks with only some 100 branches—and in products offered, with a large number of specialized nonbank institutions coexisting. In part to circumvent these restrictions, banks organized holding companies, which could acquire other banks, including banks in other states, and engage in basically any type of activity they wanted. However, because holding companies did not become highly popular, it is unlikely that substantial economies of either scale or scope were obtainable at that time.

After the turn of the century, in part because of improvements in communications and transportation, the drive for broader branching powers, including interstate branching, accelerated. This was particularly true for national banks, which were prohibited from any branching even in states that permitted their state banks to branch. In addition, national banks were more restricted in their investment banking activities than state banks were. Thus, they viewed themselves as competitively disadvantaged to state-chartered banks. They were opposed by groups that feared the emergence of a smaller number of large, universal, nationwide banks. In 1927, the national banks won a partial victory. They were permitted by the McFadden Act to branch within their home city, if such branching was permitted to state-chartered banks. However, they could not branch outside their city even if state banks were permitted to do so.

By 1930, the number of branches had increased to 3,500 operated by 750 banks. Of these, 166 national banks operated some 1,000 branches. In addition, the McFadden Act permitted national banks explicitly to engage in securities underwriting and trading within the bank itself, subject to approval by the Comptroller of the Currency. The Comptroller authorized all such activities except for underwriting of equities. Before this act, the authorization for national bank securities activities was fuzzy, and many banks engaged in these activities in affiliates and subsidiaries. State banks had greater explicit freedom. At the same time, investment banks had begun to accept deposits. By the end of the 1920s, commercial and investing banking were almost fully integrated.

The Great Depression brought massive failures of commercial banks that reduced the number from near 25,000 to less than 15,000 and, to a lesser extent, of savings and loan associations and mutual savings banks; this changed the banking landscape substantially. The Banking Act of 1933, popularly referred to as the Glass-Steagall Act, was enacted in the activist first 100 days of the newly elected Franklin Roosevelt Administration in an attempt both to repair the damage and to appease public pressure to "do something, don't just stand there." The Act was blatantly anticompetitive and placed safety well ahead of efficiency. Interest payments on demand deposits were prohibited altogether and those on time deposits banks restricted (Regulation Q). Margin requirements were imposed on the financing of security purchases, commercial and investment banking were partially separated, new bank charters were made more difficult to obtain, and federal deposit insurance was introduced. Only the branching powers of national banks were liberalized; they were given the same branching authority as state banks in their host state.

For the next 30 years, through World War II, economic forces did not challenge the regulations severely. When they did, the regulations were generally relaxed, such as the relaxation of Regulation Q ceilings whenever market rates of interest rose sufficiently above the old ceilings. This was a period of substantial growth in financial intermediation, which was participated in to varying degrees by all financial institutions except life insurance companies. There were few bank failures or failures of any type of financial institution. The period represented the "golden days" of federal deposit insurance. Only the good aspects of the program were visible—the devastating runs and failures of the early 1930s were not repeated, even to a minor degree. But, in retrospect, this period was the eye of the storm. Conditions would soon change for the worse.

Starting in the 1970s, the financial system was hit by two forces: first, an increase in the instability of the macroeconomy characterized by a sharp acceleration in the rate of inflation and then an equally sharp increase in interest rates in the 1970s; second, in the 1980s, by a dramatic slowing in the overall rate of inflation and even sharper declines in the prices of energy and agricultural products and significant advances in telecommunication and computer technology. The first force provided the incentive for market participants in the 1970s to bypass regulations that did not permit competitive rates to be paid by some depository institutions on some types of activities, and severely damaged depository institutions that had assumed significant interest rate risk exposures either voluntarily or by regulation. The second force allowed the participants to bypass the restrictive regulations by transferring funds around geographic and product barriers easily, quickly, and cheaply.

Thus, market forces had significantly weakened many binding regulations, and those that remained had put the affected institutions at a serious competitive disadvantage. That is, *de facto* market deregulation had occurred in a number of important and visible ways:

1. The inability of restricted institutions to pay competitive rates for funds resulted in disintermediation from depository institutions, particularly thrift institutions. The higher interest rates first increased the relative attractiveness of primary or direct financial instruments on the private

financial market and then gave rise to innovations on the intermediation market in the form of new institutions (e.g., money market funds), and new instruments by existing institutions (e.g., repurchase agreements and sweep accounts).

2. The rapid and low-cost availability of credit information on computer systems lowered the cost of direct sales of debt by large corporations in the form of, say, commercial paper, bypassing underwriting by the banks.

3. The ability to maintain and analyze large numbers of records made possible pooling and securitization and the development of mortgage-backed and other asset-backed securities.

4. Improved communication systems lowered the cost of locating non-full-service banking offices at greater distances from the home office and encouraged the development of regional and even nationwide non-full service banking through the holding company format. (The Bank Holding Company Act of 1956 had restricted the ability to expanded full service banking offices interstate.)

De jure financial deregulation legislation was enacted in response both to the economic and technical changes and to the *de facto* deregulation. In contrast to the changes in the 1930s that emphasized safety, the legislative and regulatory changes in the early 1980s emphasized efficiency and attempted to provide thrift institutions with a "level playing field" on which to compete and survive:

1. States enacted legislation that conformed to the provisions of the Douglas Amendment to the Banking Holding Company Act of 1956 and specifically permitted out-of-state bank holding companies to acquire domestic banks. By early 1990, only a small handful of states had not enacted such legislation on, at least, a regional basis. This permitted the first widespread full-service interstate banking in U.S. history and made nationwide banking a distinct likelihood by the mid-1990s. Interestingly, although nationwide banking has important federal implications, it is being enacted without any specific federal legislation. The liberalization of the laws to permit interstate banking reflects (1) the reduced fear of excessive concentration in banking because of freer entry both by banks and by nonbanks offering banking-type products: (2) the need of some states to attract buyers for their larger, failing banking institutions; and (3) the observation that non-full-service bank offices were already operating freely across state lines. If interstate holding company banking is a reality, can interstate branching be far behind? This, however, would require federal legislation to amend the McFadden Act of 1927.

2. States enacted more liberal intrastate branching legislation. While in

1960, about one-third of the states permitted only unit banking (Midwest), one-third permitted limited branching (East Coast), and one-third permitted statewide branching (West Coast), by 1990 less than five states maintained unit banking restrictions and more than one-half permitted statewide branching.

3. Regulation Q was phased out by federal legislation for all time and saving deposits. On the lending side, most usury laws were dismantled.

4. Restrictions on nearly all securities activities were phased out, particularly for very large banks. Surprisingly, these new powers were introduced without new legislation. Rather, they occurred because of regulatory and judicial reinterpretation of the Glass-Steagall Act, particularly by the Board of Governors of the Federal Reserve System. The public acceptance of these reinterpretations reflects reduced fears of excessive concentration, conflicts of interest, and excessive risk. Increased competition and alternatives reduce the likelihood that conflicts of interest would harm consumers, and the enhanced ability to diversify and reduce risk should offset the possible greater risk of any security activity in isolation. In addition, the new powers were authorized to compensate banks for the loss of traditional markets in financing large corporations. Last was the attempt to keep U.S. banks competitive with those overseas that generally permit greater investment banking activities. These changes give very large banks the approximate securities powers they had before the Glass-Steagall Act of 1933.

5. Restrictions on nonresidential mortgage lending were liberalized substantially for thrift institutions by the Depository Institutions Deregulation and Monetary Control Act (DIDMCA) of 1980 and the Garn-St. Germain Act of 1982, and even more so by some states for state-chartered institutions. In particular, thrifts were granted power to shorten the duration of their assets and reduce their interest rate risk exposure.

But *de jure* deregulation was both too late and too poorly designed to prevent the severe problems in the banking and thrift industries of the late 1980s. The introduction of federal deposit insurance in 1933 had permitted institutions to operate with substantially lower capital than they had before. For example, commercial bank capital-to-asset ratios declined from more than 20 percent in the early 1900s with double liability for shareholders of at least national banks to only 7 percent without double liability. In addition, for thrift institutions, most of which were mutuals at the time, the elimination of favorable tax treatment discouraged the buildup of capital. Banks and thrifts effectively substituted public capital for private capital and made the taxpayer an unlimited liability shareholder. While the low levels of private capital were sufficient for the "calm" macroeconomy and precomputer technology environment of the 1950s and 1960s, they were not sufficient for the wilder 1970s and, particularly, 1980s.

As a result, the sharp rise in interest rates superimposed on the large interest rate risk exposure forced on thrift institutions through the 1970s by regulation caused some two-thirds of the thrift industry to be economically (market value) insolvent by 1982 with aggregate negative net worth of almost \$100 billion (Benston and Kaufman, 1990; Brumbaugh, 1988; Kane, 1985; 1989; Kaufman, 1990). In addition, 85 percent of the institutions recorded losses for the year. (It should be noted that this debacle occurred without the benefit of fraud and deregulation, two of the main culprits blamed for the second phase of the debacle in the mid and late 1980s.) Instead of reorganizing and recapitalizing these institutions when their net worth dropped to zero or below, the regulators, with the encouragement of Congress, took advantage of federal deposit insurance, which effectively guaranteed the par value of all the deposits and prevented a deposit outflow, and chose to permit most of the institutions to remain open in the hope that they would regain profitability and solvency. And the bet nearly paid off!

Interest rates declined sharply from 1982 through 1984, and the economic net worth of the industry recovered sharply, nearly becoming positive again. But a number of things went wrong. The interest rate decline resulted primarily from a sharp slowdown in the rate of inflation, which was led by unusually sharp declines in energy and agriculture prices. The latter declines, in turn, triggered downturns in the economies of the regions in which they were important, that is, the Southwest and farm belt. The price declines came on the heels of rapid run-ups in these prices and projections that the prices would continue to rise almost indefinitely. Because of the restrictions against geographic expansion, many commercial banks and thrift institutions located in these regions concentrated their lending in their local communities. They justified their loans on projected continuation of the price increases and their incorporation into income, real estate values, and the demand for labor. The institutions were caught up in a stereotypical boom-period psychology. When the prices turned around and began to drop, income, real estate values, and employment all dropped and loan defaults increased sharply.

For many savings and loan associations, the resulting losses more than offset the positive effects on their net worth from the decline in interest rates and returned them to insolvency. For some commercial banks in these areas, the loan losses wiped out their net worth and drove them into insolvency for the first time. As their capital decreased, many owners/ managers increased their risk exposure in the hopes of recouping. If the gamblers won, they received all the gains; if they did not, the losses were borne by the insurance agencies.

At the same time, the thrift regulators attempted to increase capital in the industry by encouraging institutions to convert from mutual form of organization to stock form. In the process, many insolvent or barely solvent institutions were purchased with small amounts of capital by individuals who, because of the federal guarantee of deposits, viewed the highly leveraged institutions as a means to quick and large profits by providing an almost unlimited source of funding for their own real estate or other projects and those of their friends. Traditional credit analysis was neglected, and potentially high-yielding but risky loans extended. In addition, some new owners used the funds of their institutions to finance large personal expenditures. They treated the institutions as their own "piggy banks." The greater risk-taking was frequently accompanied by outright fraud and attempts to discourage regulators and legislators from taking corrective actions. In time, the new "high-roller"-type owners were joined in excessive risk-taking by some more traditional owners, who had lost their capital in perceived less risky ventures and had modified their behavior in last-ditch efforts to retain control.[1]

Where were the thrift regulators at these times? They were unprepared and understaffed for these problems. The regulators were accustomed to the calm days of the 1950s through the mid-1970s. In that period, savings and loan associations were primarily long-term, fixed rate, residential mortgage lenders on local real estate in an environment of relatively modest interest rate swings, particularly in relation to their capital base which had been built up through favorable tax treatment of earnings, restrictions on interest payments on deposits, a mutual form of organization that did not require dividend payments, and restrictions on entry that enhanced franchise values. Only a few associations failed each year. This environment simply required mortgage-lending expertise and not many examiners.

Suddenly the world changed. New powers were authorized to reduce interest rate risk exposure, powers competition increased, restrictions on deposit rates were removed, market areas for loans and deposits were no longer local, capital was impaired, and two-thirds of the industry was insolvent. In addition, the philosophy of deregulation was erroneously interpreted as implying not only less government regulation but also less government monitoring and supervision. This was particularly erroneous when the government is also the insurer of deposits and the insurance has permitted the institutions to operate at greatly lower private capital levels than otherwise.

Deregulation is only effective in increasing efficiency if the reduction in government discipline is replaced by a compensating increase in market discipline. The strongest form of market discipline is potential losses to shareholders, managers, and creditors when an institution becomes economically insolvent. But both regulators and policy makers were not ready to permit institutions to fail or to permit uninsured bank depositors and creditors to incur losses. At first, the regulators were overwhelmed by the sheer number of insolvent and near-insolvent institutions. How could they "close" two-thirds of the industry? Then, they became concerned that the institutions provided money and credit to the community that could not be replaced by other sources if the institution failed, and that failures, particularly of large institutions, could spill over and cause runs and eventual failure of other institutions, ultimately affecting the macroeconomy adversely.

Subsequent research has shown that only the large numbers were a legitimate concern in the current environment. Even these were the result of self-inflicted regulatory breakdowns that permitted institutions to operate at risk levels that were too high for conditions and did not impose sufficiently costly sanctions as an institution's performance deteriorated toward insolvency. An ounce of prevention is worth a pound of cure as much in banking as in medicine. The banking doctors were caught napping!

Money and credit are provided in the 1980s by a large number of nonbank suppliers. That explains why banks have lobbied so vigorously for additional powers that could help them offset the losses in market share in their traditional activities. Money market funds, investment banks, insurance companies, finance companies, and many others now provide one or more products that banks and thrifts have traditionally provided. Moreover, most bank customers, even households, have more than one "banking" connection and can switch suppliers without too much cost. In addition, insolvent institutions rarely disappear through liquidation. Rather, they are sold and recapitalized by new independent owners or merged into another banking organization. They reopen under a new name, but frequently with the same personnel except for the most senior officers. Thus, the bank–customer relationship need not be damaged severely when an individual institution fails.

Nor is the failure of one or a group of institutions likely to spill over to other institutions that are not subject to the same state of nature. Runs are generally considered the germs that spread bank contagion. But most runs primarily redistribute existing deposits within the banking system and cause relatively minor harm on net. Indeed, any damage produced must be netted against the benefits produced from the threat of runs in encouraging banks to operate more safely. That is, the threat of bank runs is a major source of market discipline. This is the primary reason that, before the establishment of the FDIC (Federal Deposit Insurance Corporation), banks had both capital ratios four or more times their current values and far less risky asset portfolios.

Depositors run on a bank when they perceive the bank to be unable to repay their funds in time and in full (Benston, Eisenbeis, Horvitz, Kane and Kaufman, 1986, ch. 2). They are most likely to transfer their funds to another bank that they perceive as safe, either in the same country or abroad. If they perceive no bank in their market area to be safe, they are likely to flee into safe Treasury securities—a flight to quality. But the sellers of the securities are likely to redeposit the proceeds in a perceived safe bank. Otherwise, why else would they have sold the securities? Neither of these scenarios causes any loss of reserves or deposits in the domestic banking system. Rather, they primarily cause churning and uncertainty and, if the funds are transferred abroad, a change in exchange rates, or, if they flee into Treasury securities, a relative change in interest rates on private and public securities. None of these effects is positive, but neither do they comprise the much-feared collapse of the banking system or macroeconomy. The Comptroller of the Currency attributed only 16 of the more than 350 national bank failures between 1921 and 1925 to bank runs (Schwartz, 1988).

However, if neither depositors nor the sellers of the Treasury securities perceive any bank anywhere to be safe, they will run into currency or, in the old days, gold. Such a run will drain reserves from the banking system as a whole and provide both a multiple contraction of money and credit and larger "fire-sale" losses on even "safe" assets sold to meet the deposit losses. The run on individual banks will have been transformed into a run on the banking system as a whole, and the problems in the banking system will spill over onto the macroeconomy. But, of course, the initial runs may have been ignited by problems in the nonfinancial sector, so that the direction of causation in such runs is unclear.

How frequent are these latter runs? A review of U.S. history before the establishment of the Federal Reserve System suggests that they probably occurred only once between 1870 and 1913, in 1893–1894, and possibly for very brief periods of time also in 1873 and 1907. Moreover, losses to depositors were small, averaging only about 0.2 percent of deposits at all banks over this entire period and even less than 1 percent in crisis years. The runs were stopped, in part, by the actions of local private clearing-houses in temporarily suspending convertibility, issuing temporary clearinghouse notes as substitutes for currency, and disclosing data about the financial health of all their banks in the aggregate (Benston et al., 1986, ch. 2)

After the establishment of the Federal Reserve in 1914 to prevent such crises, runs on the banking system occurred on and off between 1929 to 1933, culminating in a major run in early 1933, when states began to close banks completely in bank "holidays." These runs persisted until President Roosevelt closed all banks for at least one week in a national bank holiday in March 1933. But the effects of these systemic runs could have been prevented had the Federal Reserve acted to inject sufficient reserves to offset the reserve loss from the currency drain, as it was created to do.

Since the adoption of federal deposit insurance as a result of the Federal Reserve's failure to act in 1933, there have been no significant runs into currency—even during the major S&L crises in Texas and elsewhere, or the failure of large banks, such as the Continental Illinois in 1984, and the First Republic, M-Corp., and other large Texas banks in 1987 through 1989. Smaller depositors were convinced that the federal government would support their deposits at face value regardless of the financial condition of their particular banks, and therefore had no incentive to flee. Larger depositors could not operate using currency. Indeed, to the extent that there were runs in this period, they were primarily perverse runs from good institutions to bad institutions which offered above-market rates on federally insured deposits. Because of the advances in telecommunications technology these institutions could now attract deposits quickly from all parts of the country to fund their risky ventures.

The adverse effects of the existing deposit insurance system in encouraging excessive risk-taking had surfaced and become visible alongside the longer visible beneficial effects of preventing runs on the banking system as a whole! Interestingly, these problems with federal deposit insurance were well known in 1933, when Glass-Steagall was enacted (Barth and Bartholomew, 1991). But the crisis environment demanded strong and quick action by Congress to improve safety immediately. Without the full market penalties for failure permitted to operate for most institutions by the forbearance policies of the regulators and policy makers, the experiment in deregulation was effectively doomed to failure. With neither government nor market discipline in effect, many institutions quickly realized that the penalties for risk-taking had decreased and increased their risk exposures commensurately. The $100 billion deficit in FSLIC (the Federal Savings and Loan Insurance Corporation), which led to the restructuring of the entire thrift industry regulatory structure, and the severe problems currently confronting many large commercial banks were the result.

In particular, forbearance toward the largest banks, or a too large to fail (TLTF) policy, is too costly to continue (Kaufman, 1990). Few large banks failed before the introduction of federal deposit insurance. The incentives of the marketplace were even more effective for larger banks than smaller banks. Despite dire warnings, no catastrophe occurred in terms of either contagion or shortage of money and credit, when, after the complete bailout of the Continental Illinois Bank in 1984, bank holding companies were first permitted to fail with pro rata losses to general creditors in 1986; when the large First Republic Bank of Texas was permitted to fail legally in 1988; and when some interbank deposits of solvent banks in Texas were allocated pro rata losses when their larger affiliated banks in the holding company were declared insolvent in 1989. The last type of action is now codified in the Financial Institutions Reform, Recovery and Enforcement Act (FIRREA) of 1989.

The role of the Federal Reserve as lender of last resort (LLR) through the discount window in assisting TLTF also needs to be reexamined. Because the Fed fully collateralizes its loans to banks so that it will not experience a loss if a bank becomes insolvent, it effectively gets a free ride in supporting large banks that are legally solvent but economically insolvent. Such action gives uninsured depositors time to flee at face value. If the bank is eventually declared legally insolvent, losses are transferred from the uninsured depositors to the FDIC. The Federal Reserve is thus an important, although less visible, partner in providing the federal safety net under, at least, large banks. But its incentives differ from those of the FDIC. It has little if anything to lose from keeping insolvent large banks afloat. At times, this has put the Fed in conflict with the FDIC. Reform of deposit insurance thus requires reform of Fed LLR operations as well as those of the FDIC (Kaufman, 1991a, 1991b).

The public policy challenges for the 1990s and beyond are clear—how to redesign the banking system to increase both its competitiveness domestically as well as internationally and its safety, so that it does not adversely impact the taxpayers either by requiring subsidies or by disrupting the economy.

Ironically, each of the two structures previously introduced specifically to correct the weakness of the existing structure and to improve its safety not only failed in time but contributed to costly financial crises. Whether or not the Federal Reserve could have prevented the Great Depression in the 1930s, it could have prevented the run on the banking system by injecting sufficient reserves. When it did not, the FDIC was born. When the increased instability in the macroeconomy, in part ignited by poor Federal Reserve monetary policy, and advances in telecommunications and computer technology increased both the incentives for capital-short institutions to "game" the FDIC and FSLIC and the means to do so, the regulatory agencies, in particular the deposit insurance agencies themselves, failed to respond adequately. As a result, the thrift and banking failures of the 1980s multiplied in both scale and scope beyond what would have occurred in a more efficient structure.

Rather than having a few failed institutions, by early 1990, more than 400 savings and loan associations with some $175 billion in assets were effectively nationalized through being operated by the Resolution Trust Corporation (RTC). Another 300 associations with assets of nearly $200 billion were insolvent on the basis of tangible net worth and likely to be taken over shortly by the RTC. If one assumes that associations with less than 3 percent tangible net worth are economically or market-value insolvent, then nearly 1,000 associations, or one-third of the industry, with total assets of more than $500 billion, or nearly one-half of the industry, are economically insolvent (Barth and Bartholomew, 1991; Atkinson, 1990; Ely, 1990). Directly as a consequence of their ineffective actions, both the FSLIC and its parent Federal Home Loan Bank Board were reorganized out of existence and their powers transferred elsewhere. In addition, FIRREA may have begun a formal retreat from deregulation by restricting the nonresidential mortgage powers of savings and loans.

How can we cope with these challenges? If the system can be restructured to improve its efficiency and safety and rescue it from the trend toward reregulation and nationalization, the future for financial intermediation in the United States looks bright. The demand for financial services promises to expand at least as rapidly as nonfinancial income as per capital personal income grows (financial services are a superior good), more countries adopt market economies, and international barriers are removed, encouraging economies of scale and scope. Of course, a healthy outlook for the industry as a whole does not imply a healthy outlook for each and every segment, firm, or market. Indeed, throughout the post-World-War-II period, some types of financial institutions have expanded faster and were presumably more profitable than others, and some expanded slower and were presumably less profitable. This reflects differences in the demand for their products and in their ability to provide the products demanded at reasonable costs.

Although commercial banks are by far the largest type of financial institution in the United States in terms of assets, their market share has been steadily eroding, even after adjustment for the sharp rundown in aggregate liquidity immediately after World War II. As can be seen from Table 6–1, the total assets of commercial banks declined in the 1980s from

Table 6–1.   Asset Size, Relative Importance, and Growth Rate of Major Financial Institutions on the Intermediary Financial Market from 1950–1988.

Intermediary	Asset Rank	1988 (Billions of Dollars)	% Growth 1950–1988	Percentage of Total Assets				
				1950	1960	1970	1980	1988
Commercial banks	1	2,938	1,865	52	38	38	36	31
Savings & loan assoc.	2	1,360	7,950	6	12	14	16	15
Private pension funds	3	1,140	16,055	2	6	9	11	12
Life ins. companies	4	1,113	1,678	22	20	15	12	12
State & local pension funds	5	610	12,466	2	3	5	5	7
Finance companies	6	489	5,188	3	5	5	5	5
Mutual funds	7	478	14,203	1	3	4	2	5
Casualty ins. companies	8	434	3,598	4	5	4	5	4
Money market funds	9	338	—	—	—	—	2	4
Savings banks	10	280	1,147	8	7	6	4	3
Credit unions	11	196	20,423	—	1	1	2	2
Total		9,378	9,377	100	100	100	100	100

Source: Board of Governors of the Federal Reserve System, *Flow of Funds Accounts Financial Assets and Liabilities Year-End, 1965–1988*, September 1989; and Board of Governors of the Federal Reserve System, *Flow of Funds Accounts 1949–1978*, December 1979.

36 percent of the assets of all financial institutions to 31 percent by the end of 1988. The major gainers of market share in the 1980s were regular and money market mutual funds. Both broadened their product lines considerably. Regular mutual funds developed more specialized investment vehicles that permit investors to participate in newer financial instruments and strategies, such as mortgage-backed securities and futures and option contracts, and in overseas markets. But, because unlike most other types of financial institutions the assets of regular money market funds are valued at market prices, their rapid growth reflects primarily the sharp rise in both stock and bond prices in the United States and abroad. Pension funds, both private and public, continued their speedy upward climb.

Reflecting their serious financial problems, thrift institutions slowed their rapid growth in the late 1980s and actually declined in absolute dollar size in 1990. After increasing their market share from 6 to 16 percent between 1950 and 1990, savings and loan associations declined to near 1 percent in 1988. It is interesting to note that the rapid growth in asset size occurred despite a sharp reduction in the number of savings and loan associations. At year-end 1989, there were fewer than 3,000 associations in operation, including those under the control of the RTC. In contrast, ten years earlier at year-end 1979, the number was 4,500 and in 1965, only 25 years earlier, it was 6,000, or more than twice as many. Indeed, the number of S&Ls had peaked in 1927 at nearly 13,000. Savings banks continued their post-World-War-II downward drift.

Unless the thrift institutions are able to shed their high cost structure built up over years of regulatory protection and reverse the recent attempt at reregulation, their relative, if not absolute, importance may reasonably be expected to continue to erode. Despite the increased absolute demand for financial services overall and in almost every sector, inefficient and unlucky firms may be expected to fall by the wayside. Moreover, the number of depository institutions at least, may be expected to decline significantly. The continuing liberalization of laws governing intrastate branching and interstate banking through hold-company expansion may be expected to reduce both the overall number of banks and, in particular, the number of independent banking organizations. The continuing resolution of the problems in the thrift industry will see an acceleration in the rate of mergers among associations, as well as acquisitions of associations by bank holding companies with the association offices being converted into bank-. ing offices. Credit unions also are undergoing a period of rapid consolidation. However, despite the reduction in the number of providers, almost all users of financial services should benefit.

If the system is not adequately restructured to improve its safety in an efficient way, then safety will be enforced in inefficient ways, such as it was in the 1930s. Reregulation will replace deregulation. The more efficient suppliers of financial services as well as the users will be the losers. Moreover, it is likely that such reregulation would reduce the international competitiveness of major U.S. banks and encourage the bypassing of the United States as a major international financial center.

On net, it would appear that the present time is relatively favorable for effective restructuring. The large and progressively increasing dollar cost of the current thrift crisis and the possibility of serious problems in commercial banking have made the U.S. policymakers and public more receptive to new and perceived radical proposals. Public fears of excessive concentration in banking and of large banks per se have diminished. As a result, banking is less fragmented and segmented either geographically or in terms of powers than at least since the Great Depression.

Increased safety can be introduced efficiently in the financial system by combining the best features of the pre-FDIC and post-FDIC periods: that is, by combining effective market discipline and deposit insurance immunization against systemwide bank runs. My preferred solution is one proposed by the Shadow Financial Regulatory Committee (1990; also see

Benston and Kaufman, 1988). This plan focuses on preservation of current *de jure* deposit insurance coverage limits, substantially higher capital ratios, market value reporting, progressively more restrictive and mandatory sanctions and regulatory discipline on poorly performing institutions as they deplete their capital, and mandatory reorganization and recapitalization of institutions before their capital-asset ratios decline below zero at some low but positive value (e.g., 3 percent).

The program corrects the perverse incentive in the current structure both for bankers to take excessive risks and for regulators to forbear and give insolvent bankers a second chance rather than to force recapitalization. How many banks and even thrifts would have failed if the pre-FDIC capital need had been maintained? The Continental Illinois failure cost less than 5 cents on the dollar and the Texas banks about 10 cents on the dollar. FDIC Chairperson William Seidman had estimated that recent bank failures produced losses of some 30 cents on the dollar, including the markdown from book to market value. Most thrift failures were of similar magnitude. Thus, even without assuming that the institutions would have reduced their risk exposures as a result of the higher capital rates, as they probably would have, at even a 15 percent capital level most bank losses would have been absorbed by capital and far fewer institutions would probably have failed with far fewer losses to depositors. At a 35 percent capital level, hardly any institutions are likely to have failed. In contrast, the equity-asset ratio for nonfinancial firms is more than 35 percent and, because it is declining, has raised concern.

But would such levels of capital be too costly? Not necessarily. Capital is more expensive than deposits as a source of funds because deposit insurance has been subsidized and equity capital is more costly because dividends are not tax deductible. But the elimination of the deposit insurance subsidy is desirable and debt capital does not carry the tax disadvantage. The debt permissible to be included as capital must be subordinated to the deposit insurance agency. Thus, this effectively represents an increase in truly uninsured deposits.

Moreover, by increasing the cost of poor performance and recapitalizing institutions that insist on performing poorly before their capital becomes negative, losses to uninsured depositors and the insurance agencies are minimized and would result only from fraud, insufficient diversification, and inadequate monitoring. Market discipline would be exerted by subordinated debt holders and by uninsured depositors, who will share pro rata in any losses if the institution's capital is permitted to become negative. The program has a number of advantages. It would: (1) be relatively simple to understand; (2) keep federal deposit insurance but make it effectively redundant; (3) reduce deposit insurance premiums; (4) greatly reduce the incentives for depositors to run; (5) reduce the need for intense and burdensome regulation; (6) permit expanded powers; (7) not diminish the international competitiveness of banks by permitting tax-favored subordinated debt to be included in the definition of capital; (8) eliminate any need for TLTF policies and for Federal Reserve lender of last resort assistance to such banks; and (9) be reasonably easy to implement now.

Because it requires that poorly performing institutions be reorganized and recapitalized before their capital is completely depleted, the proposal has been criticized as confiscating or expropriating private capital. It does not. Current shareholders are given first opportunity to recapitalize their institutions. If they do not do so and walk away, it most likely indicates that there is actually less capital in the institution than the regulators estimated. Any proceeds from reprivatization through the sale, merger, or liquidation of an institution after it is taken over by the regulators would be returned to the former shareholders. Moreover, deposit insurance could be voluntary, so that an institution would not need to agree to such provisions if it did not wish to do so. Acceptance of these standards would be a tradeoff for receiving federal deposit insurance.

It should also be noted that by imposing a series of well-defined tranches through which a bank passes as its performance deteriorates and in which the regulators impose progressively stronger sanctions, such as restricted powers, dividend payments, and intercorporate transfers, the proposal establishes a paper trail of both the bank's deterioration and the warnings issued by the regulators. This trail should make easier any court's decision on the legality of the reorganization when the bank breaches the final recapitalization tranche and challenges the action, as many will. The tranches also require increasing mandatory action by the regulators to reduce the incentive for forbearance. The breach of the final reorganization tranche requires immediate mandatory action to recapitalize the institution.

If this or a similar program that efficiently stabilizes the banking structure is adopted, public policy can consider each challenge on its own merits without overriding concern for safety. International competitiveness should be encouraged, but not at the expense of matching inefficient and costly subsidies that other countries may choose to provide their institutions in short-run attempts to increase market shares. If some countries confuse bank size and bottom line and pursue policies that deliberately increase individual bank size without consideration of efficiency, there is no reason for the United States to follow blindly. Likewise, if some countries wish to subsidize risk-taking by their banks and shift losses to their taxpayers, as occurs in "too large to fail" policies, the United States could resist such temptation. Removal of restrictions on geographic and product expansion could be considered within the context of the existing antitrust legislation, just as for any other industry, without introducing questions of bank uniqueness or risk. It is interesting to note that, despite the severe geographic and product restrictions of yesteryear, U.S. banks were dominant among the largest 10 and 20 banks in the world. The significant liberalization of these restrictions since was insufficient to prevent the much-publicized decline in the relative size of U.S. banks. This suggests that U.S. banks may be more concerned with efficiency than banks elsewhere or subsidized less. If asset growth per se were a gauge of success, then the performance of the thrift industry through the mid-1980s would be viewed quite differently than it currently is. Moreover, the rapid asset growth of some money center banks in the late 1970s, which was in part fueled by LDC loans, did not enhance their long-run viability.[2]

History has also shown that the financial system is not an efficient transmitter for social policies. Political interference with unconstrained market allocations will "work" in the short run by raising barriers. However, it will break down in the longer run by encouraging circumvention through innovation in the form of new instruments and institutions that are also likely to result in a less efficient overall structure. In an efficient, deregulated environment with appropriate market discipline, financial institutions will structure themselves voluntarily to accommodate the perceived needs for financial services and their own perceived managerial skills and objectives, much as is done in the majority of industries that are not "regulated". *De jure* separate, protected, and subsidized financial industries are not required for separate customers or sectors, such as housing, agriculture, or small business. If these sectors are to be subsidized, it would be far more effective to do so with direct outright payments or tax credits.

Notes

1. See, for example, Carson (1990, p. 2) and Stein (1989, pp. 6, 7, 22, 24, and 26).

2. Similar views are expressed by Federal Reserve Chariman Allan Greenspan, "Testimony before Financial Institutions Supervision, Regulation and Insurance Subcommittee, U.S. House of Representatives," Chicago, May 14, 1990.

References

Atkinson, Bill. 1990. Ryan of OTS Sees 300 S&Ls Sure to Fail. *American Banker* (May 24), 1, 17.

Barth, James R., and Bartholomew, Philip F. 1991. The Thrift Industry Crisis: Revealed Weaknesses in the Federal Deposit Insurance System. In James R. Barth and R. Dan Brumbaugh, Jr., eds., *The Reform of Deposit Insurance: Disciplining the Government and Protecting the Taxpayer*. New York: Harper-Collins Business.

Benston, George J., Eisenbeis, Robert A., Horvitz, Paul M., Kane, Edward J., and Kaufman, George G. 1986. *Perspectives on Safe and Sound Banking*. Cambridge, MA: MIT Press.

Benston, George J., and Kaufman, George G. 1988. *Risk and Solvency Regulation of Depository Institutions*. New York: Salomon Brothers Center for the Study of Financial Institutions, New York University.

Benston, George J., and Kaufman, George G. 1990. The S&L Debacle: Causes and Cures. *The Public Interest* (Spring), 79–95.

Brumbaugh, R. Dan Jr. 1988. *Thrifts Under Seige*. Cambridge, MA: Ballinger.

Carson, Teresa. 1990. Financial Corp. Chairman Laments Failure of Thrift. *American Banker* (May 2), 2.

Ely, Bert. 1990. FIRREA: Implications for the U.S. Financial System. *Game Plans for the 90s*. Chicago, Federal Reserve Bank of Chicago.

Gorton, Gary. 1985. Clearing Houses and the Origins of Central Banking. *Journal of Economic History* (June) 277–283.

Kane, Edward J. 1985. *The Gathering Crisis in Federal Deposit Insurance*. Cambridge, MA: MIT Press.

Kane, Edward J. 1989. *The Savings and Loan Mess: How Did It Happen?* Washington, DC: Urban Institute.

Kaufman, George G. 1990. "The Savings and Loan Rescue of 1989: Causes and Perspective." In G. Kaufman, ed., *Restructuring the American Financial System*. Boston: Kluwer Academic Publishers.

Kaufman, George G. 1991a. Lender of Last Resort: A Contemporary Perspective. Research Paper, *Journal of Financial Services Research* (June).

Kaufman, George G. 1991b. Lender of Last Resort, Too Large To Fail, and Deposit Insurance Reform. In James R. Barth and R. Dan Brumbaugh, Jr., eds., *The Reform of Deposit Insurance: Disciplining the Government and Protecting the Taxpayer*. New York: Harper-Collins Business.

Schwartz, Anna J. 1988. Financial Stability and the Federal Safety Net. In William Haraf and Rose Marie Kushmeider, eds., *Restructuring Banking and Financial Services in America*. Washington, DC: American Enterprise Institute.

Shadow Financial Regulatory Committee. 1990. An Outline of a Program for Deposit Insurance and Regulatory Reform. Statement No. 41, February 21.

Stein, Benjamin J. 1989. On the Junk Heap. *Barron's* (October 9), 6, 7, 22, 24, 26.

7 FINANCIAL INTERMEDIATION AND LIBERALIZATION IN JAPAN[1]

Shoichi Royama

Institutions, markets, and regulations make up the financial system of a country. The system facilitates various economic functions, the most notable and important of which is transferring funds from surplus to deficit units of the economy. In contemporary Japan every component of the financial system is undergoing restructuring—more precisely, a process of liberalization. The term *financial deregulation* may be more familiar to non-Japanese. However, liberalization means not merely doing away with some regulations but also changes in the structure of financial institutions and markets.

Financial restructuring in Japan became an ongoing process during the second half of the 1970s. Government bond issue to fund the large deficits that emerged after 1975 was the major force pressuring the regulatory authorities to initiate a series of reforms that started this restructuring process.

In 1976 the Ministry of Finance (MOF) officially recognized an existing competitive money market for repurchase agreements in government securities known as the *gensaki* market. *Gensaki* transactions (repurchase agreements) had been in existence since the late 1940s, though it was a relatively small market until the early 1970s when volume expanded in response first to the surge in the interbank market rate of interest and then to the growing volume of government bonds. The Bank of Japan (BOJ) altered procedures in 1978 for purchasing government bonds held by financial institutions at favorable prices and, in so doing, removed an important subsidy to holding government bonds. This and other considerations forced the MOF to become more sensitive to market forces in funding the growing budget deficits. The monetary authorities as well as financial institutions and markets adapted themselves to the new financial environment.

The first part of this chapter outlines the most important features of the Japanese financial system prior to the initiation of reforms to provide background for a better understanding of the financial restructuring process and changes in the structure discussed in the latter part of the chapter.

When we examine the specific features of the Japanese financial system in the high economic growth period before 1975, we have to consider the following points carefully: (1) the dominant role of intermediation finance in the total flow of funds and the dominant role of the banking system within intermediation finance; (2) the flow of fund patterns between the personal, corporate, and government sectors; (3) the undeveloped state of direct finance; (4) the importance of customer relationships; (5) the prevention of financial instability and the allocation of financial resources toward economic growth as a foundation for regulation; and (6) the structure, form, extent, and objectives of financial regulation and supervision.

Indeed we have to consider intensively each of these six features in order to make clear how financial intermediaries have changed in Japan. Because of space limitations, however, I will take up only one of the six—the dominance of intermediation markets.

The Dominance of Intermediation Finance

The most remarkable feature of the Japanese financial system prior to reform is, needless to say, the dominance of bank intermediation in a system dominated by intermediation in general. Direct finance in Japan played a minor role in the flow of funds.[1] Has this characteristic changed since liberalization started? This question is the most important when we consider Japan's intermediation market.

The role of intermediation finance in the Japanese financial system is revealed by the flow of funds accounts published annually by BOJ. These show three things. First, intermediation markets dominated the flow of funds. During the period 1970–1975, private and public financial institutions provided 92 percent of the total flow of funds (compared to 76 percent in the United States). Second, the banking system dominated intermediation. During the period 1970–1975, the banking system provided 61 percent of the total flow of funds to the nonfinancial sector (31 percent in the United States). Third, public financial institutions played an important role in Japan's flow of funds. During the 1970–1975 period, public institutions provided 19 percent of the total flow of funds to the nonfinancial sector in Japan (10 percent in the United States).

Characteristics of Liberalization Since the Mid-1970s

The Japanese financial system was heavily regulated in the decades of the postwar period. The working of free market mechanisms was restricted either by monetary authorities or by industry self-constraint. However, since the mid-1970s, when MOF started to issue a huge amount of government bonds under the new economic circumstance of lower economic growth, financial liberalization has evolved and market mechanisms have resumed their role in Japan's financial system.

The money market has expanded to include the *gensaki*, large certificates of deposit, Euroyen deposits, yen-denominated bankers acceptances, commercial paper, and six-month Treasury bills. Money markets have unregulated interest rates and wide participation.

The interbank market has been a focus of separate regulatory reform. In 1978 BOJ ended the "quotation system," which limited movements of interbank rates, and has permitted increasing access to the market. There was a debate as to whether BOJ should continue to exercise administrative guidance over the market; however, in November 1988 BOJ introduced new rules regarding monetary control so interbank rates are more flexible than previously. Now BOJ regards this market as completely liberalized.

The capital market has expanded significantly as a result of the growth of government bonds. Both the new issue and the secondary markets have expanded, with the exception of the corporate straight bond market. The reasons for the exception include: collateralization requirements limit the flexibility of primary issues; cartel-like agreements among banks and securities companies impose a variety of restrictions on bond issues that limit their flexibility as a funding source for corporations; some, not all, large corporations continue to value customer relationships with city banks and other big financial institutions; and corporations can now borrow in foreign markets, to which they have resorted increasingly. The equity market, despite being the largest in the world, is still not regarded as a flexible source of funds.

A variety of new financial instruments and services have been introduced since the mid-1970s. Most of the money market instruments have been introduced since 1979, when certificates of deposits (CDs) were initiated. Banks have been permitted to issue combination-type deposits, resident foreign-currency deposits, and money market certificates (MMCs) with interest rates tied to the CD or other rate. Investment trust companies and trust banks have been authorized to issue investment funds of various types. Nonbank financial institutions also have provided varieties of new assets to investors. Financial future, options, swaps, and other derivative markets have been introduced with great success in almost all cases.

Along with domestic liberalization, Japanese financial institutions and markets have been internationalized. Internationalization of finance became official policy in 1980 when the Foreign Exchange and Foreign Trade Control Law was amended to incorporate the principle of liberalized capital flows. As a result, a large number of restrictions on the cross-border flow of funds and capital have been relaxed. There now exists a close relation between domestic money markets and international interest rates. Japanese financial institutions, investors, and corporate borrowers have taken advantage of this connection, and their presence in every international financial center has become very noticeable.

Gradually foreign institutions have been given greater access to Japanese financial markets; for instance, foreign securities companies have been admitted to the Tokyo Stock Exchange. In December 1986 the Tokyo International Banking Facility opened. Tokyo has indeed become a major world financial center. While the yen does not yet play a role in international finance consistent with Japan's role in international trade, there is little doubt that it will become a more widely used international reserve and investment asset.

Interest rate liberalization has occurred in selected areas of the financial system. Interest rates are essentially unregulated on money market instruments, the new issue market for medium and long-term government bonds, the secondary bond market, the six-month Treasury bills, foreign currency deposits, investment trust funds, and large-denomination time deposits. In addition, loan interest rate restrictions have been relaxed. Deposit rate ceilings still affect a considerable portion of total deposits, though the percentage has declined drastically, from 90 percent at the end of 1985, to 64 percent in 1988, and to 49 percent in March 1990. Also, the ceilings have been adjusted more frequently. Regulatory authorities have accepted the principle of first liberalizing interest rates on large deposits, with small deposit liberalization to be considered later.

Monetary policy has not been as big an issue in the reform process in Japan as it has in the United States; however, BOJ has been required to adjust its operating procedures in response to the changing financial environment as part of its goals of maintaining low and stable inflation and a stable exchange rate for the yen. In 1978 BOJ began announcing money supply projections for each quarter about one or two weeks before the quarter. These are not annual monetary aggregate targets as in the United States but instead are projections or forecasts of future money supply growth. The announcement is made to highlight BOJ concern about the money supply and price stability. In 1979 BOJ added CDs to the official money supply measures.

BOJ has gradually shifted emphasis from credit allocation controls such as "window guidance" to instruments more in tune with a liberalized financial environment. In particular, BOJ has made efforts to develop open market operations as a major policy instrument.

The recent evolution of free market mechanisms in Japanese finance may be summed up in the following way: (1) it has been primarily incremental; (2) it has been relatively smooth and lacking in disruptions to the financial system such as those in the United States during the 1970s and early '80s; and (3) to all appearances, the process seems to have been characterized more by regulatory rather than by market innovations. It lacks the intense regulatory-market conflicts common in the United States. This means that regulatory authorities have taken the role of intermediary to mitigate the regulatory-market confrontation that surely would have occurred otherwise.

Liberalization and Securitization

The transition in Japanese finance can best be thought of as a process of securitization of the financial system in a broad sense.[2] Then a question comes to mind quite naturally: Has the intermediary finance that dominated Japanese finance in the past declined in importance in the process of liberalization? For a considerable period of time, few Japanese financial economists were convinced that securitization was the essential phenomenon in 1980s Japan. They believed the role of once-dominant intermediary finance declined in importance. However, careful examination of recent flow of funds data (BOJ in 1989) shows that the development of securitization itself has helped in preserving the dominance of intermediation finance. The essence of recent Japanese flow of funds can be summarized in the following way.

To begin, we should clarify the concept of securities. In examining the recent remarkable phenomenon in the flow of funds, we have to go beyond the concept of securities defined by Article 2 of the Securities and Exchange Law, which designates securities as a limited number of financial instruments. Rather, we have to define "securities" in a broader sense to include such instruments as domestic commercial paper."Securitization" in a financial system is a phenomenon of the emergence and development of public offering, and brokerage of, funding by, and investment in such broadly defined securities.

With this view of securitization, we can observe some remarkable features in the recent flow of funds data.

Funds supplied through financial institutions to primary borrowers have increased from 88 percent in 1987 to over 90 percent in 1988 relative to the total funds raised by nonfinancial sectors as a whole. This shows that indirect (or intermediation) finance is still dominant in Japan. (Among forms of supply broken down into bank loans, new securities issued, and "others," the weight of "others" has increased because of the growing supply of funds in the form of nonsecurities to overseas borrowers through offshore markets.)

Net issue of government bonds is falling year by year. Their percentages relative to total funds raised by nonfinancial sectors were 38 percent in 1986 and 32 percent in 1987. However, owing to an increase in new issues of domestic commercial paper, total securities newly issued represented 33 percent of the total supply of funds in 1988. This suggests that a new development in securitization is under way regardless of the decline in the issue of government bonds.

During the period of high economic growth, securities accounted for less than 20 percent of total funds raised by nonfinancial sectors. It is from 1975 on that the role of securities has grown, initially as bonds to fund government deficits. In the late 1970s, securities' share rose to about 40 percent. Since 1980, however, as the government moved toward more balanced budgets, the pace of government bond and other securities issue began to shrink relatively. Meanwhile, equity stock and commercial paper offered by business corporations increased sharply, boosting the proportion of securities in total funds raised to more than 30 percent.

Indirect finance through financial intermediaries has persistently carried the dominant weight in the Japanese system. The bulk of funds raised in the form of securities are held by financial institutions. This suggests that securitization in the Japanese financial system has actually brought about a qualitative change in portfolios of financial institutions, rather than shifting the flow of funds from indirect to direct financing. Securities holdings of ultimate lenders have not yet increased.

These recent changes in flow of funds mean that the penetration of securitization into financial intermediation (particularly banking) is through the existing Japanese financial system. Securities markets in a broad sense have become more important in the working of the whole system, but this does not mean that intermediation finance has declined in importance.

We need some analytical concept to describe the financial system other than the concept of "direct" versus "indirect" (intermediated) finance. I would like to propose for this purpose "negotiated debt transactions" versus "open market transactions" to make clear the analysis of the working of the system.

Negotiated Versus Open Market Transactions

Negotiated debt transactions are "customer relationship" oriented, multi-dimensional in terms of the services provided, long term, and frequently implicit rather than explicit. In negotiated transactions the actual transfer of funds and the price at which funds are exchanged represent only two specific aspects among many of the relationship between borrower and lender.

Open market transactions, in contrast, are essentially defined by price and quantity; they are limited in terms of the services provided in the borrower–lender relationship; they are short term and generally explicit rather than implicit.

The distinction between negotiated and open market transactions can be understood by considering a basic function of the financial system, the supply of liquidity to every economic entity in an imperfect information environment. Individuals and corporations seeking to sell assets or issue debt to get liquidity can do it in two ways: in a transaction with a specific counterpart (especially a financial intermediary) or by going into an open market.

In the case of transactions with a specific counterpart, the two sides negotiate the terms of the transaction (price, collateral, period, and so on). The more imperfect the information retrieval system and the more arcane the characteristics of the financial instrument, the greater the tendency for this form of obtaining liquidity to become the basis for establishing

a long-term relationship between the parties. Hence, bilateral or negotiated forms of providing liquidity provide a foundation for customer-
relationship-based financial transactions. In addition, the greater the costs
of obtaining information, the more likely the customer relationship will
evolve into a long-term relationship that covers services other than the
provision of liquidity.

Liquidity can also be obtained in an open market where the borrower
sells financial instruments in an open market composed of a large number
of participants. While this open-market method requires a mediator, that
is, a broker and/or exchange agent, there are many potential sellers and
buyers. Open markets require some commonly agreed upon method for
judging the quality of financial instruments and some method of obtaining
information in a cost-effective manner. But, in general, in this setting there
is little interest in, or need to know, much in the way of specifics about the
two parties to the transaction. The participants' concern is entirely with the
price, quantity of funds, and asset quality.

Cargill and Royama (1988) decompose the Japanese and U.S. flow of
funds in the period 1954–1985 in terms of a four-part taxonomy: indirect-
negotiated, indirect-open market, direct-negotiated, and direct-open market. Our analysis suggests that negotiated transactions played a far more
important role in Japan compared to their role in the United States. While
negotiated transactions in Japan have declined since 1975 as a result of the
liberalization process, they continue to dominate Japanese finance and
remain a significant distinction between the financial structures of Japan
and the United States.

Securitization means a shift is occurring from bilateral, negotiated, or
customer-based ways of obtaining liquidity to methods relying on the open,
less regulated markets with wide participation. This is the basic nature of
the financial transition in Japan after 1975.

By definition, increased securitization implies the decline of negotiated
transactions. Related to the overall decline in negotiated transactions,
securitization has also weakened the once dominant long-term customer
relationships between a bank and a corporation characterized as the main
bank system. Horiuchi and associates (1988) tell us that the percentage of
funds obtained from their main bank by major corporations (defined as a
company listed in the first section of the Tokyo Stock Exchange) steadily
declined over the period 1962–1983.

The securitization process has had fundamental effects on the structure
of Japan's finance. However, the transition has been fairly steady and
gradual since 1975, and we should not expect to see dramatic changes in
Japanese finance over short periods. The incremental approach has been

effective because of BOJ's successful price stabilization policies. BOJ has maintained a small gap between regulated and unregulated interest rates that would otherwise have been incentive for institutions to introduce money substitutes.

Implications of Securitization in Japan

The securitization of finance in Japan has raised a number of issues regarding banks and other financial institutions. Three of the more important issues are: (1) conflicts arising from legally mandated separation of different types of financial activity; (2) increased risks for individual financial institutions and hence for system risk; (3) the influence of global financial markets on Japanese banks and other financial institutions.

Specialization and Securitization

Since the late 1980s MOF has been exploring ways to deal with conflicts between the institutional specialization and the securitization process, which by its nature requires ease of substitution among different financial channels. The Financial System Research Council (created in December 1987) has considered a number of possibilities and, in May 1989, it summarized two possible and desirable policies that could be undertaken to restructure the system. Both are designed to enhance competition by permitting financial institutions to enter other businesses as long as the entry is made by their subsidiaries. This will eventually reduce the degree of specialization of financial institutions established during the Meiji era a century ago. The proposal of the Financial System Research Council, although its May 1989 report was interim, was followed by discussions in every group concerned. Among official advisory bodies, the Securities and Exchange Commission published interim reports in May 1990, while the Insurance Council also summarized its reactions. It will take several years to implement any revisions in the legal system of finance. During the discussion, conflicts among vested interests will surely hinder restructuring. However, discussions so far appear to have some points in common based on three generally accepted principles.

1. Enhanced competitiveness in the financial services industry is a necessary condition for improving the availability of assets and services to

the economy. As part of this, the potential for unfair trade practice should be reduced.

2. Japan's financial structure must be internationally compatible, especially with the financial structures of major industrial powers.

3. The system must be able to deal with risk in a manner that does not increase system risk.

System Risk

In the past, Japanese financial institutions operated with limited portfolio flexibility and, hence, has restricted opportunities to assume many types of risk. Fundamentally their risk was the credit risk of each customer-borrower, which could be easily managed through long-term relationships. As the transition toward securitization and open markets continues, however, individual institutions are faced with new portfolio choices that involve more risk not only in degree but in variety; interest rate risk, new types of credit risk (such as sovereign risk), liquidity risk, exchange rate risk, and so on. This added risk to banks is reflected in the fact that bank stock price variation has increased in the past decade—such volatility being itself considered a risk measure.

Sovereign risk, in particular, has become a more serious problem as a result of lending in international markets and the decline in the importance of the main bank system. The close relationship between banks and their borrowers and the main bank role as spokesperson for the business provided an efficient form for assessing and monitoring credit risk. As this system declines in importance, publicly available financial disclosure frameworks become more important.

While the need to monitor and regulate financial institution risk has been more recognized than previously, regulatory authorities have accomplished some monitoring and risk-sharing control in the real world. In this respect, there has been a considerable amount of debate over deposit insurance as well as under what circumstances the monetary authorities should undertake bailouts.

A deposit insurance system was established in 1971, modelled after the U.S. system, with some notable exceptions. The differences are that in Japan membership is compulsory for almost all private financial institutions offering banking services. Private financial institutions have management representation on the Deposit Insurance Corporation (DIC), and the DIC is capitalized in equal parts by the government, BOJ, and private financial institutions. Even though the vice-governor of BOJ is governor of

DIC, other officers and management appointments must be approved by JOF. And while DIC is permitted to borrow from BOJ, such borrowing is subject to approval by MOF. However, the most remarkable difference between the Japanese DIC and the U.S. FDIC is that JDIC has never made any payouts. Although there have been several failures in Japan, the monetary authorities made every effort to get other banks to absorb the bank having problems. The trump card of deposit insurance has never been played.

Globalization of Finance

Increased internationalization has been a major feature of Japan's financial system during the past decade. Some of the indices of internationalization include:

1. In 1986 the volume of foreign exchange transactions in the Tokyo market ($48 billion) almost equalled the $50 billion volume in the New York market. By 1990, foreign exchange transactions in Tokyo exceeded those in the United States; Japan has assumed second place behind London.

2. Despite unattractive tax and regulatory constraints, the Tokyo offshore market has grown rapidly. As of the end of 1986 the Tokyo offshore market held assets of $94 billion dollars, about one-third those of New York's International Banking Facility. By the end of 1987, however, the two markets were about equal in size, and at year end 1988 the Tokyo market exceeded the New York market.

3. Japanese banks and other financial institutions are far more dependent on international activities than previously; this is especially the case for the city banks and other large financial institutions. For example, all banks (city, long-term credit, and trust) received 42 percent of their revenue from international activities in 1987, and the largest of these institutions was even more dependent on international activities.

4. Japanese financial institutions have expanded the activities to a number of overseas markets. International banking business in the past was confined to supporting Japanese trade in manufactured products; however, these institutions now engage in a wide variety of activities. At the same time, the Japanese financial system has become more open to foreign entities. After 1985 the number of foreign institutions operating in Japan increased greatly, as did the number of Japanese institutions operating abroad.

The globalization of finance reinforced the securitization process in two ways. First, it has brought increasing pressure to establish an open short-term government securities market. Such a market is deemed to be an important component to the free flow of funds in and out of Japan and the efforts to "internationalize" the yen. MOF in 1987 began to issue six-month Treasury bills as a step toward a short-term securities market; however, there is considerable debate about the speed with which such a market will be established in Japan. MOF has shown considerable resistance to a short-term market because BOJ traditionally purchases almost all short-term government debt at subsidized prices.

Second, globalization has forced the regulatory authorities to place banks and other institutions conducting international transactions on a basis more comparable with institutions in other countries. In July 1987 the Bank for International Settlements established uniform capital ratios that all major international banks in the G-10 countries and Luxembourg must achieve by the end of 1992. This has created some problems for Japanese banks because of the higher collateral requirements imposed by Japanese banks compared to their counterparts and because Japanese banks are permitted to hold corporate equities as part of their asset portfolio, though in amounts limited to 5 percent of the outstanding stock of any given company.

Conclusion

The Japanese financial system has relied extensively on negotiated debt and less on open market transactions than has been the case in the United States. In the mid-1970s, however, new economic and technological forces generated pressure on the Japanese financial system to increase the role of financial transactions in open markets. As a result, the financial system is now more open and more competitive in terms of price competition than previously.

This transition in finance has reduced the role of the banking system in the flow of funds in two ways. First, banks now provide a smaller percentage of funds to the nonfinancial sectors of the economy than they had previously. Instead, financial intermediaries other than banks are gaining share, even as intermediation finance as a whole is expanding. Second, there is evidence that the main bank system, with its long-term relationships, is less important than it was even in the early 1980s.

Whether banks and other financial institutions can maintain their present market share or even enhance it remains uncertain in this newly evolved competitive market system. It depends partly on how innovative the behavior of individual institutions is toward the financial needs of end-users, and partly on how the regulatory framework is reformed. Regulatory authorities are in the process of deciding fundamental structural questions about the future financial system. If the past regulatory attitude is any indication, banks and other financial institutions, including securities houses, will be allowed considerable flexibility in providing financial services, which will at least permit them to maintain current market share levels.

In any event, there is little doubt that the role of negotiated transactions has become less and less important. Japanese finance is moving toward the type of open market environment of the United States; however, this is a slow process and likely to evolve into something much different in its form of competition than in the United States.

The Japanese financial system has taken a key role in the working of the world financial and economic systems.

Since 1985 Japan has been the biggest net creditor country in the world, while the United States has become a net debtor. Net claims of Japan against overseas borrowers reached almost $300 billion at the end of 1988, 25 times as much as at the end of 1980. This means Japan's money and the savings behind it are now used extensively for capital formation outside Japan.

The relatively stable performance of the Japanese market up to the end of 1989 contributed much to the stability of the global financial system. This was evident in the case of the movement of stock markets on October 16, 1989, after the mini-crash in New York. The quickest recovery from the crash in October 1987 was also found in the Tokyo market. Indeed, the role of the Japanese financial system seemed to be as an anchor for the global system. Conversely, volatility in the Japanese markets will surely have a serious influence on other markets. Whatever happens, it is a consequence of the natural evolution of the Japanese financial system's role in the world.

The global financial system as well as the world's economy as a whole is facing a new era. It is not precisely clear how European economies, including those in Eastern Europe, will be confederated. We are now in a decade of greater uncertainty. However, there are some areas of certainty. One of these is that Japan's money will be a key factor. To meet new and stronger financial demands, Japan must restructure its financial system towards a more efficient, open, and fair system in a global perspective.

Acknowledgments

This chapter is based on joint work with Thomas F. Cargill (University of Nevada, Reno), titled "The Evolution of Japanese Banking and Finance" which is prepared for George G. Kaufman, ed., *Banking Structures in Major Countries* (Boston: Kluwer Academic Publishers, forthcoming). It should be mentioned that some basic analytical concepts in this chapter are more precisely explained in T.F. Cargill and S. Royama, *The Transition of Finance in Japan and the United States: A Comparative Perspective* (Stanford, CA: Hoover Institution, 1988). I appreciate Professor Cargill's permission to use the works. However, opinions expressed here are mine alone, as are any errors. I am also grateful to the Osaka Stock Exchange for financial support.

Notes

1. According to Gurley and Shaw (1960), if primary securities issued by ultimate borrowers to finance their deficits are acquired by ultimate lenders in the financial system, it is direct finance. If they are purchased by financial intermediaries that issue their own debt to cover the acquisition of primary securities, it is indirect or intermediation finance. Note that it is direct finance when some corporate bonds newly issued are subscribed and held in the portfolio of a financial institution such as a commercial bank.

2. The term *securitized* is often used in a narrow sense to describe assets held by financial institutions transformed into negotiable assets that anonymous investors can buy. However, securitization also describes a process in which borrowers shift their source of funds more toward the issue of securities. Thus, *securitization* means disintermediation in cases where new issues of securities substitute for bank loans. However, this is not the general case. It is conceivable that banks acquire newly issued securities in place of loans, so the level of financial intermediation remains unchanged. See the Bank for International Settlement (1986).

References

The Bank for International Settlement. 1986. *Recent Innovations in International Banking*. Basel: BIS, April.

The Bank of Japan. 1989. Showa 63 nen no Shikin Jyunkan [Flow of Funds in 1988]. *Monthly Review* (June).

Cargill, T.F., and Royama, Shoichi. 1988. *The Transition of Finance in Japan and the United States: A Comparative Perspective*. Stanford, CA: Hoover Institution Press.

The Financial System Research Council. 1989. *On a New Japanese Financial System, Interim Report by the Second Financial System Committee*, May.

Gurley, J.G., and Shaw, Edward. 1960. *Money in a Theory of Finance*. Washington, DC: The Brookings Institution.

Horiuchi, A., Packer, Frank, and Fukuda, Susumu. 1988. What Role has the Main Bank Played in Japan? *Journal of Japanese and International Economics* (June), 159–180.

The Securities and Exchange Council. 1990. *Restructuring the Japanese Capital Market: Toward an International Market and Improvement of the Legal Framework in Response to Securitization*. Interim Reports by the Fundamental Research Committee (May).

III SECURITIES MARKETS

8 INTERNATIONALIZATION AND REGULATION OF THE WORLD'S SECURITIES MARKETS

Joseph A. Grundfest

Growth in the internationalization of world securities markets in the 1980s has been remarkable. Aggregate foreign purchases and sales of securities in the United States grew from $75.1 billion in 1980 to $416.3 billion in 1989—a cumulative annual growth rate of 21.0 percent maintained over a full decade.[1] Meanwhile, aggregate U.S. purchases and sales of foreign securities grew at an even more rapid 32.8 percent cumulative annual growth rate, from $17.9 billion in 1980 to $230.3 billion in 1989.

Foreign direct investment in the United States grew at an annual cumulative growth rate of 22.3 percent from $65.5 billion in 1980 to $400.8 billion in 1989. The only international investment category involving the United States that showed significantly lower growth was direct foreign investment abroad by U.S. investors. In that category, investment activity grew at a much more moderate cumulative annual growth rate of 6.3 percent from $215.4 billion in 1980 to $373.4 billion in 1989.

The reasons for this growth are several. Most notably, the growth in internationalization can be traced to fundamental imbalances in the world's supply of and demand for capital. Simply put, at various points in time, nations will have differing comparative advantages in their ability to generate investable capital. Similarly, the best investment opportunities at

123

any one point in time will not necessarily be found in the same nations that generate investable capital. For a variety of reasons, the imbalance between sources of capital and the locus of investment opportunities grew throughout the decade. In order to employ the capital generated by surplus providers, which were located away from the most promising investment opportunities, the world's securities markets inevitably had to become more internationalized—otherwise, there was simply no way the world's investable capital could have been matched up with the world's best investment opportunities.

The trend toward internationalization was also fueled by developments in technology, finance theory, derivative markets, and deregulation. The costs of telecommunications and computations plunged through the decade, thereby sharply reducing the costs of developing international investment and trading linkages. Progress in our understanding of finance theory also contributed to internationalization as investors began to diversify across international marketplaces and to develop refined techniques for valuing and hedging instruments that present international risk and return characteristics.

At the same time that technology and understanding of finance advanced through the decade, the world evolved a complex series of options and futures markets that facilitated hedging and reallocation of international as well as domestic investment risk. Finally, throughout the decade, markets in New York, Tokyo, London, and elsewhere experienced a wave of deregulatory initiatives that swept away barriers that had limited both domestic and international competition in the world's securities markets.

Regardless of specific developments in the world's financial markets over the coming years, it seems relatively safe to predict that internationalization of the world's securities markets is here to stay. Imbalances between the sources of investable capital and the location of investment opportunities will continue—and may well grow in magnitude as a consequence of developments in Eastern Europe and elsewhere. The pace of technological progress will not slow. Advances in finance theory have still not spread as widely as they could through the financial marketplace, and as they spread they will provide further incentives for international investment. Further derivative product markets continue to introduce new international investment products that expand the scope of international investment, hedging, and speculation opportunities.

Only in the area of regulation can one find fundamental forces at work that could significantly impede the further internationalization of the markets. If political forces induce regulators to reverse field and to

introduce new restrictions that increase domestic or international investment and trading costs, then the growth of internationalization can be
impaired. Predicting the activities of politicians and regulators is, however,
an exceedingly dangerous exercise, and one can only hope that reason will
prevail on this score as well as others.

Given the rapid internationalization of the world's securities markets,
and the likely continuation of this trend, it is important to recognize that
internationalization will present serious challenges on the enforcement
front for all the world's regulators. Simply put, in this new environment, no
nation will be able to enforce even its most basic antifraud strictures
without the cooperation of a substantial number of its trading partners. As
one illustration of this new reality, consider the following example: a
Japanese subject violates Japanese law in the course of trading Japanese
securities with other Japanese citizens in Japanese markets. The violative
trades are, however, channeled through the United States, Britain,
Switzerland, or other foreign jurisdictions. Under these circumstances,
Japan will not be able to enforce its own rules against its own subjects
trading its own securities in its own markets without the active cooperation
of its international financial market trading partners.

This example is more than hypothetical. The recent revelation of the
"Quinn scandals" in Europe suggests that tens of millions of dollars have
been stolen from European investors as the result of a scheme based on
transactions in the United States securities markets.[2] Without the active
cooperation of U.S. law enforcement agencies, European authorities
would be hard pressed to develop a case against a fraud that occurred in
their own back yard.

In a similar vein, a recent study by the General Accounting Office
determined that trades originating abroad represented more than one-third
of all cases of suspected insider trading referred to the United States
Securities and Exchange Commission in 1987.[3] As several cases have
demonstrated, such trading can be generated by United States nationals
electing to trade from foreign locales for the express purpose of evading
detection by U.S. authorities.[4]

Significantly, no nation need impose its philosophy of market regulation
on any of its trading partners in order to successfully address this level of
fraud. Each nation can continue to define fraud as it likes; each can adopt
its own approach to insider trading regulation; and each can set whatever
penalties it deems appropriate under the circumstances. All that is needed
is a common understanding that the purpose of internationalization is to
facilitate legitimate trading. The purpose of internationalization in the
world's securities market is not to provide a means of evading the domestic

regulations of participating markets, nor is it an excuse for one nation unilaterally to impose its standards on trading that does not involve its own markets.

The problems posed by international fraud can be addressed by cooperation rooted in the simplest form of enlightened self-interest. Putting aside rogue jurisdictions that perceive little benefit from assuring that their market facilities are not used to shelter illegal offshore trading, each jurisdiction has a legitimate interest in maintaining its ability to enforce its domestic regulations in its domestic markets. This enforcement capacity can be maintained only if cooperation is forthcoming among trading partners. But cooperation will be forthcoming only if the favor is returned.

This rather straightforward fact of modern commercial life explains a great deal of the success achieved by the Securities and Exchange Commission in negotiating its network of memoranda of understanding, treaties, communiques, and accords. These bilateral understandings today exist between the United States and agencies of the United Kingdom, Japan, Switzerland, France, the Netherlands, Brazil, Ontario, Quebec, Canada, Italy, Turkey, the Cayman Islands, and the International Organization of Securities Commissions. Together they create an effective network through which foreign jurisdictions can obtain information from the United States about activities that might constitute violations abroad.[5] Similarly, they create an effective network whereby U.S. authorities can obtain information about violations in domestic U.S. markets resulting from foreign trades.[6]

In order further to enhance the ability of U.S. authorities to cooperate in investigations of foreign securities law violations, Congress adopted the Insider Trading and Securities Fraud Enforcement Act of 1988.[7] That statute contains a provision empowering the Securities and Exchange Commission to conduct investigations on behalf of foreign securities authorities, even if there is no allegation that U.S. law has been violated. This provision was adopted both in order to assist investigations of foreign securities law violations and to provide an inducement for foreign trading partners to adopt reciprocal cooperative provisions.[8]

The value of a cooperative approach to international enforcement issues is particularly striking in light of the SEC's (Securities and Exchange Commission's) experience in the early part of the eighties. At that time, the Commission relied primarily on unilateral attempts to obtain foreign-based evidence. Those efforts were often fruitless. In addition, the efforts were "time consuming, expensive, and strained international relations."[9] In contrast, having invested the effort of explaining to foreign jurisdictions the value of a bilateral understanding that allows each party to protect and promote the interests of the other, the Commission is now reaping the rewards of its more cooperative approach.

Indeed, the value of international enforcement cooperation extends far beyond the operation of the world's securities markets. In late April of 1990 representatives of the Group of Seven (Britain, Canada, France, Italy, Japan, the United States, and West Germany) met with representatives of eight other nations, some of which are known for their bank secrecy laws (including Switzerland, Austria, and Luxembourg), to discuss problems raised by money laundering arising out of international narcotics traffic.[10] The meeting led to the proposal of a broad set of regulatory and banking reforms designed to pierce through the shield erected by bank secrecy laws (Labaton, 1990, C1, col. 3) Evidently, the benefits of international enforcement cooperation are not limited to the world's securities markets, and progress in this direction can be expected along many different fronts.

No doubt, some market participants might object to even this level of enforcement cooperation on the ground that certain domestic regulations are inefficient. By prohibiting foreign trading in violation of these strictures, international enforcement cooperation could thus reduce market efficiency. The difficulty with this argument, however, is that it is essentially lawless. No legal regime can operate in an environment in which compliance is voluntary. Indeed, even when regulations properly address market externalities, some traders will perceive that their interests are adversely affected and will attempt to evade domestic regulations on the premise that those regulations are inefficient. If avoidance can be justified on this rationale then compliance becomes discretionary and domestic legal regimes lose their force.

Thus, unless one believes that regulation of capital market transactions is suspect in all circumstances, provisions to protect the enforcement integrity of the legal regime are, at some level, necessary. The socially accepted means of expressing objection to an inefficient regulation is to work within the system to change the regulation and not to evade the regulation through illegal means. Furthermore, if a regulation is in fact inefficient, it creates opportunities for other markets to establish trading systems that do not suffer from the same inefficiency and through which traders can legitimately interact. International competition thus acts as a potential safety valve governing the extent to which local regulators can impose inefficient constraints without forcing transactions offshore.

In summary, the world's securities markets have been forever changed as a result of internationalization. The world's enforcement mechanisms are lagging behind, and in order to provide basic assurances that each nation can enforce its own laws in its own markets against its own citizens, new modes of cooperation will have to evolve among the world's regulators.

Notes

1. These and other statistics cited in this chapter are compiled in Grundfest (1990).

2. *SEC v. Arnold Kimmes, et al.*, 89 C5942 (N.D. Ill. 1989).

3. *Problems With the SEC's Enforcement of the Securities Laws as to Suspicious Foreign Originated Trades*: Hearings before the Subcomm. on Commerce, Consumer, and Monetary Affairs of the House Comm. on Government Operations, 100th Cong., 2nd Sess. (1988) (Opening statements of Hon. Douglas Bernard, Jr., and Gary Montjoy). See also Torres and Salwen (1990, A3, col. 2), noting spate of insider trading inquiries in connection with foreign acquisitions of publicly traded U.S. firms.

4. See Levine, (1990, p. 80). To maintain secrecy, Levine explains that he opened a numbered Swiss bank account and "went to great lengths to avoid creating a paper trail for investigators to follow. . . . [The bank] sent me no bank statements. I called in my trades from public phones—collect."

5. For an excellent summary of the current state of SEC enforcement efforts on the international front, as well as a summary of international information sharing arrangements, see Mann and Mari (1990).

6. Interestingly, this degree of cooperation is forthcoming even from countries that have a long history of bank secrecy. These jurisdictions often recognize that their secrecy statutes were adopted for reasons that have nothing to do with the facilitation of illegal commerce, whether in the form of securities transactions or the laundering of drug money. Thus, in circumstances where sufficient evidence can be presented that a secrecy jurisdiction is being used for purposes inconsistent with the host jurisdiction's purpose in protecting depositor confidentiality, the host can be persuaded to lift the veil of secrecy.

7. *See* H.R. 5133, 100th Cong., 2d Sess. (1988), Section 6.

8. *See generally*, Theodore Levine and W. Hardy Caldicott, *The SEC and Foreign Policy: The International Securities Enforcement Cooperation Act of 1988*, 17 Sec. Reg. L.J. 115 (Summer 1989).

9. See Levine and Caldicott (1989, p. 3). See also Rider (1990) for a review that is critical of U.S. attempts to extend the scope of its international securities jurisdiction, particularly as reflected in the SEC's "waiver-by-conduct" proposal (Exchange Act Release No. 21186, 1984). "When somewhat presumptuously questioned as to how far his writ ran, Henry II responded, as far as his arrows reached! Given the developments that have since taken place in ballistics, such an approach to jurisdiction might even accommodate the extraterritorial zeal of our North American cousins."

10. See, generally, Walter (1990).

References

Grundfest, Joseph A. 1990. *Internationalization of the World's Securities Markets: Economic Causes and Regulatory Consequences—or—Beware the Über-Regulator. Journal of Financial Services Research* 4, 349–378.

Labaton, Stephen. 1990. Group of Seven Asks Money-Laundering Curbs. *The New York Times* (April 20), C1, col. 3.

Levine, Dennis B. 1990. The Inside Story of an Inside Trader. *Fortune* (May 21), 80.

Mann, Michael D., and Mari, Joseph G. 1990. *Developments in International Securities Law Enforcement*. Washington, DC: U.S. Securities and Exchange Commission.

Rider, Barry A.K. 1990. Policing the International Financial Markets: *An English Perspective, Brooklyn Journal of International Law* 16, 179–221.

Walter, Ingo. 1990. *The Secret Money Market: Inside the Dark World of Tax Evasion, Financial Fraud, Insider Trading, Money Laundering, and Capital Flight*. New York: Harper & Row.

9 JAPANESE SECURITIES MARKETS AND GLOBAL HARMONIZATION

Takashi Kato

Global harmonization of securities regulation is beneficial to efficient international transfers of funds, and thus contributes to optimum global allocation of resources. Where harmonization is difficult, "transparency" should be increased so that differences are clear. I believe that Japan should assume a positive attitude toward realization of harmonization and transparency as a means of promoting international coordination. Indeed, many of the changes in both the regulation and the structure of Japanese securities markets have been based on this approach, and I believe it will be pursued in the future.

Japanese Globalization

In Japanese securities markets, globalization has been taking place in the area of market participants, data processing, and flow of money. Three factors have contributed greatly to globalization: increased domestic and overseas capital transfer, accumulation of financial assets and changes in the flow of funds, and technological innovation in communications.

Increased domestic and overseas capital transfer was concomitant with the rapid accumulation of current account surpluses, and this encouraged

131

liberalization of cross-border and cross-currency transactions. In particular, through the complete revision of the Foreign Exchange Control Act in 1980, external trading was liberalized in principle and simplification of trading procedures advanced. Progress in market globalization has been pronounced. The move is being promoted primarily through arguments put forward by the U.S.-Japan Ad Hoc Committee for the Dollar-Yen Exchange Rate.

Overseas securities investment in 1989 amounted to $1790 billion, while domestic securities investment in Japan totaled $480 billion. Securities companies worldwide are progressing toward globalization. As of March 1989 Japanese securities houses had 231 overseas branches in 22 countries, including 119 subsidiaries, 25 subsidiary branches, and 87 representative offices.

In Japan, 53 branch offices belong to 48 foreign securities companies from six different countries. Although their trading accounted for only 1 percent of the Tokyo Stock Exchange (TSE) total at the beginning of 1988, the ratio exceeded 7 percent in 1989 and is continuing to expand.

Second, Japan has changed from an overinvesting economy to an oversaving economy. At the same time, the ratio of overseas fund procurement to total fund procurement by Japanese corporations was 42 percent in 1989. This has led to intensified diversification and expansion beyond national borders in terms of fund procurement and fund management. This was brought about by a change in financial flows and the accumulation of financial assets in both the corporate and individual sectors.

Third, technological innovation in communications has led to a decline in costs. Combined with the trend toward computerization of both back office operations and actual decision making, the communications innovations have facilitated formation of a global information network.

Regulatory Trends

Insider Trading

The Japanese Securities and Exchange Act was written along the lines of the U.S. Securities Act of 1933 and the Securities Exchange Act of 1934. Article 58 of the Japanese Securities and Exchange Act was established with a purpose similar to that of Article 10(b) of the U.S. Insider Trading Regulations. However, in Japan few legal proceedings have ever been instituted based on Article 58 because of its equivocal nature. This is also because Japan has a different culture as far as legal proceedings are concerned.

Insider trading regulations have been strengthened overseas, particularly in the United Kingdom and the United States. In the light of these new regulatory trends, the Securities and Exchange Act was amended in Japan. In the amended Act, material facts constituting insider trading are defined concretely. Thus the Japanese Act differs from its U.S. counterpart, which does not set forth the definition of insider trading, but instead rules on cases based on judicial precedents. For example, in Japan a decision to change a dividend by 20 percent or more is by law a material fact, so an increase from 10 to 11 yen per share is not governed by the rule, but an increase from 10 to 12 yen is deemed a material fact.

Another feature of Japanese regulations on insider trading is a system intended to prevent such trading before it happens. The Japan Securities Dealers Association instituted detailed rules under which all securities firms prescribe their own in-house trading regulations.

A number of listed corporations also established in-house insider trading rules according to their own requirements. The company rules are, in general, more extensive than the relevant provision in the Act. For example, short-term (swing) trading (defined as less than six months) by directors is prohibited regardless of whether a trade makes a profit or a loss.

An offender will be judged by his company's in-house rules before he appears in court. A penalty of this kind can be much heavier than a legal one in Japan, where life-long employment is established in society. The maximum legal penalty is six months imprisonment or a ¥500,000 fine. On the other hand, if an offender is discharged from employment, he loses his job as well as large retirement allowances.

The former chairman of the U.S. Securities and Exchange Commission, David S. Ruder, made a comment to the effect that Japanese insider trading regulations are, in substance, as effective as those in the United States. However, some concerned people doubt the effectiveness of the Japanese regulations because not one case has been prosecuted under them since their introduction in April 1989. One possible answer to such doubts is that the purpose of the Japanese regulations is to prevent insider trading before it takes place, rather than merely to prosecute offenders.

Options and Futures Trading

Liberalization and internationalization of financial and capital transactions have increased price fluctuation risks with regard to assets such as stocks, and a growing number of institutional investors are believing it necessary to seek hedges and other forms of risk management. Under these circumstances, Japan amended the necessary laws in May 1988 in order to introduce stock index futures as well as option trading. These efforts were made not only to provide institutional investors a means of hedging but also to bring Japanese securities markets in line with those in other economically advanced countries.

Since stock index futures began trading in September 1988 the functions of both stock and bond markets have been improved and expanded significantly. In particular, the bond market was expanded to include cash and government bond futures, and then OTC (over-the-counter) bond option trading. At the end of 1989, U.S. Treasury bond (T-bond) futures were listed on the TSE, marking the first time a foreign-currency-denominated futures contract has traded in the Japanese capital market. Further improvement and expansion of the bond market is under way, and government bond futures options trading was introduced on the TSE in early 1990.

Strengthened Disclosure Requirements

Inherent in internationalization is expanded participation by various investing members of a worldwide public. Although measures have been instituted to promote healthy development of Japanese securities markets, a further amendment to the regulatory Act is being examined by the authorities so that, on behalf of investors, it will be able to require timely disclosure of information regarding acquisition, holding, and liquidation of sizable positions of a stock. The disclosure of information such as stock distribution and holding will certainly introduce greater transparency, which is important for Japanese securities markets in order to develop further internationally.

An example of why disclosure is important is the case of large purchases of listed shares, a phenomenon frequently noticed in Japanese securities markets. The aim has varied from a desire to participate in management, forge closer business connections, reap capital gains, or collect greenmail. Large-scale acquisition of shares is not illegal in Japan unless it involves the manipulation of prices or other forms of unfair trading, such as insider trading. However, recent cases are often accompanied by wild price fluctuations, and investors at home and abroad become more vulnerable to unexpected losses unless they are fully informed of the fact large purchases of the shares of a certain company are being made.

Five Percent Rule. The United States, the United Kingdom, France, and West Germany have already introduced systems to obligate the disclosure of information with regard to the holding of sizable positions in a stock. These systems have been put to practical tests for years and obtained a high level of consistency. Japan introduced a disclosure system in 1990, taking into account past overseas legislation and other factors peculiar to Japan such as its unique stockholding structure. The system requires a designated person or its group to report in writing to the Ministry of Finance, the securities exchanges (Japan Securities Dealers Association in the case of OTC registered companies), and the issuing company within five days if they purchase more than 5 percent of the equity, including stock, convertible bonds, and warrants, of an issuing company.

Japan follows the United States and other countries in having a 5 percent holding threshold. The United States allows ten days to report, but there is a strong advocacy for reducing it to five days. Japan decided arguments for the shorter period are persuasive, and thus has implemented a five-day rule.

Tender Offer Bid Regulations.   Regulations on tender offers have been invoked only three times in Japan since they became effective in 1971. This is primarily because the Japanese dislike hostile takeovers, and even in friendly bids, shares are acquired through exchange or party-to-party transactions and there has been no need to acquire shares, especially from stockholders outside the exchange.

Taking into consideration increased mergers and acquisitions activities by Japanese corporations, the Japanese tender offer system must be reviewed from the viewpoint of international regulatory coordination. The Japanese authority concerned is working toward amendment of the system. What has been studied is the abolition of the proxy requirement system (a registration attorney is required when a nonresident conducts a tender offer), the abolition of the ten-day prior filing requirement, the extension of the offer period from "over 20 days to 30 days" to "over 20 days to 60 days," and a reduction of the holding ratio (trigger) from 10 percent to 5 percent.

Securitization

Financial securitization can be categorized into the securitization of both corporate finance and corporate assets, and progress can be seen in both. When we consider the fact financial securitization is inevitable, the consolidation and securitization of related markets emerge as an important issue. Securitization is making steady progress throughout advanced economies against the background of financial liberalization and increased capital adequacy requirements. Japan is not an exception. Thus, the commercial paper and mortgage securities markets have recently been improved.

With the aim of promoting the healthy and smooth development of capital markets in Japan, the Fundamental Research Committee of the Securities and Exchange Commission is studying appropriate systems and administrative measures to respond appropriately.

Progressive securitization in Japan has given rise to arguments questioning the exclusive powers of securities companies. Corporate bonds are analogous to bank loans, while the liquidation of bank credit is increasing in an effort to satisfy Bank for International Settlements (BIS) regulations. This factor is behind requests that banks be authorized to deal in securities. Therefore, the issue of financial securitization is closely related to the issue of segregation of the securities business and the banking business.

Segregation of Banking Institutions from the Securities Business

The segregation of banking institutions from the securities business and vice versa has been an issue in Japan. Thus, the Financial System Research Council, an advisory arm of the Ministry of Finance, faced up to the task of studying fundamental financial system reform and presented, via an interim report, five alternative methods to allow banks and securities firms to participate in both areas. The five methods are: investment bank, subsidiary, mutual participation, universal bank, and holding company. Of these, the investment bank method and the subsidiary method are deemed most practicable.

The investment bank method allows banks and securities firms to establish an investment bank subsidiary that can engage in all areas of the wholesale securities business, such as underwriting corporate bonds, corporate finance, foreign exchange, and trust services. The subsidiary method allows banks and securities firms to establish subsidiaries that can participate in a particular area of banking or the securities business.

It is still unpredictable how this issue will finally be resolved in Japan; the same issue is yet to be solved in the United States, and the future course of European Community integration must be taken into consideration as well. Several key factors must not be overlooked in the solution of the problem.

First, a conflict of interest exists between the banking business and the securities business. For example, a bank extends a loan to an underwriting client to avert a default on bonds or prop up management. In such a case, depositor interests are jeopardized to protect investors in the corporate bonds, despite the fact that protection of depositors should naturally be a major concern of the bank. It should be remembered that the intention of the Glass-Steagall Act was to eliminate such conflicts of interest.

Maintenance of sound bank operations is the second point. Since this is indispensable in keeping the credit and financial systems in order, it touches on the fundamentals of the national economy. Bank participation in risky securities business, therefore, should be questioned from the viewpoint of what is prudent for a banking institution.

The third point relates to the elimination of monopolies and the promotion of fair competition in the financial industry. A policy of segregating the banking business from the securities business has the same role as the antitrust law in eliminating monopolies. An economic framework built on fair competition must be observed under all circumstances, with a view to an appropriate distribution of national resources. The point is even more important in Japan since a bank is allowed to have, and in fact many banks hold, up to 5 percent of the equity of a corporation.

Fourth, as financial and capital markets become internationally integrated, the banking and securities businesses in the major countries should be harmonized internationally. However, I think this harmonization should be realized on the basis of accepting each country's history and own institutional arrangements.

The interests of the users of financial services is the fifth point. Enhancing the benefits to users will contribute to an efficient allocation of resources.

The opinions of Japanese banks with regard to the issue of separation are in general as follows. First, the purpose of Article 65 of the Securities and Exchange Act, which stipulates the segregation of banks from the securities business, is to protect and develop the securities business. It is not reasonable that this Article should be maintained. Second, the securities business is not necessarily a risky one for banks. Third, if the present system of separation remains in force, it could cause friction with Europe, where a universal banking system (combining both banking and securities business) has long been established. The international competitiveness of Japanese banks would eventually be weakened.

In the debate over an appropriate separation of the banking and securities businesses, the purpose of the present system—the prevention of conflict of interests, the maintenance of healthy banking operations, the elimination of monopolies, and the promotion of competition—must be emphasized to keep the segmented system in force. Based on the present system, banks and securities firms must remain completely competitive and maintain a mutually indispensable relationship.

Amended Commercial Code

I want to consider briefly the amendment to the Commercial Code scheduled for 1990. The amendment most likely to affect the securities market is the easing of regulations governing the issuance of preferred stock. Only preferred stock can be issued without voting rights. Despite this advantage, few corporations have issued preferreds in Japan because of the complicated procedures. (Until the amendment, issuance of preferred stock had to be stated in the articles of incorporation prior to actual issuance, thus hindering fitting issuance to prevailing economic conditions.)

According to the amendment draft, once a general outline of issuance terms is given in the articles of incorporation, the board of directors can fine tune the terms, and corporations can time issuance. The amendment also contains an increase in the maximum level of nonvoting preferred stock from one-fourth of the total outstanding shares to one-third. Under the amendment, a growing number of corporations are expected to issue preferreds as a measure to counter acquisition.

The second point of the amendment is to increase the amount of corporate bond flotation. Japan is one of a few countries that sets a ceiling on corporate bond issuance, and opinions have been strongly voiced urging abolition of the ceiling. Abolition was postponed, but the ceiling was raised from "an amount two times capital and legal reserves" to "two times net assets." In this respect, the amendment failed to meet international regulatory standards, but it will certainly contribute to an active primary market for corporate bonds in the future.

Major International Problems

National Treatment of Foreign Firms

Since the securities market has become increasingly internationalized, the integration of domestic and foreign securities firms has become active. In regard to the entrance of foreign securities firms into Japan, Japan has assumed a positive attitude, based on the principle of treating them in the same way as domestic companies (national treatment).

In 1971 the Law Governing Foreign Securities Firms was enacted, paving the way for these firms to open branches. Under this Law, foreign firms were permitted to engage in the securities business at branch offices in Japan, as licensed by the Minister of Finance. Various types of licenses were granted, using almost the same standards and grounds for refusal as for Japanese firms. However, the foreign firms could not trade directly on Japanese exchanges because they were not able to become members of the exchanges.

Tokyo Stock Exchange (TSE) membership was gradually opened to non-Japanese entities, again on the basis of national treatment. A system allowing foreign firms to obtain TSE membership was established in the 1982 revision of the articles of incorporation of TSE. In practice, however, obtaining membership was almost impossible as there were no vacancies. However, in 1985 the number of members was increased, and six foreign firms obtained membership at that time. In 1987 the number was again increased, and 16 more foreign firms were granted membership. In 1990 it was decided to effect a third increase, including three foreign firms. Consequently, TSE membership now includes 25 foreign securities firms.

Net Capital Adequacy Standards Requirement for Securities Firms

Ever since Black Monday 1987, the capital adequacy of securities firms has been an international concern. U.S. SEC rules and U.K. TSA rules have already mapped out regulations requiring comprehensive evaluation of the risks to which securities firms are exposed.

In Japan, following the licensing system adopted in 1968, minimum equity, maximum debt ratio, and maximum holdings of each investor were set depending on the type of license and type of business. Since then, however, regulations on investment instruments have been considered insufficient because various new instruments have been introduced—including options and futures. Thus, the capital adequacy standard was studied in Japan and a revised framework was established in March 1989. These regulations were based on a comprehensive survey to evaluate the degree of overall risk that securities firms are exposed to by assigning risk weights to each type of asset held by the firms. These new regulations were effected in April 1989 as an experiment and fully enacted in April 1990.

International unification of the regulations concerning securities firm equity capital has been studied by IOSCO (International Organization of Securities Commissions) and other organizations. Meanwhile, the

European Community adopted legislation in December 1989 to regulate the equity capital of banks in the EC, and it is expected that securities firms will come within the scope of this legislation. I think it is necessary for Japan to participate positively in discussions in order to promote international cooperation. In addition, if there is to be international agreement on unified standards, Japanese regulations should be adjusted accordingly.

Cross-Border Insider Trading

As securities markets internationalize further and attract a wider range of participants, the markets must develop in ways that gain the trust of investors by ensuring fairness and transparency. From this viewpoint, in recent years many countries, including Japan, have strengthened their regulations on insider trading. However, where markets have become internationalized and geared toward unification, the independent regulations of a single country are not sufficient. International cooperation is now paramount.

The Japanese Ministry of Finance (MOF) prepared a memorandum in 1986 regarding information exchanges with the U.S. Securities and Exchange Commission, and periodic discussions have been held. In 1987 Japan exchanged a similar memorandum with the U.K. Ministry of Trade and Industry. In addition, at the July 1989 "Arche" summit meeting and at the September 1989 IOSCO general meeting, Japan declared its intention to continue cooperation to regulate insider trading.

At the fourth regular meeting of MOF's Securities Bureau and the U.S. SEC, held in January 1990, it was decided that a working committee would continue studying revision of the 1986 memorandum, aiming to improve the flow of information and investigation with regard to international unfair trading practices. Since legal systems differ from country to country, it may be impossible to improve everything immediately, but it is important to continue making efforts.

Disclosure Systems

It is now common for a single investment instrument to be accessible to the public in more than one country. Furthermore, investment and trading have passed national borders and are carried out on a global basis. Under such a situation there is a tendency for business to concentrate in markets with looser disclosure standards. As a result, an international harmonization of the disclosure system has become mandatory. Moreover, unification of accounting standards is essential since it forms the basis for an appropriate disclosure system.

An effort for a unified accounting standard has begun at IOSCO and the International Accounting Standards Committee has been formed to meet this need. Japan strongly supports such efforts and regards it of utmost importance to study the matter positively. In line with this, it has been decided Japan will introduce segment accounting, as practiced in the United States and elsewhere, from the business term ending March 1991.

However, since the social and economic environment and legal systems differ from country to country, it is very difficult from a practical standpoint to unify various country systems any time soon. It is desirable, therefore, first to establish an obligatory unified standard for offerings in the international market, or listing in a foreign market, and thereafter gradually to unify the domestic standards of each country.

International Unification of Settlement Systems

To address the expanded cross-border trading of securities, unification of settlement systems is being studied by IOSCO, the International Federation of Stock Exchanges (FIBV), and the G-30. Several proposals have already been offered. It is very important and significant that international cooperation toward establishment of common settlement systems be promoted. The linkage of settlement institutions in various countries is to be promoted in order to minimize the risk regarding settlement at times of market turbulence, such as a stock market price plunge.

The Bond Issuance Primary Market

The report by Japan's Securities Exchange Council has made some important proposals for the reform of the Japanese corporate bond issuance (primary) market. The first is revision of the principle that bonds should be backed by mortgages (the original idea of a bond narrowly defined). The basic underlying concept of this revision is that the market itself should decide whether a debt instrument needs to be a (mortgage-backed) bond, some other secured debenture, or an unsecured debenture.

The second is the trustee system. In Japan it is usual for trustee companies to be so closely involved in corporate bond issuance that the division of roles between trustee and underwriter is unclear. Consequently, the structure of issuance is rather opaque to outsiders. The revision is designed to improve the current situation and make the Japanese market free and transparent.

The report also recommends an increase in the types of corporate debt. This will enable debt issuance to better satisfy both issuers and investors.

Conclusion

As cross-border securities trading grows, the harmonization of the regulations and systems of each country through cooperations has become increasingly important in order to achieve efficient and fair international trading of securities. In promoting harmonization, the greatest emphasis should be on investor protection. To this end, it is important to maintain the stability of the international market as well as the domestic market of each country. In addition, fairness and transparency regarding capital transfers to ensure competition among the markets and securities firms of various countries should be studied. As I have noted several times, I believe that, naturally, Japan needs to participate positively in international discussions on cooperation and to assume a positive role in the realization of international harmonization of regulations and systems.

10 REFLECTIONS ON THE CFTC/SEC JURISDICTIONAL DISPUTE

Philip McBride Johnson

Perhaps it is time to revisit who regulates what in the securities and futures world. Not because the futures markets are harming the securities markets (there is no evidence of that), or vice versa, but simply for the fun of kicking dirt on the other fellow's shoes. Baseball season opened on the day when this article was written. But the new debate should at least be conducted with a fair knowledge of how the exercise came out the last time, and why. It is neither a lengthy nor a complicated story.

Far from wishing to create a "fragmented" regulatory environment, the objective of the 1981 Jurisdictional Accord was to avoid that result by applying a "goal test." For example, it is the predominant goal of securities regulation to facilitate capital formation and capital flows in an efficient and fair environment. Accordingly, it is logical that activity that raises or reallocates capital, regardless of the industry involved, should be central-ized in a regulatory agency such as the Securities and Exchange Commis-sion (SEC). Similarly, the main goal of futures regulation is to facilitate the shifting of price risk ("hedging"), and this responsibility has been assigned by the Congress to the Commodity Futures Trading Commission (CFTC) regardless of what industry the hedging function may serve. To illustrate the difference in goals more concretely, mortgages are a vehicle for providing funds to home buyers, while the attendant transaction risks are covered by mortgage and homeowners insurance. The former provides the capital; the latter provides the hedging. And yet, even though mortgages are a critical focus of both businesses, no one would seriously suggest that Citibank and Geico should be regulated under a single scheme.

What the 1981 Jurisdictional Accord sought to avoid is name fixation. This is an intellectual malady that causes the listener to hear only the first part of a phrase, such as *Treasury bond* futures, *soybeans* futures, *oil* futures, and so on. Without treatment, this can lead the patient to think that the futures should be regulated by the same agency that supervises the *name*. The consequences, of course, are preposterous:

Name	"Proper" Agency
Gold futures	Department of Interior
Gasoline futures	Department of Energy
Wheat futures	Department of Agriculture
Yen futures	Federal Reserve Board
U.S. stock index futures	Securities and Exchange Commission
Treasury note futures	Department of the Treasury
Nikkei index futures	Japanese Ministry of Finance
European currency unit futures	European Monetary System

Name fixation, as illustrated above, causes fragmentation to a fare-thee-well. Since no one proposes to redistribute all futures to like-sounding governmental departments and agencies, I can only assume that a new strain of name fixation virus has developed, to be known as "selective name fixation" or SNF.

But new strains of virus, like SNF, are usually caused by violent events that force adaptation. While stock index futures have been blamed for most modern ills, there is general agreement that empirical evidence to support those claims is sorely lacking. Turning to the literature, however, I find several arguments why securities-named futures, but no others, should be regulated by the same agency that oversees the *name*.

First, it will *avoid unseemly and wasteful court battles* between the agencies. In answer, the CFTC and the SEC were in court against each other in 1981, too, and resolved their problems without any shift of jurisdiction.

Second, it will *allow innovation* to flourish. The terms *innovation* and *futures markets* are practically synonymous. The futures exchanges have designed hedge tools for the grain, perishables, livestock, financial, energy, mining, and service sectors and today offer the richest menu of products in the financial community. In my lifetime, the securities exchanges' only major new product has been standardized stock options, thanks to the Chicago Board of Trade—a futures market—which organized the Chicago Board Options Exchange in the early 1970s. Even there, the equity option markets were not required to compete for listings until this year.

Third, it would break the jurisdictional bondage for so-called "*index participations*" or IPs. It has never been a question of whether IPs can trade but only where that activity should be conducted. The federal court decision that cash-settled IPs belong on futures markets could easily have been accommodated by listing them on a futures exchange. After all, every one of the major U.S. stock exchanges has created a futures market of its own. In fact, both losers in the recent IPs court test, the American and Philadelphia stock exchanges, simply chose not to list on their own ready-made futures subsidiaries. Thus, the IPs "crisis" is a staged incident, nothing more.

Fourth, the IPs' *business is going abroad* due to the CFTC/SEC bifurcated jurisdiction. It is true that the Toronto Stock Exchange has launched what is at least initially a successful IPs product, not because of the U.S. court decision but rather because the Toronto Exchange designed an ingenuous stock trust to avoid any legal challenges. The U.S. securities markets have every bit as much talent and ingenuity as our brethren to the North, without needing to restructure the national government.

Finally, a jurisdictional shift will *eliminate disagreements between the agencies*, lack of coordination, and policy differences. From every indication, these have not been a problem even during the hottest crisis to date: October 19, 1987. Sure, having only one decision maker eliminates any chance of a quarrel but, if that is inherently good public policy, we have two branches of government too many.

A third consideration that went into the 1981 Jurisdictional Accord was the ugly subject of cost. It seemed clear that any jurisdictional shift would involve governmental expense of ill-defined proportions. But that number would likely be dwarfed by the private sector expense as the two industries made the necessary internal and external adaptations. Curiously, very little has been said of late about the cost of shifting securities-named futures from the CFTC to the SEC, let alone the cost of some of the broader proposals being floated.

In 1981, we recognized that there were four basic choices: (1) the status quo; (2) full agency merger (or a new "super-agency"); (3) redistribution of all futures to the regulator of the named item (discussed earlier); and (4) redistribution of securities-named futures only. Other than the status quo, the seemingly simplest solution would be to transfer to the SEC only securities-named futures, such as stock index futures, and the seemingly simplest way to achieve that end would be to redefine the term *security* under federal law to include those futures contracts.

However, the cost of this step could be staggering. If products such as stock index futures were reclassified as securities, CFTC-regulated entities dealing as either broker or trader in those futures could suddenly be in the securities business and subject to all applicable provisions of the federal securities law. CFTC-registered futures commission merchants might automatically become securities broker-dealers requiring both SEC and up to 50 state "Blue Sky" registrations; their CFTC-registered associated persons would need to register again with the SEC and the states and complete a different qualification exam; CFTC-registered commodity pools (CPO's) could become SEC-regulated investment companies; and CFTC-registered commodity trading advisors (CTA's) could find themselves to be "investment advisors" subject to SEC rules.

Moreover, the SEC's rules would not necessarily be compatible with the entity's duties to the CFTC. For example, the CFTC's required "disclosure document" for CPOs and CTAs is not the same as the document that the SEC requires of its investment companies and advisors. And, while CTAs may (and commonly do) charge fees based upon portfolio performance, the SEC severely restricts the ability of an investment advisor to do so.

The exchanges where the newly transferred futures contracts are traded would presumably have to qualify and register with the SEC as national securities exchanges. Here, the requirements of the CFTC and the SEC are dramatically different, not only as to trading procedures (block trading, specialists, and so on, versus open outcry) but even regarding internal structure and governance. If securities-named futures were deemed to be "securities" like any other, they could presumably be issued and traded outside an exchange, such as by private placement, over the counter, or other direct means, quite opposite the CFTC's steadfast on-exchange requirement. Similarly, it is unclear whether the transferred futures could continue to be cleared at the futures clearinghouse or would need to be cleared at a separate 1934 Act-registered entity. Would the futures positions be insured by the Securities Investor Protection Corporation (SIPC) and, if so, what adjustments would SIPC need to make in order to administer and underwrite this new exposure? Would the futures be margined as if they were equity securities, as equity options, or on some other basis? In case of bankruptcy, would the provisions of the Bankruptcy Code governing securities brokers be applied, or should the commodity broker sections be invoked?

Most of these questions, among others, were identified in 1981 when we reviewed the "simplest" way to shift jurisdiction from the CFTC to the SEC. My personal conclusion was that, for many scores of CFTC-regulated entities, the only practical course would be to create a new and separate business for securities-named futures. The aggregate cost of such a step would run into the many millions of dollars in transitional expense, and years of future operating costs as well. My negotiating counterpart, as shrewd a businessman as I have ever known, probably had the same concerns.

One might argue that the trauma of transition, and perhaps some of its cost, could be moderated by allowing a period of time for the CFTC-regulated entities and individuals to come into compliance with the securities laws. While such a proposal might make the transition appear less catastrophic, it also acknowledges a lack of urgency in carrying out the jurisdictional transfer. If the industry is to be burdened with the need to restructure itself, at great cost, and despite a lack of urgency, there should be a compelling reason for taking even the first step in that direction. None has been articulated in a clear and persuasive manner, just as the circumstances of 1981 argued for a retention of the jurisdictional status quo.

An outright merger of the two agencies, or their absorption by a new agency, would pose the same problems unless, of course, futures and securities continued to be regulated as before, a result that would place the entire exercise in question. In my experience, even in nations that have a "unitary" regulatory program covering both types of markets, the agency staff is often divided into specialist groups that concentrate on one or the other area. Sometimes, about the only thing that the two staffs have in common is the same employer. While this bifurcation of functions is not practiced in all agencies, it is common enough to raise doubts whether a single regulatory body can or will in fact operate as such.

And so, if there is no clear consensus that any jurisdictional change is needed at this time, and movement in that direction is certain to be a costly and disruptive affair, why is it under consideration at all? I cannot address present circumstances with authority but it might be of interest to understand the climate when the preceding jurisdictional assault was launched.

There was, first of all, a general public bias against the futures markets as a virulent form of gambling that denies producers a fair price while, by some wizardry, inflating prices for the consumer. In this respect, I doubt that times have changed very much.

Second, regulatory agencies that oversee unpopular industries tend to become unpopular as well—just ask the Nuclear Regulatory Commission.

Third, the CFTC sustained two major blows in the first five years of its existence. Fraud in the sale of so-called "London options" reached such proportions that the CFTC effectively conceded defeat in regulating them and proceeded to ban nearly all forms of options, foreign or domestic. The Hunt family provided further drama in the silver futures markets as the 1970s became the 1980s. Those events drew as much attention in Congress and the media as the indictment of Chicago futures traders last year.

It was a time when sentiment ran so deep against the CFTC, from so many sources, that nearly everyone in and around the government was looking for some vehicle—any vehicle—to formally register their "no confidence" vote against the agency. The jurisdictional issue was simply as good a way as any to vent that displeasure. The 1981 Jurisdictional Accord, by restoring confidence that the CFTC could deal on equal terms with institutions that were older, larger and very highly respected, seems to have relieved that pressure, at least for awhile.

But let us step back for a moment from the parochial issue of CFTC/ SEC jurisdiction to reflect upon the broader human condition. Certain truths about no humans are self-evident, one of which is that the human being is the only species that deliberately makes work for itself. How else can the planet sustain an ever-increasing population? Because work is the art of problem-solving, vast numbers of people would perish if there were no problems. Accordingly, troublemaking is essential to the economic and physical well-being of humankind. On this analysis, we should be grateful that the CFTC/SEC jurisdiction debate did not die in 1981. And we should be appreciative of what the combatants are doing for the betterment of the world. Whether or not greed is good, it seems *a priori* that turmoil is terrific.

IV FUTURES MARKETS

11 REGULATION OF FUTURES MARKETS IN THE UNITED KINGDOM

Phillip A. Thorpe

In looking at the background to the present regulation, now principally found in the Financial Services Act 1986, the emphasis must inevitably be on the securities industry. While London has been the home to a substantial futures industry for over 100 years, the changes that occurred in the City of London in the 1970s and '80s, and the events and debates leading to the Act, almost exclusively related to other markets.

The Traditional City of London

The British financial services industry, with its focus on the "square mile" within the City of London, developed within a closed and intimate environment. At the senior levels of the various institutions and professional firms there was a degree of homogeneity through shared backgrounds and common values, reinforced by the informal codes within which this society conducted its business. This was reflective of and underpinned by a class system which, with its institutions of social control, subtle and exclusionary in their operation, allowed the City to function with a predictability and efficiency that rivalled any formal system of legal regulation. It was in the nature of the City that self-regulation should develop and attain a degree of respect unmatched in any other set of financial markets. It did this substantially to the exclusion of any governmental regulation, and this persisted, largely unchallenged, until the 1970s. It is difficult to understand the structure and workings of the present system of control and supervision without fully appreciating this background.

Competition and Restrictive Practices

In developing a perspective on the evolution of City regulation, it is also necessary to look at the economic events affecting the financial services industry in the City of London in the last few years.[1]

For the securities industry in particular, substantial change was in store when in 1976 the Labour Government issued the Restrictive Trade Practices (Service) Order extending the scope of the restrictive trade practices legislation to the financial services sector. The Stock Exchange was not exempted from this, and its worst fears were realized in February 1979 when the Office of Fair Trading (OFT) formally referred the Stock Exchange rule book and certain practices (including the setting of minimum commission levels) to the Restrictive Trade Practices Court. A new Conservative Government refused to interfere, despite urging from the Bank of England; Mrs. Thatcher has never been a supporter of the "club mentality" and also disliked the too frequent association of fraud and abuse with capitalism. She may have also wondered about the efficiency of the market for digesting great chunks of the public sector when it came to her plans for privatization.

The Stock Exchange attempted to establish that a system of minimum commission was vital to the maintenance of a structure of separate capacity that emphasized the strict segregation of broker and jobber functions. Under a certain amount of pressure from the Bank of England and with a more sympathetic attitude within the Department of Trade and Industry (DTI), an accord was arrived at between the Government and the Stock Exchange in 1983. In an exceptional piece of legislation, the Restrictive Trade Practices (Stock Exchange) Act 1984, the litigation between the OFT and the Stock Exchange was discontinued on the basis that the Stock Exchange agreed voluntarily to introduce a package of changes. Hence commissions became negotiable between brokers and their clients, and the Stock Exchange developed a new trading system which in effect provided for dual capacity trading, much in line with the practice in North America and other developed markets. "Big Bang" was the phrase used to describe the effect on October 27, 1986, when the Stock Exchange brought in these reforms. Further changes took place with great rapidity, not least being the abandoning of the Stock Exchange floor, marking a fundamental change in the way business would henceforth be conducted in the City. A tougher, more energetic, more competitive City emerged.

Members of the Stock Exchange had also discovered in the early 1980s that in order to compete with overseas dealers and because of the demand of institutional investors and companies seeking to raise long-term funds, they needed substantially more capital than they possessed. The need for outside capital proved irresistible, and in March 1986 restrictions were removed so that member firms could be entirely owned by a nonmember. As a result many leading member firms were acquired by U.K. merchant and clearing banks, overseas commercial and investment banks, and securities dealers. Consequently there has been a noticeable growth in the United Kingdom of financial conglomerates on the American pattern, many of whom have moved to acquire financial and commodities futures operations to support their other activities.

In 1986 legislation to bring about the regulation of financial services was going through Parliament. Although this coincided with Big Bang, and the media naturally linked the two, they were distinct events, and it is important to recognize that the revitalization and restructuring of the City's financial institutions brought about by Big Bang originated more from political and economic considerations than from any admitted deficiency in regulation and supervision. For all that, the debate on whether and how to regulate the financial services industry in Britain can be traced back to well before Big Bang and, as in many other countries, was dominated by recurring scandals and abuses.

Frauds and the Adequacy of Traditional Regulation

Responding in part to concerns over growing abuses, in 1974 the Government division responsible for financial services, the Department of Trade and Industry, sent out questionnaires inquiring as to the adequacy of supervision and regulation of the securities market. The predominant response at the time was that the self-regulatory system then operating was likely to be as effective as any other. The City has always harbored an almost paranoid fear that it would have a governmental body imposed upon it similar to the United States' SEC, a view which can still be heard expressed today. The DTI review did show, however, that some new legislation was required, and consequently a committee consisting of officials from the Bank of England and the DTI was set up; the City, not to be outdone, set up the ill-fated Council of the Securities Industry (CSI).

The DTI committee, in delivering its report in 1980[2] and to the surprise of many, was prepared to give the existing system of self-regulation a clean bill of health. Although it did recognize the need to improve certain aspects of the system, on the whole it thought that it worked tolerably well. Unfortunately, the scandals continued and some assumed proportions that were impossible for the Government to ignore. In 1981 in particular a number of financial failures occurred (such names as Norton Warburg and Halliday Simpson took the headlines); collapsed companies were found variously to have used clients' funds for their working capital, or to have invested clients' money in their own group companies, or to have used the firm's accounts to transfer money to various clients on the basis of fictitious transactions. In his annual report for 1981 the Commissioner of the City of London police referred to the inadequacy of the existing legislation in protecting depositors and controlling firms which handled funds for the investing public. He noted that the principal piece of relevant statute, the Prevention of Fraud (Investments) Act 1939 (the PFI Act) focused on the regulation of a limited class of securities dealers, but even then the procedures for vetting firms were inadequate and there was a total lack of continuing supervision. The Commissioner was moved to observe, "The result is that the Fraud Squad has been called upon to investigate the failure of investment companies whose financial difficulties [sic] would have been observed at a much earlier stage by a competent authority making standard supervisory checks."[3] At the end of 1982, reports of city fraud had increased by 42 percent and the Fraud Squad was investigating 96 cases involving alleged losses of some £100 million.

The City's defense against change or interference was based on the strength of its self-regulatory bodies. The Stock Exchange was at this time, as it had historically been, the most important of them. Stockbrokers were obliged to conduct their business in accordance with the rules of the Exchange, its codes of dealing, and to follow its guidance. It had a disciplinary function with an appeals procedure and a capacity to impose a range of penalties. It undertook financial surveillance and required member firms to maintain a minimum solvency ratio, to submit annual statements, and to make quarterly unaudited returns. Rules existed in respect of client monies, and there was in place a compensation fund for clients and a fidelity insurance requirement on members.

The other body of note was the City's answer to the earlier DTI initiatives, the CSI, but this never proved itself a competent or even efficient body. Its creation had been something of a "pre-emptive strike" by the industry, to avoid having less palatable regulatory alternatives thrust upon it, but the attitude of many in the City toward it appeared ambivalent, and there was a distinct lack of authority that reduced it to no more than a talking shop. It lacked virtually every characteristic that would have enabled it to solve the many problems and tensions that were fast developing in the City. Its mandate was unclear, it lacked leadership, its composition was inappropriate, and it could never find the resources and support it needed to enable it to operate effectively.

It was readily apparent that the CSI was not going to meet the Government's need for an effective, independent self-regulator, and despite the Exchange's regulatory efforts, and even with the improvements it made as the various scandals and failures occurred, it did not have the regulatory reach to deal with the problems that were emerging. A substantial, and probably statutory, solution was required to the increasing problems and, in due course, the Government reacted.

The Government's Response

The unique quality of British financial regulation is nowhere better illustrated than in the manner in which the onus of developing a comprehensive scheme for supervision and regulation was placed on the aged shoulders of a single eminent academic. In July 1981 the Government appointed Professor L.C.B. (Jim) Gower, the former Vice Chancellor of Southampton University, to undertake a review with the following Terms of Reference: (1) to consider the statutory protection now required by private and business investors in securities and other property, including investors through unit trusts and open-ended investment companies operating in the United Kingdom; (2) to consider the need for statutory control of dealers in securities, investment consultants, and investment managers; and (3) to advise on the need for new legislation.

In addition, and if this was not enough, Gower was asked to take into account any relevant developments in the European Economic Community (EEC). What in most countries would have been no modest task for a team of experts with competent and adequate support, Gower was required to do alone. He published a discussion document[4] in January 1982 and then invited comments.

Gower recognized that one of the most serious problems was simply to determine the scope of his review and thus the extent of his proposals. He decided that it should cover all forms of investment other than those in any form of property over which the investor has exclusive control after its acquisition. Gower considered that there were four main ways of protecting investors: (1) by regulating the *modus operandi* of the body in which the investor invests; (2) by regulating the terms of investment; (3) by providing for full disclosure about what those terms are; (4) by regulating those who act as intermediaries.

Gower considered that it was not practical for him to look at (2), which was really a matter for company law, but that he could attempt the others. He also considered that self-regulation and Government regulation should complement each other, and he was convinced that the Government should be the decider of major questions involving public policy. He thought that the "ideal would be to weld self-regulation and governmental regulation into a coherent statutory framework which would cover the whole field that needs to be regulated and in which each would perform the role which it does best, working harmoniously together."

In developing his proposals, Gower was circumscribed by a number of practical and political considerations. First, he was aware of the Government's desire to see a substantial reduction in the number of "quangos."[5] Second, while Gower recognized that *caveat emptor* was a discredited policy, there were serious differences in the nature and character of both investors and securities. He thought that it was desirable to "adjust" regulation to reflect this and the differing expectations associated with each. Third, he acknowledged the "cost-benefit" balance necessary in regulation. It would be self-defeating to introduce regulation that could only be complied with at considerable expense. "The likely effect would be to drive out the scrupulous who would be unwilling to continue to practice in breach of regulations, and leave matters in the hands of the unscrupulous." Fourth, prevention was both in principle and practice better than cure. However, breaches were to some extent inevitable, and "the only effective ultimate safety net for investors is some form of compensation fund." Finally, Gower was also mindful of the need to ensure that in the international arena London was regarded as sufficiently well regulated to promote confidence in its integrity, but that it was not excessively onerous in its conditions.

Considering various approaches to regulation, Gower indicated a preference for the logic of setting up of an all-embracing "securities commission." However, due to the political constraints, he emphatically dismissed this alternative as viable. In the practical world, Gower considered that the most likely and profitable approach was to adjust the existing balance between governmental and self-regulation. In this process Gower recognized that the collaboration of the City was imperative. Indeed, it was largely because he recognized the City's extreme dislike of securities commissions that he accepted the inevitability of the political reaction to a recommendation to establish such an organization.

Gower considered that effective self-regulatory authorities would be required in the following areas: (1) issues and distributions of securities, acquisitions, and takeovers; (2) operation of the securities markets; (3) broking and jobbing on or off the market, in securities; (4) investment management and advice; (5) operation of unit trust and pools.

In a more popular move with the politicians, Gower advocated that the cost of this new scheme of self-regulation should be borne by the users and investors, who were to be the beneficiaries. He also advocated that laws and rules seeking to ensure honesty in the markets were probably not sufficient and that regulation should be devised to ensure the competence of those entering the industry. Gower's proposals met with a mixed reception which was divided along the expected lines of tradition and self-interest. Most in the City thought that his ideas were interesting, but many dismissed them as academic.

The Gower Report

His subsequent report, "Review of Investor Protection," was published in two parts, the first in January 1984 and the second in March 1985.[6] In the first part of his report, Gower had obviously taken account of many of the points raised. While the essentials remained the same, although refined, there was in some respects a change of emphasis. In any event, during the course of his review there had been a number of significant developments. The DTI itself published new rules[7] in 1983 which introduced into British securities regulation a number of novel and potentially far-ranging provisions. It also significantly tightened up its procedures for licensing and monitoring dealers under the PFI Act. Furthermore, legislation was passed that implemented three EEC directives on listed securities, and, as noted above, the issue of restrictive practices and the Stock Exchange was resolved.

Gower felt it necessary to restate his philosophy in his report. In something of what may now be interpreted as an apologia, he stated that "logic and tidiness. . . are of importance only insofar as they contribute to a legal regime which can be understood, which will be regarded as fair by those who it affects and which, as a result, would be generally observed and can be effectively forced." Gower emphasized that unintelligibility and the failure to treat alike would undermine enforcement and credibility.

In assessing the optimum degree of regulation, Gower did not consider that it was practical or that he was sufficiently well qualified to attempt any formal cost-benefit analysis. He accepted that "there is a tension between market efficiency and investor protection which often pulls in different directions." In the end, it had to be a value judgment as to how much weight is given to a free market and how much to investor protection. His much quoted judgment was simply that regulation should be "no greater than is necessary to protect reasonable people from being made fools of." He offered no greater science than this to the measure of the cost or efficiency of his proposals.

Gower also persisted in his view that the basic principle of a comprehensive system of regulation within a statutory framework, based as far as possible on self-regulation subject to government surveillance, was desirable. Professor Gower had to accept, however, that self-regulation based purely on a functional division of investment business was unworkable and that instead it had to be built on present professional commercial groupings.

The pace of development both in the City and in Government continued, and Gower and his Parliamentary Council, who were also attempting to prepare a draft bill based upon the reports, were overtaken by events. The second and final part of Gower's report was accordingly confined to a commentary on the Government's own White Paper on financial services which had been rushed through and published a couple of months earlier in January 1985.[8] In his second report Gower acknowledged that there had been a change of heart in the City, and that there was an increasing feeling that a proliferation of small self-regulatory organizations without oversight or coordination might not be beneficial. He also noted that while there was still little real support for a securities commission, most took the view that the DTI would not be capable of effectively discharging such an oversight role. Consequently, and somewhat tentatively, many were coming around to the notion that a new "super" self-regulatory agency should be established.

To put these events in context, it should be noted that shortly after the publication of Gower's First Report in May 1984, the Governor of the Bank of England had appointed a high-powered practitioner-based advisory group mandated to advise him urgently on the structure and operation of self-regulatory agencies, and whether a practitioner-based system could be fashioned in the near future. Under pressure from the DTI, another such group was formed to advise on the prospects for practitioner-based regulation in the marketing of life assurance and unit trusts. These committees concentrated essentially on the issue of whether a new institutional structure was required. They decided it was, and considered it would be preferable to have the Government delegate powers to a private body resembling a more powerful version of the CSI. The Bank of England and the Stock Exchange must have preferred this solution to the "dangerous logic" of Gower. This was pressed on a tolerably receptive DTI, and a White Paper was rushed to the printers in time to cause Gower to have to abandon his own bill. Professor Gower had put ministers in a difficult position by so blatantly arguing in terms of a securities commission but stating that it was impossible on the grounds of political expediency. In his First Report he had presented the arguments with a disturbing polarity, a commission or alternatively a large role for the DTI; there was no middle road.

The Government's White Paper, while adopting most of Gower's detailed recommendations, departed in several important respects from his view. It underlined the clear national interest in a healthy and well-run financial services industry. While accepting the need to improve laws relating to investor protection which were "outdated and incomplete," the White Paper emphasized that the Government was well aware of the dangers of excessive regulation. Regulation should be no more than the minimum necessary to "protect the investor." The Government also made it clear that "regulation cannot eliminate risk" and that an element of risk is inherent in investment as distinct from savings. In developing its new framework the Government stated its objectives as: the promotion of efficiency in the financial services industry, promoting competitiveness both domestically and internationally, and inspiring confidence in issuers and investors that the financial services industry is a "clean" place to do business.

What the White Paper managed was to accommodate the interests of the City and the preference for self-regulation with the need to see increased powers and discipline. If this smacked of compromise it is hardly surprising. The City had substantial influence with the Government (a significant number of members of Parliament were stockbrokers or members of Lloyds) and this, taken with the Government's own policies (of privatization and a reduction of central government functions) made the final proposal almost inevitable.

In large part it was the structure envisaged in the White Paper that subsequently found its way onto the statute books. The Government succeeded in enacting the Financial Services Act in 1986 but refined its "super" SRO proposals with the result that a single Securities and Investments Board was to play a central and coordinating role amongst the host of self-regulators. As has been mentioned earlier, the achievement of this new regulatory structure coincided closely with Big Bang and meant 1986 marked the start of a period of rebuilding, reflection, and debate within the financial services industry. Continuing collapses and scandals added further flavor to the process.

The Futures Industry

From the above it is apparent that events of the early 1980s were almost exclusively related to happenings in the securities industry. Gower, in his first discussion paper and in the subsequent reports he published, omits almost entirely any reference to the futures markets and futures brokers. Indeed, his suggestions for a new structure involved listing five potential SROs, none of which was to have anything to do with the futures industry and may have reflected his intention to regulate only that which required regulation. Gower's disinterest was mirrored in press and public comment where, again, the City's reaction was very much tied to the securities industry and the Stock Exchange. Even when matters reached the House of Commons, many hours were spent arguing the merits of the White Paper, but not more than a minute or two of that time was devoted to the futures markets.[9]

Nevertheless, those markets did manage to make themselves known during this period of change, and in much the same way that the securities industry had done in establishing the need for that change. In 1980 and 1981, a number of frauds were perpetrated by commodities brokers, with large losses resulted for small investors, and 1985 brought to light serious problems for the London Metal Exchange with the Tin Crisis. In the securities industry this gave rise to questions about the effectiveness of existing regulation, while in the futures industry, it revealed that, outside of that provided by the exchanges, there was no regulation to speak of. It wasn't a matter of whether it was effective; it simply wasn't there.

In the U.K. the futures industry had largely gone about its business untouched by regulators. Since the industry's inception in the last century, what regulation there has been has come from incidental sources and it was never intended to be or required to be comprehensive. To appreciate why this is so, and was able to remain so, it is important to note that, far more than the securities industry, the futures markets in London have traditionally operated at a distance from the investing public. They were originally, and to a large degree remain, mercantile markets. They were established by merchants and dealers in the numerous commodities which the United Kingdom bought, bartered, or broked from the far-flung corners of its empire. The world's principal commodity houses had trading offices in London, regardless of the decline of London as a port, and the futures markets were an important part of a huge international commodities business. A wide variety of commodities markets and associations proliferated through the hundred years prior to Gower's report[10] and with the growth of commodity trading in other centers, such as Chicago and New York, London's markets increasingly specialized their business to cater to particular commodity sectors. Thus they provided producers, merchants, and users of a wide variety of commodities with facilities for hedging the risks inherent in the forward sale or purchase of supplies. The markets gave rise to competition between the brokers and ensured that their customers had access to facilities and a quality of service that was equal to or better than anything offered anywhere else in the world. London's arbitration procedures meant that there was an established capacity to resolve disputes, English law provided certainty and protections, and by and large the trade proceeded with a minimum of difficulty.

The make-up of the present markets illustrates the antecedents of London's commodities business; the London Metal Exchange providing the principal world market for base metals, the Futures & Options Exchange (known as London Fox) trading cocoa, sugar, and coffee, the Baltic Futures Exchange trading a mix of traditional agricultural and novel freight-oriented contracts, the International Petroleum Exchange trading oil-based products, and most recently established, the London International Financial Futures Exchange (LIFFE) principally offering hedging mechanisms for other financial markets. It is worth noting again that this was, and remains, essentially a users' market. While increasing amounts of private investor speculative interest is to be seen in some markets, that is not the rule in the United Kingdom, and in the traditional commodities futures markets that speculative interest can be measured in single figures percentages. This contrasts sharply with the customer mix in other financial markets in other jurisdictions.

Historical Regulation of the Futures Markets

Regulation of London's futures markets has, as stated, been minimal. The only independent regulation prior to the Financial Services Act came from the surveillance undertaken by the Bank of England. For the remainder, the markets have been dependent on self-regulation but not nearly to the degree developed by the securities industry and the Stock Exchange. There has been no specific body charged with regulating the industry as a whole (and this remains so) and up until the advent of the Financial Services Act, no one charged with looking after the interests of the customer in those markets.

Only four pieces of legislation prior to the Financial Services Act had any connection with the futures industry, but in keeping with the now established theme, this was either minimal or indirect. The Exchange Control Act 1947 was relevant insofar as London's futures brokers dealt with customers worldwide and their business thus involved frequent foreign exchange remittances. During the period when exchange control was in place (until shortly after the election of Mrs. Thatcher's Conservative Government in 1979) the Bank of England required the reporting of these transactions to it and had an approval function over them. It also developed a system of regular reports upon which it assessed, *inter alia*, customer exposure and concentration risk and set requirements accordingly. In doing so, it developed close contacts with the commodities brokers and thereby the futures markets.

The Banking Act also had some effect in that it prohibited a firm from undertaking deposit-taking business unless it was either a recognized broker or a licensed deposit taker,[11] and it is in the nature of futures trading that a futures broker will be engaged in a form of deposit-taking. The Bank of England requested the Government include an exemption in the regulations made under the Banking Act so that members of listed markets (which included all of the futures markets mentioned above) could accept deposits from clients without fear of contravening the Act. This meant that only members of listed exchanges could safely take margins in respect of trading, and it raised serious questions as to the validity of off-exchange futures, this being an important part of London's derivatives business. The Financial Services Act resolved this point in favor of continuing off-exchange business.

The third piece of legislation which, again, had some minor effect, was the PFI Act, but its focus was essentially on securities and it is doubtful whether it had material impact on futures trading. It, too, ceased to be relevant with the passing of the Financial Services Act. The one other notable piece of legislation was the Gaming Act of 1845 which, in common with its equivalent in a number of other jurisdictions, raised doubts about the validity of contracts that provided for cash settlement. Again, the Financial Services Act has clarified the position and ensured that futures contracts with cash settlement are enforceable.

The Role of the Bank of England

The Bank of England, regardless of the minimal direct statutory connection to the futures markets, has nevertheless been seen as the traditional regulator of those markets. Users of the markets themselves have pro-moted this idea, and since the introduction of the Financial Services Act some continue to express an enthusiasm for the Bank retaining that role.

As with much that the Bank does, information about its functions is hard to obtain, and no doubt this can be advantageous in that the belief that it has oversight alone is often a disincentive to bad behavior. Its actual involvement, particularly after the abolition of exchange control, appears to have been slight, and largely associated with its continuing and general concern over the well-being of London's wholesale financial markets. Prior to the Financial Services Act, the Bank maintained a small division specifically devoted to monitoring the futures markets, but that supervision did not convert into substantial or definable accountability for the events within those markets. The Bank had a team of people, probably less than 20 persons in total, who received and analyzed trading information from the markets, and who would contact the exchanges and those involved in trading the markets from time to time to gauge their well-being and, as and when circumstances directed, to suggest where closer attention or action was necessary. The Bank operated by virtue of its established contacts and through its ability to obtain action from the banks it supervised more directly, many of whom were closely involved in the financing of commod-ities trading or in backing the clearing arrangements for the markets. The Bank most emphatically was not responsible for ensuring that the markets were undertaking supervision of their members, or for undertaking that supervision itself. In this regard there was no control other than the control imposed by the exchanges on the admission requirements for membership or on the monitoring of their subsequent behavior.

The role of the futures exchanges and the clearinghouses therefore was of great materiality to the regulation of the markets. Much in the manner of the Stock Exchange, they operated on the basis of "club" principles, entry being limited, and discipline being meted out to those members who broke club rules. The clearinghouse provided an element of financial regulation, monitoring the solvency and exposure of those participating as clearing members of the markets.

While Gower did not appear to pay much attention to futures markets in his analysis of the City, nevertheless he did notice them enough to recommend that dealing in futures and options should be regulated as "investment business." This recommendation achieved recognition in the Financial Services Act, despite lobbying by sectors of the futures industry that their inclusion was inappropriate. Prior to the 1986 Act, and driven by the likely inclusion of futures in any new regulatory scheme, and also as a reaction to the continuing abuses that were emerging from the futures markets, the industry established the first of London's new self-regulatory organizations in the shape of the Association of Futures Brokers and Dealers Ltd. (AFBD). The AFBD adopted, with the agreement and support of London's futures exchanges, a nonstatutory regulatory function in respect of the markets, and it was empowered in such a way as to ensure that it did not become another CSI. Understandably, given the parties establishing the AFBD and the enthusiasms of Government at that time, the focus of its regulatory function was the protection of the private investor as an adjunct to the goal of promoting efficient and well-run markets where professionals could trade with the minimum of inter-ference. This happily coincided substantially with the intentions of the Financial Services Act, though its role expanded somewhat as a result of that legislation.

Equally fortunate was that the Financial Services Act anticipated the establishment of such an SRO, and in due course the Secretary for State recognized the AFBD in terms of that legislation. The legislation also provided for recognition of investment exchanges and clearinghouses, and all of London's exchange and clearinghouses achieved that recognition in due course.

With the introduction of these new aspects to the structure, the role of the Bank of England altered noticeably. There appeared to be a recogni-tion within the Bank that it could no longer undertake oversight of the futures markets without devoting considerably more in the way of resource and requiring more extensive and formal powers. The problems arising from the Tin Crisis in 1985 helped crystallize this concern and no doubt generated some enthusiasm for ridding the Bank of its previous connec-tions with the futures markets. The Bank could thereafter rely on the primary responsibility for the regulation of the industry being upon the Securities and Investments Board (SIB), as recognizer of the exchanges and clearinghouses, and on the AFBD, as authorizer of the users of those markets.

The Bank now has a small section of no more than two or three people watching futures markets, and they provide a source of information on those markets for use by other parts of the Bank, a coordinating link for other regulators when problems of mutual concern arise, and allow for the Bank to undertake work on projects of intermarket significance where a familiarity with the futures markets is of assistance.[12] The Bank does, however, continue its traditional and effective behind-the-scenes role as a facilitator and arbitrator between the various institutions in the markets. Recently this has been witnessed in respect of the proposed link-up between LIFFE and the London Traded Options Market. However, it is very clear that the Bank is in no sense a regulator of the futures markets, although this is something with which some within the markets have yet to come to terms.

The Financial Services Act—Two Years On

The Financial Services Act was heralded in the White Paper issued prior to its enactment in 1986 as "self-regulation within a statutory framework." Gower (1988) himself described this presentation as almost amounting to a confidence trick. He suggested a more accurate description of the system as being "statutory regulation monitored by self-regulatory organizations recognized by, and under the surveillance of, a self-standing commission." That he managed to sound pleased in describing it thus perhaps explains why such complexity emerged from his proposals.

What his design had achieved was the establishment of the Securities and Investments Board, ultimately accountable to Government in the shape of the Secretary of State, through the efforts of the Department of Trade and Industry. Under the Securities and Investments Board there ranged five SROs,[13] a number of recognized investment exchanges (RIEs), a brace of clearinghouses (recognized clearinghouses or RCHs), and several recognized professional bodies (RPBs). Thus, at launch, the Financial Services Act envisaged about 20 bodies with varying regulatory roles. This assorted troupe went forth to meet the Act's requirements. All firms engaged in "investment business" had to obtain authorization through a recognised SRO or be a member of an RPB (e.g., a solicitor in good standing with the Law Society could give investment advice); the SROs and RPBs, in turn, had to be recognized by the SIB. For the SRO to be recognized, it had to show a rule book equivalent to that promulgated by the SIB. The process of rule writing, revision, comparison, and resolution absorbed a vast amount of SIB and SRO time over that introductory period, which extended through to 1988. Equally time consuming was the induction process for the members of the SROs, with an entire industry queuing up to show itself as "fit and proper" and to gain admission.

Two years after the commencement of the Act proper, that induction process and the bedding down of the rule books have largely come to a close. Amid a modest amount of second birthday fanfare about the number of persons barred or brought to book thus far, the actual business of regulating those involved in "investment business" in the City has finally got under way.

However, even in the process of implementing the Financial Services

Act, problems emerged which have led to proposals for adjustment to the structure. Those problems have focused, not surprisingly, on the question of the division of regulatory tasks among the various participants in the system, and on the cost-effectiveness of the system as a whole.

The "New Settlement"

The need for some adjustment was first identified in the middle of 1989, and the present Chairman of the Securities and Investments Board, David Walker, has subsequently promoted his solution to these problems as "The New Settlement." His New Settlement is perhaps best regarded as recognition of the fact that Gower's intentions for the system have not made it through the implementation process unscathed. Gower (1988, p. 17) has subsequently stated that he saw the rules and regulations upon which the actions of SIB and the SROs were to be based as having five main aims:

1. Since prevention is better than cure, to ensure that people do not undertake investment business unless they are fit and proper and have satisfied the regulatory body that they are.
2. To ensure that, once authorized, firms become subject to rules and regulations, providing protection for their clients both as regards client money and the firm's conduct of business.
3. To provide clients with known and adequate channels of complaint.
4. To provide clients with the ultimate safety net of a compensation fund should the firm become insolvent.
5. To ensure that firms are put out of business as rapidly as possible if they transgress and, if their offence is sufficiently grave, that they are prosecuted.

These very sensible investor protection measures have been obscured by the volumes of detailed and often confusing rules that have emerged from both the SIB and the SROs. Practitioner reaction has been inevitable, and for Walker, with a background in the "raised eyebrow" world of the Bank of England, the move away from the detailed legalistic approach to regulation is unsurprising. His approach calls for a lack of detailed prescription, and hopefully, therefore, the better tailoring of regulation to the markets: a complementarity between the need for basic governmental regulation in a statutory framework and flexible practitioner-based self-regulation. In some senses, therefore, Walker's New Settlement is a reassertion of those original objectives of the Financial Services Act as espoused by Gower.

The New Settlement has a number of component parts. Firms doing "investment business" are now to be subject to a three-tier system of regulation. The top tier is a list of ten clearly stated principles, since April 30, 1990, binding for disciplinary purposes, but not available as a basis for any action for damages against authorized firms. The second tier is to be composed of more detailed "core rules," designated as such by the SIB and applying directly to authorized firms. The third tier is the rules of the SROs themselves. In practice there are likely to be additional tiers, made up of codes of practice, guidance notes, interpretative opinions, and so on.

Given that the New Settlement aims for simplification, and that the existing system is anything but simple, the wish to introduce additional layers of regulation is hard to understand. The tier structure means that a single business activity will be potentially subject to at least three different layers of regulation, each with a different legal weighting and significance. The potential for tensions and conflicts between the tiers is a real one and already emerging is a body of opinion that the core rules in fact add nothing to the system other than a capacity for the SIB to impose its will in rule making.[14]

Of greater merit is the SIB proposal that SROs be judged by a new standard of "adequacy," rather than by the previous standard of "equivalence." The new adequacy test is intended to lay to rest the much debunked view that equivalence means the SROs achieving a line-by-line equivalence with the SIB rule book if they are to be "recognized" under the Financial Services Act. This had led to a dogmatic approach to rule writing and, in the case of the futures markets, a rule book containing inappropriate securities concepts. Since the coming into force of this new standard, the AFBD's rule book has adjudged adequate rather than equivalent.[15] This transformation has occurred by default, that is, the AFBD by beatific statutory action is now adequate. Finally, the recent changes to the Financial Services Act have introduced the concept of cost consciousness into regulation. This is widely thought to be a Government reaction to mounting criticism of Gower's neglect of this topic and the increasing costs of compliance with the Financial Services Act. Cost containment is not helped by SIB's old equivalence approach which did little to allow for variations in practices within the financial services sectors, and is also not helped by the sizable duplication and wastage inherent in the present structure. Under the New Settlement regulatory costs will not be subject to a full cost-benefit analysis, but the statute does require the costs of the regime to be taken into account by an SRO in framing its rules or any of its amendments.

The statutory changes necessary to bring into being these aspects of the New Settlement occurred earlier this year, but full implementation has yet to be achieved.

Reaction to the proposals has been mixed. Many members of the SROs welcome the initiative if it will result in a simpler, more comprehensible, and more flexible regime. Others have expressed concern over what may amount to a substantial revision of the Financial Services Act structure at a time when firms are only now coming to terms with the original structure. How much impact the new approach will have will only be determined in 1990–1991. Also, the SIB's commitment to the themes of the New Settlement is yet to be tested, in that the SROs are now bent on rewriting their rule books to make the most of the adequacy test, while the SIB has yet to fully formulate its own requirements for adequacy. It has, however, restated its wish to see consistency between different rule books, and has already taken to itself the drafting rights for certain sections relating to financial resources. For the moment, the only certain fact about the New Settlement is that it has generated considerable debate and a large amount of work for all of those involved in the present system.

The Failures of the Financial Services Act

What the preceding material is intended to provide is an explanation for the focus of the current legislation and a guide to the interests that predominated in its production. The Financial Services Act is quite clearly designed as a piece of investor protection legislation, and with a heavy securities emphasis. It reflects the interests of the City during the 1970s and '80s, and its present form owes much to the relative influence upon Parliament of the City, the Bank of England, and the DTI. It is in no way a piece of legislation that was tailor-made to the futures industry, or even legislation designed to offer comprehensive regulation across all financial services sectors.

Even Gower (1988, p. 19), as the author of the report upon which the Financial Services Act was based, found that it was deficient in its coverage. While he believed that the scope of the Act was wide, certainly much wider than the PFI Act which it replaced, and while he viewed it as covering all business relating to investments (defined to include life assurance and futures, options, and contracts for differences), nevertheless he noted, in particular, that banking continued to be regulated by the Bank of

England under the new Banking Act 1987 and there remained two "thoroughly anomalous" exclusions. Gower viewed the nonapplication of the legislation to Lloyds as unsatisfactory, and also indicated a preference to see the Takeover Panel brought within the scheme of the legislation, or at least within secondary legislation. Despite these reservations, Gower's answer to the question "Will it work?" was "Well, I can't see any reason why it shouldn't. It is, basically, a tried system which has worked pretty well elsewhere." This hardly amounts to a ringing endorsement, and, in any event, it is difficult to understand why he assumed that it replicated a system working elsewhere. The British "solution" is without precedent.

Failure #1: The Monitoring and Control of Risk

Gower's coverage in his report, and his subsequent identification of the areas he felt had been omitted, confirmed that his focus on investor protection ensured that, in regulatory terms, he missed a great deal. This singular and rather blinkered focus on investor protection has been accepted by the markets and their users and has meant a minimizing of the interference that regulation causes to their business. Nowhere is this more apparent than in the futures markets, where the concept of professional or experienced customers is used to modify and limit the regulatory requirements for a large proportion of the users of those markets.[16]

It is undisputed that regulation may have several potential objectives, among which investor protection is but one. Professor Goodhart, a leading commentator on the Act, confirms his view that the emphasis of the Gower Report, the Financial Services Act, and SIB has all been on investor protection, protection against fraud, negligence, conflicts of interest, mismanagement, and so on (Salden, 1988; Goodhart, 1988). Goodhart's purpose is to make convincing arguments regarding the excessive cost of regulating for investor protection, but he is as guilty as Gower in neglecting the other regulatory objectives.

It is an inevitable part of being involved in the futures industry that one is required to look beyond investor protection and recognize the aspects that affect the financial safety of the markets. Market operators, market participants, and regulators have traditionally concerned themselves with systemic risk, market risk, broker risk, and client risk, and the trading, clearing, and regulatory systems that have developed have aimed to address each of these. Not so in the case of the United Kingdom. Goodhart himself acknowledges that regulation's objectives may include protection against the risk that some sizeable parts of the system as a whole may collapse. He also recognizes that some aspect of SIB's regulations may bear on potential systemic risk—for example, in its approval of rules for exchanges and for the clearinghouses and settlements systems connected with such markets. However, the regulatory scheme is only barely concerned with systemic risk and only marginally more concerned with market risk. It is in this area that the Financial Services Act shows a significant failing. The failing has come about both in theoretical terms, that is, in the narrow and imperfect scope of the Financial Services Act, and in practical terms in the way in which SIB has chosen to implement the even minimal requirements that relate to markets and systems.

In part this is because the primary focus of the SROs is their membership, and is thus upon the integrity of behavior and financial soundness of those members. The SROs have little capacity to influence risk management in any one market, or systemwide, and accordingly set their requirements and monitor them only so as to try and ensure that those who operate as members are doing so honestly and within their financial capacity. As to market risk, as mentioned above, the Financial Services Act has some impact (but indirectly) and only because exchanges must seek recognition for the carrying on of their business. In practice, this means exchanges having sets of rules to ensure the conduct of an orderly market, governing floor behavior, and for the admission and discipline of its membership. In practice, this has also meant very little supervision of the exchanges by the SIB and, as a result, standards vary greatly. The SIB has only one or two people involved in exchange or clearinghouse oversight and then only from the perspective of the requirements for continuing the recognition of those bodies, and the exchanges themselves have relatively few people undertaking compliance functions. There is no body anywhere charged with undertaking the broader oversight of systemic or intermarket risk under the Financial Services Act structure.

It has been explained above that in the past systemic risk was at least monitored by the Bank of England and that there remains a perception that this is still the case. It must be concluded that this is not so and that, in any event, there is a great difference between monitoring, and monitoring and intervention. From recent examples of market disturbances, it is clear that, while the Bank is an interested party, it plays a minor role in their resolution. Solutions in such circumstances are very much ad hoc and responses from among the exchanges and other bodies also vary greatly.

The AFBD, as the principal SRO regulating firms trading futures and options, has to be concerned at the lack of supervision of both systemic and market risk. It does not have oversight of exchanges or clearinghouses, and it cannot rely upon the SIB or any other body to provide that oversight. Thus the AFBD finds itself in the invidious position of trying to offer effective regulation of its membership in an atmosphere that is otherwise incompletely regulated. This problem is compounded by factors which, in other circumstances, have been described as the benefits of the Financial Services Act. A former director of policy of the SIB promotes the virtues of the Financial Services Act by stating:

> It should be noted that, unlike, say, the U.S. CFTC, the SIB is not going to vet new products or new contracts or require anything more of their producers than that they describe them fairly, promote them reasonably and do not sell them to those for whom they are manifestly unsuitable. It is not the case that all deals will have to go through our RIEs or designated exchanges overseas and as mentioned above, U.K. exchanges will not be able to prevent their members dealing off exchange (Salden, 1988; Mortimer, 1988, p. 45).

While this may indeed allow for innovation and free entry to London's markets, it allows also for the relatively unrestricted entry of risk into any AFBD members' books. There are no prohibitions or even substantial controls on the type of futures and options business an AFBD member may do other than by AFBD-imposed financial requirements attaching to such business. Off-exchange futures products (OTC futures) are expanding and form a significant part of many AFBD members' business, whether it is in the more traditional areas of bullion or forex, or in new "bespoke" financial products. There is almost no analysis in London of the cumulative effect of this off-exchange business, and for reasons that will be detailed below, the split of regulatory functions between SROs makes this almost inevitable.

Equally, in respect of on-exchange business, while the clearinghouse performs risk assessment procedures, there is little coordinated analysis of concentrations in the system, or even of the open positions in any one contract market. Thus, while some exchanges do monitor closely the levels of business and open interest in their market, others do nothing at all; yet those markets may well have overlapping memberships. As indicated above, this leaves the AFBD in a position of incomplete knowledge, and when problems do emerge it has proven difficult to assess the degree of risk that might flow from one particular failure through to other AFBD members or to other markets.

As stated, the conventional defense to the charge that London's futures markets lack sufficient regulation has been that the Bank of England performed an oversight function. A more recent suggestion, that the exchanges and clearinghouses perform a regulatory function, is in practice only partially true. The legislation as it now stands does not address the problem, and in its present form does not easily allow for participants to devise their own solution.

Failure #2: Structural Overlap and Underlap

To compound the difficulties described above, even the present and imperfect scope of SRO regulation is open to question. While it may appear that, for instance, the AFBD is the regulator for futures and options, to assume it is the only regulator is somewhat misleading. While the AFBD is the principal regulator overseeing the investment business of about 400 firms, nevertheless the SIB undertakes a minor degree of direct regulation of futures and options brokers (well, one to be exact), and other SROs also have it within their scope to regulate futures and options business, usually when it is done as an ancillary part of their members' principal business.[17] However, in the case of the Securities Association (TSA), this concept has been so stretched as to mean that TSA has some 50 members who do nothing but futures and options business, and a further 250 members who do a significant amount of such business (this out of a total membership of around 900). The Investment Management Regulatory Organisation (IMRO) also regulates futures and options business where it is ancillary to the main business of its members, though it is unclear what the extent of this regulation is or the numbers involved.

Accordingly, even if the AFBD were asked to take initiatives to try and address Failure #1 and offer more comprehensive regulation of the futures industry, it is beyond its capacity to do so while a significant proportion of the trade in derivatives in the U.K. is done by firms who are not its members. A conventional justification for this overlap of regulatory jurisdictions is that it would be anticompetitive for any one SRO to have a monopoly on the regulation of one sector. In addition to being unhelpful in addressing systemic or market risk, it also means that there are potentially several standards of regulation that may apply to firms doing derivatives business. While SIB has endeavored to address this in the context of the New Settlement, and to a degree rule books can be harmonized, in terms of the practical business of regulation, differing standards are likely to continue. The AFBD, for instance, takes a view on regulation that is largely evolved from doing nothing else except regulating futures and options business, dealing with brokers in those products, and forming liaisons with the markets and others concerned with them. IMRO, by contrast, looks upon the use of derivatives largely as a portfolio hedging device and in the context of its primary concern of regulating investment management businesses. A similarity of approach to regulation, regard-less of the internal and organizational differences between the AFBD and IMRO, is in the circumstances, highly unlikely. This enshrines the potential for regulatory arbitrage; it does nothing but reduce effective regulation.

The overlaps are apparent and aside from diminishing the opportunity for coordinated or consistent regulation, they must generate unnecessary costs and general waste (see below). The plethora of "regulators," still some 20 at last count, also serves to disguise the gaps in the system. In the preceding paragraphs the absence of a mechanism for monitoring and assessing risk in the futures markets has been described. The reliance upon a large number of bodies, primarily representative of pre-Financial Services Act interest groups, means that similar shortcomings in other parts of the financial services regulatory scheme may also become evident. The sheer number of bodies may also make unconscripted coordination unlike-ly and diminish the enthusiasm for expanding existing roles to cover the gaps or for creating new bodies to fill them.

Failure #3: The Unnecessary Costs of Regulation

While in the preliminary discussions and debates on Gower's reports, views were expressed regarding the excess cost that would be generated by statute-backed regulation, nevertheless very little was devoted in Gower's report itself, or in the White Paper, to this problem. This has led to subsequent and strident criticism of Gower with suggestions that his report lacked fundamental economic understanding (Salden, 1988, p. 8). Commentators have remarked that "the Gower report is indicative of the narrow approach characteristic of the English lawyer." Gower, as a professional company lawyer, had little familiarity with economics. He may therefore have felt confident in dismissing consideration of the economics of his proposals; this approach was continued by the consequences of the early interpretation of "equivalence" by the SIB.

As the City came to terms with the requirements of the Financial Services Act, and the need for in-house compliance officers, legal advisors, staff manuals, and the fees that had to be paid toward the running of the SROs and the SIB itself, calls for recognition of the cost element have grown. These calls received attention in the shape of amendments to the Financial Services Act mentioned above (regarding the New Settlement) which require SROs to have a means of judging the costs of any regulatory initiatives they take. How this will translate into practice is yet to be seen, but it is likely to require some form of self-certification by the SROs when proposing rule changes or changes in practice, confirming that they have examined and taken into account the costs of the actions or changes they are intending to pursue. Unlike the United States, the U.K. does not possess a history of cost-analysis, and a long learning period should be anticipated before this provision is likely to have real meaning. The introduction of the test also comes at a point when SRO rule books have been written, establishments have been fixed, and standing costs are unlikely to diminish. Thus any application of the test is likely to have only peripheral effect in the short to medium term.

An awareness of the need for cost-efficiency in regulation is a useful improvement; however, the structural defects in the Act mean that even the best-intentioned application of this discipline will fail to reduce all wastage and duplication. The number of regulatory bodies is high, the potential for and actual duplication is equally high, and this diminishes both regulatory effectiveness (as described in Failure #2) and cost effectiveness. For the SIB to maintain an ability to regulate one futures firm, for the TSA to have resources sufficient to regulate a further 50, and for the AFBD to then undertake similar tasks for some 400 firms, means unnecessarily high organization costs and the loss of potential economies of scale that might otherwise emerge if combined, specialist regulation were to be pursued.

The Future of Futures Regulation in London

The United Kingdom's hybrid regulatory solution has left areas of the futures industry unregulated, other areas oversupplied with regulation, and an inherently costly structure. The sum of these shortcomings has diminished the effectiveness of regulation in the futures markets and may, among other things, allow the development of significant and unmonitored risk. The futures industry attracts volatility; it is an industry devoted to risk transfer and thus requires effective and comprehensive oversight to ensure that the transfer occurs in the most risk-neutral environment attainable. A realization of this is not readily apparent in the United Kingdom's legislation.

David Walker's "New Settlement" is a recognition of imperfections in the Financial Services Act, and while it makes some progress in respect of cost efficiency, it goes very little distance toward addressing the other major flaws in that legislation. Substantial change is needed, and probably this should be achieved by major legislative reform. Having only recently enacted amending legislation, it is unlikely that further or extensive amending legislation would be sponsored by the Government within the next two years.

Short of there being any Government initiative there is always the potential for the SIB and the SROs to take practical steps to correct some of these deficiencies. This is occurring in a number of areas. The AFBD is anxious to assist the futures exchanges in London to oversee their markets to the same minimum standard and has raised with the SIB and selected exchanges ways in which this might occur. These discussions are at a very early stage, but have looked at such matters as monitoring of members, competence training and testing, and improved reporting of trading information. A further area receiving attention is that of information exchange, where efforts are being made to understand better the information requirements of the SROs, exchanges, and clearinghouses, and to then ensure that there is a free flow of useful and timely information among those bodies. The wide range of markets and market practices in London, and the diversity of products, member firms, and existing information requirements means that this will be a substantial task.

In terms of regulatory overlap, the AFBD has also examined ways in which it can work toward ensuring that it offers comprehensive oversight of derivatives trading, and to this end has commenced discussions with the Securities Association (TSA). It is hoped that at the least this could lead to a single regulatory effort toward derivatives regulation, possibly by means of the AFBD contracting to provide regulatory services to the TSA in respect of their derivatives-orientated members. On a more adventurous analysis, this could also lead to more extensive cooperation that effectively sees the combining of the two regulatory bodies. Studies thus far indicate that there is a substantial potential cost-saving in some degree of combined effort, and, while less amenable to quantification, a real improvement in regulation is likely to occur. There is no reason why a similar approach could not extend to the other bodies undertaking elements of derivatives regulation, and the concept of exchanging services on a contractural basis looks increasingly attractive.

These are, however, limited and patchwork solutions and are no substitute for a full and legislative response. The severity of the present problems is difficult to assess and, like much in the way of regulation, is only likely to be fully appreciated and addressed when losses occur because of the problems or are exacerbated by them. For the moment, London's markets are in a healthy state, volumes are increasing, and there is a commitment within the markets to pursue change and improve their attractiveness, both in terms of their utility to customers and in the standards of operation and regulation. This, too, will go some way toward dealing with the shortcomings of the legislation but may also delay the pursuit of a comprehensive solution.

London in an International Context

London has been described as exhibiting a wide range of attributes that have combined to place it as a leading financial center. "Size, openness of markets, trading activity, sophistication of international investors, quality of research, transaction services, and innovative thinking have traditionally characterised London" (Levich and Walter, 1990). These factors were evident before the Financial Services Act came into effect, and to a large degree have been left unaffected by it; indeed, it was the legislative intention that this be the case. However, the nature of the markets has changed, to a degree the make-up of the users has also changed, and the requirements for operating in the international marketplace have also altered; an ability to demonstrate fairness, transparency, and orderliness is now a basic prerequisite. London does do these things, and its increasing volumes are irrefutable evidence of investor confidence. That confidence will only be retained so long as London displays those attributes and, particularly in the 1990's, shows skill and speed in its innovations and adaptations.

The structure of the regulatory scheme may, on the one hand, mean that market development is relatively unhindered, but on the other, development may proceed on a precarious basis if the regulators cannot keep pace. More fundamentally, the regulatory overlaps may introduce costs and drag that will hinder London's response time, and limit the effectiveness of those responses.

From the outside looking in, the United Kingdom regulatory scheme must appear confusing. The complexity makes regulator-to-regulator communication less efficient, and trader-to-regulator contact less clear and more costly. These results do not serve regulators well and therefore do not serve the industry. Greater rationalization of the United Kingdom regulatory scheme must be achieved if London's markets are to be allowed to operate to their full potential.

Acknowledgments

The author is the Chief Executive of the Association of Futures Brokers and Dealers, the self-regulating body primarily responsible for the regulation of firms undertaking derivatives business in the United Kingdom. The views expressed in this chapter are those of the author, and do not necessarily represent those of the Association.

Notes

1. See generally, Gower (1988), Pimlott (1985), and Fox-Bassett (1981).
2. 1980 Command Paper 7939. "The Wilson Report on the Functioning of Financial Institutions", 1980 Command Paper 7937, London, Her Majesty's Stationery Office (HMSO).
3. Gower Report 1.13(7), para 1.11 see note 4 below. LCB Gower, "Review of Investor Protection Report: Part 1", 1984 Command Paper 9125, London, HMSO, para. 1.13.
4. Review of Investor Protection—A Discussion Document (1982 HMSO). LCB Gower "Review of Investor Protection: A Discussion Document", January 1982, London, HMSO.
5. "Quasi-autonomous governmental organizations," of which the United Kingdom had developed a considerable number, many of which were viewed as having failed to perform as promised.
6. 1984 Command Paper 9125 and 1985 HMSO. Gower reference in Note 3 and LCB Gower "Review of Investor Protection, Report: Part II; 1985, London, HMSO. (*Not* a Command Paper.)
7. Licensed Dealers (Conduct of Business) Rules 1983, made pursuant to the Prevention of Fraud (Investments) Act 1933.
8. "Department of Trade & Industry, Financial Services in the United Kingdom: A New Framework for Investor Protection," (1985, Command Paper 9432), London, HMSO.
9. Hansard, vol. 77, No. 103, House of Commons Debates, April 24, 1985, pp. 920, 921. The only real comment on the futures markets was in fact contained to a discussion of the benefits of removing capital gains tax for those markets. No debate on the regulation of those markets appears.
10. The London Commodity Exchange (now trading as London Fox) represented a wide array of Commodities Associations, including: the Coffee Terminal Market Association of London Ltd.; the Gafta Soya Bean Meal Futures Association Ltd.; the International Petroleum Exchange of London Ltd.; the London and New Zealand Futures Association Ltd.; the London Cocoa Terminal Market Association Ltd.; the London Potato Futures Association Ltd.; the London Rubber Terminal Market Association Ltd.; the London Vegetable Oil Terminal Market Association Ltd.; and the United Terminal Sugar Market Association Ltd.
11. Banking Act 1979, Sections 1(1) and 11(1).
12. For instance, the Bank of England has taken a particular interest in developments in relation to screen-based trading. One of its staff, Dr. Fiona Ashworth, chairs a multijurisdictional working group looking at regulatory issues arising from such systems.
13. The five SROs are: the Association of Futures Brokers and Dealers Ltd. (AFBD); Investment Management Regulatory Organisation Ltd (IMRO); Life Assurance and United Trust Regulatory Organisation Ltd. (LAUTRO); the Financial Intermediaries, Managers and Brokers Regulatory Association Ltd. (FIMBRA); and the Securities Association Ltd. (TSA).
14. See generally, Blair (1989) and Nelson (1989).
15. Companies Amendment Act 1989.
16. Under AFBD rules, customers can be categorized as "professional, experienced or private" and treated to differing levels of, *inter alia*, disclosure, as a result. Other "advan-

tages" exist: for example, professional or experienced customers may opt out of segregation, that is, they may choose to allow their monies to be co-mingled with that of other customers and with their brokers' funds.

17. "Scope" has a technical and much-debated meaning in the context of the Financial Services Act and its rules. The statement of each SRO's scope effectively determines its regulatory territory, and during the initial period of implementation of the Act, disputes between SROs over scope were frequent and energetic.

References

Blair, M. 1989. Regulation of the Conduct of Investment Business. *Journal of International Banking and Financial Law* (September), Vol. 4, No. 9, pp. 376–402.

Fox-Bassett, N. Financial Futures Markets: London Regulatory Framework.

Goodhart, C. The Costs of Regulation. In *Financial Regulation—Or Over-Regulation*, A. Salden, (ed.), 1988, p. 25.

Gower, L.C.B. 1988. Big Bang and City Regulation. *Modern Law Review* 51(1), pp. 1–22.

Levich, R.M., and Walter, Inigo. 1990. Tax Driven Regulatory Drag: European Financial Centers in the 1990s. An International Business Area Working Paper, unpublished working paper—44 pages, November 1989 (Revised January 1990), INSEAD. Working Paper 5–90–02, Salomon Brothers Center, New York University, Graduate School of Business (1990).

Mortimer, K. The Securities and Investments Board. In *Financial Regulation—Or Over-Regulation*, A. Salden, (ed.), 1988, p. 45.

Nelson, P. 1989. Regulation Rules Too Detailed. *Financial Times* (December 7), p. 35.

Pimlott, G.F. 1985. The Reform of Investor Protection in the UK—An Examination of the Proposals of the Gower Report and the UK Government's White Paper of January 1985. *Journal of Comparative Business and Capital Market Law* 7, pp. 141–172.

Salden, A., ed. 1988. *Financial Regulation—Or Over-Regulation*. Institute of Economic Affairs.

12 THE JAPANESE FINANCIAL FUTURES MARKET: PRESENT AND FUTURE PROSPECTS

Yoshiteru Murakami

The history of the financial futures market began in May 1972 when currency futures were listed and traded on the Chicago Mercantile Exchange (CME). The success of currency futures brought about other financial futures such as bonds, interest rates, and stock indices. With each additional new contract, the market expanded rapidly, and it now far exceeds the volume of commodity futures despite their much longer trading history. Of all the futures traded on the CME and Chicago Board of Trade (CBOT), in 1989 financial futures contracts accounted for 91 percent and 74 percent of the volume, respectively.

The financial futures market owes its origin to the so-called Nixon Shock and the resultant collapse of the Bretton Woods System. As the foreign exchange market changed fundamentally from the system of a fixed rate of exchange to that of a floating rate, the need to hedge effectively against market volatility increased proportionately. Similarly, Eurodollar futures began trading on the CME in 1981 as a means to hedge against increased interest rate volatility, which was caused by the high rate of inflation following the 1973 and 1979 Oil Shocks.

Rapid growth of the financial futures market took place not only in the United States but also in other major financial centers worldwide. In the

179

United Kingdom, the London International Financial Futures Exchange (LIFFE) was established in 1982 and commenced trading currency, interest rate, bond and stock index futures contracts. Similarly in Singapore, SIMEX was established in 1984 and began trading futures in the currency and Eurodollar contracts. (A unique feature of SIMEX is that both currency and Eurodollar contracts bought or sold on SIMEX can be settled or netted against positions with the CME, and vice versa, through a mutual offset agreement between the two exchanges.)

Japan entered the era of financial futures by listing Japanese Government Bond futures on the Tokyo Stock Exchange (TSE) in 1985, followed by stock index futures in 1988, and by Euroyen and Eurodollar interest rate futures and Japanese yen futures in 1989. New exchanges with active trading in financial futures have also been established in other financial centers such as Australia, France, Canada, and Hong Kong. The financial futures market has developed rapidly and will continue to expand in response to ever-changing investor and market demands.

The History of the Japanese Financial Futures Market

In Japan, the origin of futures markets can be traced to the rice exchange in Osaka. The exchange was chartered in 1730 by the Tokugawa government and was called *cho-ai-mai-kaisho*, which literally means tally-book rice exchange. This predates establishment of the CME in 1848 by more than a century. On the Osaka exchange, members engaged in trading rice contracts that specified the grade and unit size as well as the trading period. At the end of a contract month, all trading positions were settled on a net basis in cash. Neither physical delivery nor exchange of warehouse receipts was ever made on the underlying rice. The *cho-ai-mai-kaisho* had other similarities to present day futures exchanges such as margin requirements, mark-to-market and clearinghouse systems.

Financial futures products in Japan can, on the other hand, be traced to a securities future transaction referred to as the "long-term forward settlement transaction." Through this transaction different types of securities were traded under varying terms instead of under a standard contract. This practice was suspended after World War II by the occupying U.S. Armed Forces administration as being too speculative. For the next 40 years, financial instruments were traded on a cash-only basis until the introduction of Japanese government bond futures in 1985.

Following the 1973 and 1979 oil shocks and the ensuing recessionary periods of 1975 to 1980, the Japanese government issued a massive amount of JGBs to finance its deficits. This surpassed all other bond issuances. As the volume of outstanding JBGs increased, so did price volatility. JBG futures were introduced as a means of allowing institutional investors to hedge their ever-increasing positions. This was an historic event for the Japanese financial market, particularly in a nation where cash-only trading had prevailed uninterrupted for over 40 years. Once trading was permitted, the market grew steadily, so by the third year, the trading volume in futures was in excess of the underlying cash market volume.

As far as stock index futures are concerned, rapid expansion of the cash market made it nearly impossible to hedge against the risks inherent in the market through traditional methods of risk diversification. As a result of investor demands for a method of hedging against price fluctuations, Stock Futures 50 (OSF 50) contracts were listed with the Osaka Stock Exchange in 1987. Stock Futures 50 refers to an index of 50 stocks. The contract requires final settlement by delivery of underlying stocks; practical consideration should have demanded settlement in cash, as in the case of Standard & Poor (S&P) 500 index contracts. The Securities and Exchange Law at the time, however, did not allow this. Fortunately, this restriction was soon lifted, and in 1988 Tokyo Stock Price Index (TOPIX) and Nikkei Dow 225 Average (Nikkei Average) contracts, in which final settlement could only be made in cash, were approved and listed on the TSE and OSE, respectively.

As for interest and currency futures, the enactment of the Financial Futures Trading Law in 1989 led to the opening of Japan's first exchange to deal exclusively in financial futures, the Tokyo International Financial Futures Exchange (TIFFE). Euroyen and Eurodollar interest rates and Japanese yen futures began trading on this exchange in 1989. With liberalization of the Japanese financial market came increased funding through large, money market time deposits and negotiable certificates of deposits. Euroyen contracts in particular were enthusiastically received by institutional investors as the first of their kind; they permitted hedging short-term yen interest rate exposure.

A major objective of TIFFE was to create an international exchange with as many participants as possible. To this end, TIFFE modeled its clearing system on those used by other international exchanges and relaxed membership qualifications for foreign applicants. For example, for a domestic institution to apply for clearing or non-clearing-member status, an applicant is required to have a net worth of over 50 billion yen or 5 billion yen, respectively. In the case of a foreign applicant, however, one needs only 5 billion or 1 billion yen, respectively.

Options on the TOPIX and Nikkei Averages have been listed since 1989 on the TSE and OSE, respectively. In May 1990, options on JGB futures were listed on the TSE. Furthermore, discussion is now underway at TIFFE to list options on Euroyen futures by mid-1991. Despite a later introduction and establishment of a financial futures market than in the United States and United Kingdom, a result of the pace of financial deregulation, the Japanese financial futures market has grown to become one of the major markets in the world.

Japanese participation in futures and options continues to be liberalized. In 1987, Japanese financial institutions were permitted for the first time to trade financial futures for their own accounts at overseas financial futures exchanges. Similarly in 1988, Japanese financial institutions were allowed to trade options on underlying financial instruments at overseas exchanges.

The Japanese financial market was deregulated in response to the globalization of the financial market, the increased need for Japanese financial institutions to hedge foreign currency denominated assets and liabilities, and numerous requests from overseas exchanges for Japanese participation. In 1989, Japanese financial institutions were permitted to broker financial futures traded at overseas exchanges. This has allowed Japanese corporations access to overseas exchanges through domestic banking and brokerage institutions, thereby hedging their increasing foreign currency denominated asset and liability exposures.

Characteristics of the Market

The Japanese financial futures markets has three major characteristics. First, interest rate and currency futures are traded on TIFFE, while bond and stock index futures are traded on the Tokyo and Osaka stock exchanges. This is due to the fact that interest rate and currency futures are regulated by the Financial Futures Trading Law while bond and stock indices are governed by the Securities and Exchange Law.

Second, the main participants in the Japanese market are all institutions. In Chicago, individuals referred to as "locals" engage in transactions directly for their own account as well as for institutional accounts. Participation in the Japanese market, however, is limited to financial institutions such as banks and securities firms. Even orders brokered by banks and securities firms are overwhelmingly from corporations. In other words, the Japanese market has institutional bias where orders tend to be large-lot transactions, thereby contributing to market growth in monetary terms.

Finally, the Japanese market operates on a computer-based trading system. While most overseas exchanges have adopted the open outcry method of floor trading, Japan has employed a computerized trading system, which enables rapid and accurate processing of large and voluminous orders.

Restrictions on the Market

In Japan, various kinds of restrictions have been placed on the financial futures market to keep it sound. First of all, membership is open only to institutions that meet the qualifications of each exchange. In addition, the exchanges have employed position limits on members' proprietary trading accounts, as well as price limits, all in an attempt to maintain the soundness of the market while preventing it from being impaired by excessively speculative trading. When the exchanges sense trading is irregular and it is necessary to take action to maintain market order, they may adopt further restrictive measures. These restrictions include setting and expanding price limits, raising margin requirements, and regulating the total volume of trading during a single day.

The exchanges also set various transactional restrictions on customers as well as members in order to protect them. Brokerage licenses are limited to corporations authorized by the Ministry of Finance, thus insuring that the brokerage business is properly operated. Licenses are approved based on experience in the financial market, financial well-being, and reputation in society. In order to prevent excessive trading, minimum margin requirements and position limits are based on a customer's net capital. This "Minimum Customer Margin System" has been designed to exclude investors who are not financially sound. Due to the highly leveraged nature of futures and their inherent risks, customers are required to make a minimum deposit with their broker of 6 million yen regardless of their actual trading volume.

The Effect of Futures Market Activities on the Japanese Cash Market

On October 19, 1987, also known as Black Monday, the New York Stock Exchange (NYSE) saw massive sell orders from the opening bell, thereby setting a record one-day drop. Although there was a general downward trend in the equities market just prior to the crash, a result of the large U.S. trade deficit, rising interest rates, and stiff, new taxes on corporate takeovers, program trading involving cash and futures arbitrage has been widely blamed for accelerating the fall. True or not, it is in any case recognized that futures markets have a great deal of impact on cash markets, and this can be very disruptive at times. Accordingly, various countermeasures have been adopted in the United States since Black Monday in the hope of preventing future market crashes.

One such countermeasure is the "program trading report" issued by the New York Stock Exchange. This report details all trades in an effort to avert disorders caused by cash and futures arbitrage. Furthermore, cash, futures, and options markets incorporated a new regulation called a "circuit breaker" which suspends all trading should the market fall by more than a specified amount.

As the Japanese futures market continues to develop and expand, similar problems are being encountered. The Tokyo equities market, which had been in a precarious position since early 1990 due first to the weakening yen and then to high interest rate forecasts, saw the Nikkei Average tumble 1,569 points, on February 26. This was the second largest one-day fall after Black Monday. The Tokyo stock market continued to lose ground until stabilizing in late spring. But the Iraqi invasion of Kuwait has revived the downtrend. As in the United States, some have argued program trading on the Nikkei Average has been responsible for the market instability. Take, for example, an arbitrageur with "short futures and long cash market" trade when futures were relatively more expensive than the market. If he later decides to reverse the trade as futures cheapen against cash, this may have the effect of exacerbating further sell-offs in the cash market.

In an attempt to prevent further confusion, the TSE made an unusual request to all its member firms. It requested that they restrict their arbitrage-related selling in the underlying cash market to the opening of the morning and afternoon sessions. This was in the hope that the usual high volume at the open would absorb and diffuse resulting selling pressure. Opinions are divided over this matter. Those in favor have stated that by removing the element of uncertainty regarding when arbitrageurs might sell, confidence would be restored in the cash market. Those in opposition state that this would only serve to skew the relationship between futures and cash prices.

Since then the TSE has adopted a policy similar to the NYSE. In order to make futures trading activities more visible and to maintain market stability, the TSE now releases a weekly report detailing cash- and futures-related equities trading volume and ending cash position for each securities firm. Moreover, in an event of extreme market volatility caused by cash and future arbitrage, the TSE is now empowered to restrict such program trading. For the near future, effectiveness of this new measure on the cash and futures markets will be observed. The TSE, however, is ready to incorporate additional measures to maintain soundness and stability of the market as it becomes necessary.

Issues Facing the Japanese Financial Futures Market

Although the Japanese financial futures market has grown in a short period of time to one of the major financial futures markets in the world, it still faces several issues that need to be addressed and resolved jointly by all market participants. First, the number of orders from nonmembers remains small. The breakdown of trading volume by investors shows approximately 90 percent is accounted for by banks and securities firms engaged in trading for themselves. In order for the market to have any depth, it is essential to increase the participation of institutional investors, corporations, individuals, and nonresidents.

Second, present trading hours are too short. JGB futures, for example, are traded on the TSE in two-hour sessions, for a total of four hours a day, while interest rate futures on TIFFE are traded for five hours. This is less than any other overseas financial future exchange. As the globalization of financial trading progresses, overseas events and economic indicators released abroad have an increasingly large impact on the domestic market. It has become necessary to hedge against price fluctuations on an around-the-clock basis. Trading hours have been extended in overseas markets through the introduction of night and morning sessions, as well as computerized trading systems. The length of trading hours has come to be regarded as the measure of convenience of futures exchange. Therefore, it is inevitable that Japanese hours will be extended in the near future.

Third, Japanese market transactions are concentrated on nearby contracts. Although five contract months are listed on the TSE for JGB futures, and eight contract months are listed on TIFFE for interest rate futures, trading is concentrated on the nearby contract. Trading in other contract maturities is limited, making it difficult to put a long-term hedge through the listed futures contracts.

Fourth, types of orders are limited. Specifically, there are only two ways to place orders: limit and market. In an effort to promote market activity and encourage wider investor participation while coping with various customer needs, other types of orders (such as the stop and spread) should be permitted. Furthermore, commissions should be lowered for spread or hedge orders, as in overseas exchanges.

Fifth, the hedge accounting system remains undeveloped. Although it is currently under discussion, hedge accounting is not presently recognized in Japan. As a result, even if an underlying cash is hedged with futures, the effect of the hedge on the profit and loss on cash and futures positions is not properly reflected. Given that the Japanese financial futures market was established to provide a method of hedging against underlying cash instrument price fluctuations, the lack of proper hedge accounting guidelines is a serious deficiency and must be corrected without further delay.

Sixth, many questions remain regarding the taxation of financial futures. Any tax on futures instruments would have the effect of increasing trading costs, which would discourage nonresident participation. Furthermore, domestic investors would also prefer to trade on less costly overseas exchanges, which would most certainly be detrimental to any further development in the Japanese financial futures market.

Finally, there are two regulations governing financial futures trading. In Japan, currency and interest rate futures are subject to the Financial Futures Trading Law, while bond and stock indices are regulated by the Securities and Exchange Law. The former is listed on TIFFE and the latter is listed on the stock exchange. This is highly inefficient as a method of protecting investors and ensuring adequate market control and supervision. Therefore, the Japanese financial futures market needs to be integrated under a single regulation which specifically governs financial futures instruments. This point in particular has been scheduled for a legislative review in 1991, taking both domestic and overseas market conditions into consideration.

Future Prospects

As financial market deregulation and globalization continue and communications technology becomes more sophisticated, investors will need to hedge their risks on an around-the-clock basis. In response to this, a number of financial futures exchanges are currently extending trading hours. This, however, is costly as well as logistically problematic. The best solution, therefore, would be for exchanges to cooperate with each other and make fungible all futures contracts having the same underlying cash market. This would provide investors with truly liquid hedging instruments. An availability of such contracts would make it possible for investors to manage their risks on a 24-hour basis without taking any additional risk. Investors would be able to trade during their own day as usual and then be able to trade the same contract and position with an overseas exchange. To facilitate such global trading, it is necessary to sign a mutual offset agreement between the exchanges involved.

In order for this to become reality, it is essential for the exchanges to agree to standardize some aspects of the existing financial exchange infrastructure.

In other words, it would be necessary to establish a universal system of clearing, a uniformity in marking-to-market positions, and a common margin requirement. Although it would be difficult to restructure and achieve uniformity in the exchanges of various countries due to existing, unique financial systems and market conditions, a uniformity of infrastructure must be achieved for the benefit of all market participants.

In the mutual offset system, the exchange that lists the financial contract first and succeeds in it would have control of the contract over its partner exchanges. This would mean that in order for exchanges to retain a controlling interest in a contract, the exchange must be the first to list a new product that meets investor needs. This would encourage exchanges to develop new products, which would in turn make the exchanges more convenient for market participants.

For financial futures trading to expand globally and contribute to the development of the world economy, it is vital to maintain a level of competitiveness among the exchanges within a mutually beneficial and cooperative framework. To this end, it is essential for both exchanges and market participants to establish regular forums, to discuss market developments, and exchange information. Such forums will contribute greatly in advancing product and market developments of financial futures for the benefit of all market participants worldwide.

13 THE INTERNATIONALIZATION OF FUTURES MARKETS: ISSUES FOR U.S. MARKETS

Robert K. Wilmouth

Many issues affecting self-regulators in the domestic futures industry have international dimensions and implications. This is a product, in part, of the tremendous and unprecedented growth of the futures industry and the fact that futures trading has become a trading component of virtually all types of other increasingly complex financial transactions. What affects the U.S. futures markets affects the international financial arena, and vice versa. From this myriad of interrelated issues and linkages, several topics currently facing the futures industry warrant specific attention.

Jurisdiction

The most controversial of these current issues is the question of regulatory jurisdiction between the Commodity Futures Trading Commission (CFTC) and the Securities and Exchange Commission (SEC). The dispute revolves around which agency should have jurisdiction over futures trading in general and stock index futures in particular. Some people and agencies outside of the futures industry argue that stock index futures and the relatively low margins on these contracts are responsible for increasing the volatility of the stock market and, therefore, played a substantial role in the stock market crash of October 1987, and the market drop in October 1989. Based on this misconception, the argument demands realignment of some jurisdictional lines in order to limit such drastic volatility.

The three jurisdictional changes that have received the most attention are the transfer of regulatory jurisdiction over stock index futures from the CFTC to the SEC; the transfer of regulatory jurisdiction over all financial futures from the CFTC to the SEC; and the merge of the CFTC and the SEC with the possible creation of a super-agency with jurisdiction over both the stock and the futures markets.

Numerous independent studies, including those conducted by Federal Reserve Board economists and the SEC, have concluded that there is no evidence to support the alleged connection between stock market volatility and stock index futures and their margins. Furthermore, evidence indicates that stock index futures do not increase market volatility. Additionally, no futures clearing member firm defaulted in either October 1987 or October 1989, which substantiates the fact that the current margining system works effectively.

The current regulatory system, which is organized along functional lines, is far more effective than the proposed regulatory adjustments that would place different markets with different purposes in the hands of the regulator who regulates the underlying commodity. Even shifting regulation of stock index futures alone to the SEC calls into play a vast array of problems and obstacles. If stock index futures are reclassified as securities, contract markets would be subject to oversight by two federal agencies. CFTC-regulated entities dealing in those futures would suddenly be subject to all federal securities laws. CFTC-registered entities could be required to obtain state securities registrations, and a firm's registered associated persons would probably have to pass additional securities qualification exams and become registered with the SEC. These are only a few of the expensive, time-consuming, and potentially conflicting requirements that would surface if stock index futures were transferred to the SEC, the proposal currently espoused by several Administration officials.

The U.S. Congress determined the regulatory jurisdictional alignment almost 20 years ago and should not alter it until Congress is satisfied that a system that regulates by underlying commodity will be more effective than the current system. Even though the financial environment has clearly changed, the fundamental premise that a functional approach is more efficacious than regulation along product lines remains. Unless the change will be beneficial, it is foolish to go through immense effort and expense to alter even one section of the current regulatory structure.

Electronic Trading

Another issue of particular international consequence is the notion of electronic trading. Open-outcry has been in existence for as long as the commodities markets themselves—almost 150 years. While there are merits to both sides of the debate between screen trading and open-outcry, it is certain that some degree of electronic trading is here to stay. In an effort to remain competitive and to capture more of the international market, U.S. exchanges are devoting their resources to developing their own electronic trading systems and convincing other exchanges around the world to offer their contracts for trading on these U.S. exchanges.

A number of foreign futures exchanges, such as the Tokyo Stock Exchange, the Swiss Options and Financial Futures Exchange, and the Osaka Securities Exchange, are fully automated, and a number of other exchanges have instituted screen trading systems to complement open-outcry.

GLOBEX, the joint venture between the Chicago Mercantile Exchange and Reuters, is a pure screen trading system that matches buy and sell orders. Aurora, the Chicago Board of Trade system, more nearly replicates trading pit conditions by allowing the person at the terminal to pick the trader he will sell to or buy from, with some restrictions. GLOBEX anticipates being operational by the end of 1990, and Aurora will probably follow suit shortly thereafter.

Changes in how the market operates will certainly affect how the markets must be regulated. Current regulations are based on a partially manual system and, with the recent technological advancements in futures trading, alterations will become a necessity. As with any new product, it will have to be determined which type of trading system is the most successful and is less susceptible to trading abuses. Progress in technology does not necessarily generate increases in honesty and decreases in greed. In fact, an electronic system may also allow for misuse. Only time will tell.

International Regulatory Harmonization

The U.S. futures markets are becoming increasingly globalized and therefore more competitive internationally. However, the cost of conducting business in more than one country generally depends on the similarity between the regulatory requirements imposed by the two countries. Conflicting regulatory requirements can make the cost of doing business in two different countries prohibitive, while similar but different requirements can still increase the cost of doing business.

For example, making a firm print two different futures risk disclosure statements to distribute to the same customer and even simply maintaining the staff and procedures to ensure that both sets of "similar" requirements are being followed can substantially increase the cost of doing business, and thus reduce incentive. In order to encourage international competition by reducing the cost of doing business in more than one country, regulators must work together to harmonize their regulatory requirements to avoid confusion and conflict. When it is impossible to develop complementary rules, regulators must provide clear interpretations of how compliance with multiple requirements can be achieved.

Comparable regulatory requirements also make it easier to receive an exemption from regulation in a country where the firm is not domiciled. For example, the CFTC will grant exemptions from registration and from most U.S. regulatory requirements to firms that solicit U.S. customers for transactions on foreign exchanges if the CFTC has determined that those firms are subject to comparable regulatory requirements. At the present time, the CFTC has granted exemptions to firms located in the United Kingdom, Singapore and Australia, and to several exchanges in Canada. However, since these exemptions are not available for firms that solicit U.S. customers for transactions on U.S. markets, it is still important to harmonize regulatory requirements between the United States and other countries.

Information Sharing

In order to facilitate comparable regulatory requirements, the first step must be a routine exchange of regulatory information among countries. In this increasingly global economy, information sharing among regulators from different countries has become particularly crucial. Regulators must find a way to prohibit individuals who have been put out of business in one country for unethical or fraudulent practices from just moving to another country and setting up shop there. In addition, a firm having financial problems in one country can affect the financial condition of other related firms in other countries. Frequently, knowledge of a problem early on may prevent the problem from becoming unmanageable. An example is the recent series of events involving the bankruptcy of Drexel Burnham Lambert.

Currently, an investigation into unethical practices or conversion of customer funds may be stymied by the fact that the records or funds are located in a country with a blocking statute. Even determining an individual's or firm's accurate financial condition can be almost impossible without open sharing of information. Adequate sharing arrangements can reduce, if not solve, these and other problems.

These issues are not only obstacles for the regulator who is unable to obtain specific information, and for the customers who are not adequately protected from unscrupulous firms and individuals; they are also problems for legitimate firms attempting to do business in another country. For example, because of the obstacles the National Futures Association (NFA) has encountered in trying to obtain information from countries with blocking statutes, it has become more difficult for firms in those countries to become NFA members and, therefore, to do business in the United States. Appropriate information-sharing arrangements with regulators in foreign countries with blocking statutes would make it easier for firms from those countries to become NFA members.

Disciplinary Clearinghouse

Another regulatory issue that has received much attention and interest recently is the idea of a clearinghouse of information. A central location of information would provide ready availability of the futures-related disciplinary background of individuals and firms in the futures industry. Adverse disciplinary actions taken by the futures exchanges and NFA are already public information individually, but obtaining complete background information related to the futures activities of particular individuals and firms can be very time-consuming and confusing.

NFA has taken the initiative in this area and has developed a program to provide all public information regarding disciplinary actions taken against firms and individuals by futures regulators. NFA, with the futures exchanges and the CFTC, is currently in the process of developing the mechanics of adding their disciplinary actions to the clearinghouse data base. NFA anticipates operation of its clearinghouse by the end of 1990.

NFA is developing this clearinghouse on a domestic level at present but it does have international implications as well. A clearinghouse will provide foreign regulators, firms, and individuals with ready access to complete disciplinary information on U.S. futures industry participants. The U.S. clearinghouse will provide a substantial benefit to both foreign and domestic regulators and customers because they will be able to obtain a complete picture of the disciplinary background of a firm or individual.

Once the clearinghouse has become functional and the operating procedures have been worked out, NFA would be amenable to negotiating with foreign regulators to share public disciplinary information and possibly expand the data base to include actions by foreign regulators. The possibility of an international clearinghouse of information is a long way off at this point, but the domestic clearinghouse will soon be a reality.

Industry Governance

The issue of who should serve on the governing boards and committees of futures industry self-regulatory organizations has recently received much attention. There are two aspects to this issue. The first deals with the number of directors and committee members who should come from outside of the industry as public representatives. The second problem is whether individuals who have been subject to disciplinary sanctions should be allowed to serve on governing boards, disciplinary committees, and arbitration panels.

The premise is that the greater the number of public representatives who participate in the governance of self-regulatory organizations, the greater the perception that self-regulation is objective and accountable to the public as a whole. NFA already has three seats on its Board of Directors filled by public directors and five additional seats filled by individuals representing commercial firms and banks that NFA does not regulate. NFA, then, already meets the level proposed in pending Congressional legislation for the reauthorization of the CFTC that 20 percent of the seats on the governing boards of NFA and the exchanges be held by directors without direct ties to those organizations.

The CFTC recently answered the second question by adopting Regulation 1.63, which generally bars individuals from serving on governing boards, disciplinary committees, or arbitration panels if they have been sanctioned by the CFTC, NFA, or an exchange within the preceding three years or if a sanction is still in effect. A limited number of violations, such as minor violations of record-keeping requirements, are excluded if they do not result in serious sanctions.

Conclusion

The six topics discussed are only a sampling of the current issues that must continue to be addressed as we face an increasingly international market.

The globalization of the financial markets, and the futures markets in particular, has brought many countries closer together. This greater economic proximity, however, brings challenges and obstacles to overcome. The old ways of conducting business will have to be modified and improved through greater communication and cooperation among countries. No longer is each country an independent entity with its own concerns; now each "domestic" issue has international implications and ramifications that must be considered.

V INTERNATIONAL CLEARANCE, SETTLEMENT, AND PAYMENT PROCEDURES: THE ROLE OF REGULATION

14 AUTOMATION OF THE FINANCIAL MARKETS: IMPLICATIONS FOR CLEARANCE, SETTLEMENT, AND PAYMENT PROCEDURES

Wendy L. Gramm

These are exciting times. Rapidly changing economic conditions and technological innovation have revolutionized the financial markets. In the past decade the stock market has more than tripled in value, real estate has gone through boom and bust cycles, and commodity prices are adjusting rapidly to changing fundamentals. We have also seen new markets emerge worldwide for all kinds of financial investments. Capital has become more mobile; and new products and instruments have opened new vistas for money managers, providing them with more choices and greater flexibility than ever before.

For all the changes that are occurring, two trends are dominant: internationalization and automation. These developments have been occurring for some time in the futures markets, but more recent examples include automated trading systems such as GLOBEX at the Chicago Mercantile Exchange (CME), Aurora at the Chicago Board of Trade (CBT), and ELOS at the Amex Commodities Corporation. U.S. equity markets are also developing automated trading capabilities in addition to those now in place for small orders; the government securities market in this country is considering automated trading; and automated order routing and hand-held trading terminals have been developed or are being developed in both equity and derivative markets.

U.S. companies stand to benefit tremendously from these changes, particularly those conducting business in international markets. Today, U.S. companies are better able to respond to production and marketing opportunities overseas. Automated trading systems allow firms to reduce the cost of financing such opportunities and to reduce the cost of managing risk.

Automation also has tremendous potential as far as regulators are concerned. Technology can be used to monitor risk more closely, thus improving the safety and soundness of systems. But automation can also generate new risks. These risks may be exacerbated as the international financial markets become increasingly integrated. The potential for improvements due to automation is thus contingent on our ability to maintain the integrity and security of our markets. The regulatory challenge is to ensure the safety and soundness of the clearance, settlement, and payment system, without stifling innovation.

This chapter will discuss: (1) the effect of technology on clearance and settlement; (2) the benefits and new issues that regulators must address in our review of systems; (3) the implications of automation in an international setting; and (4) the role of a regulator in the light of automation. The focus will be on the major regulatory themes that underlie these very broad issues.

Risks in the Trading Process

In order to understand the costs and benefits of automation to clearance and settlement, it is helpful to look at each step in the clearance process separately. Each step—trade entry, matching, clearing, settlement, and payment—has different risk attributes. That is, the risks to various parties shift as each step in the process is completed. Therefore, with respect to clearing and settlement risk, each party is motivated to complete its step in the process in a timely fashion and shift the risk to the next party in the chain.

The initial stage of the process—entry of the trade information into the clearing and settlement system—is crucial for those executing trades on the floor and for clearing members. Floor traders face the risk that the opposite party to the trade may submit data that do not match, leaving the trader exposed. Clearing members are at risk because they guarantee floor traders.

Without an efficient trade-data entry process, the entire clearing and settlement process is delayed and system integrity is threatened. Efficient trade-data entry is particularly important in volatile markets, when intraday financial risk assessment may be crucial. The ongoing movement toward continuous trade-data entry is a response to those regulatory concerns and to the interests of floor traders and clearing members in the efficiency of the next step in the process, trade matching.

The trade matching step of the clearance process provides for confirmation and correction of trades. Generally the trend in the futures markets is to confirm and correct trades throughout the day to minimize losses due to errors. This also is particularly important when markets are volatile; traders and clearing members may depend on the matching information to plan further trading. It also is of concern to clearinghouses, some of which effectively assume counterparty risk for trades when they are matched. Clearinghouses also want the ability to monitor trade positions throughout the day to enable them to make margin calls and assess the financial risks being assumed by individual customers and clearing members.

A trade is cleared when the counterparty risk is transferred and accepted by the clearinghouse as the "counterparty to every trade." At this point the traders no longer bear risk relative to each other; each trader depends on the financial integrity of the clearinghouse.

With the settlement of trades, the risk is transferred from the clearinghouse to the settlement banks, at which point the irrevocable commitment to make payment is made. Payment is the disbursement of funds for the agreed transfer. Generally, clearinghouses require that clearing banks obligate themselves to pay in the morning before the markets and bank payment systems open, thus transferring the risk to the bank until payment is received. Credit and settlement banks rely on the Fed-wire for the actual transfer of funds.

The clearing and settlement process can be summarized as one in which each step transfers risk from one party to the next: from the trader, to the clearing member, to the clearinghouse, and finally, when payment is made to the clearing member's account, the clearing and settlement risk to the clearinghouse is eliminated. The strength of the futures market clearing system is the predictability of the risk transfer and the fact that parties are only exposed for a short time—no more than one day, as opposed to securities markets, where settlement and payment may not occur until five or more days after the trade is executed. The widely recognized risks associated with clearance and settlement in the securities area resulted in the Group of 30 recommendations.

The Effect of Automation on Process Risks

Automation will affect each of the clearing and settlement steps. The process will be more efficient and, as a consequence, risk can be reduced. However, automated trading may also introduce new risks.

Automated trading will promote increased speed and precision of data entry, thereby reducing the risks for all traders, but particularly for floor traders and clearing members. Because automated trading systems such as GLOBEX will combine the trade execution and trade matching functions, the risks of out-trades and their associated costs will be considerably reduced or eliminated. This should reduce the costs of using futures markets to hedge investment risk in other markets. The increased automation of data entry, which will accompany automated trading, will reduce the costs of the clearing and settlement process by rendering current post-trade-data entry operations obsolete.

Automated trading offers the opportunity to shift counterparty risk from the opposite trader to clearing member to the clearinghouse more quickly. The clearinghouse is more likely to be capable of bearing the risk of counterparty default than an individual clearing firm. Although this may leave the clearinghouse exposed for a longer period of time, it provides real-time data on customer and clearing-member market positions. This improved information may permit more tailored approaches to the control of customer and clearing member exposure to the clearinghouse. As intraday margin calls become more prevalent, the clearinghouse also has the opportunity to shift risk from itself more quickly.

One of the primary new risks that automated trading imposes on clearing and settlement systems is associated with the increased potential for extended hours trading. This risk generally will be borne by the clearinghouse, which will not be able to complete the settlement and payment process when local payment systems are not operating. In its approval of the GLOBEX application, the Commodity Futures Trading Commission (CFTC) recognized that there are a number of ways to deal with this risk, ranging from obtaining binding bank obligations to pay when the payment system is not operating—which occurs now—to having money deposited in clearinghouse bank accounts overseas where payment systems are open. In addition, banking authorities in this country are currently examining ways of extending the operating hours of bank payment systems. The Commission had experience in dealing with the risk associated with extended trading hours with its oversight of the CBT's night trading session. We have been able to draw on this experience during our review of automated systems that extend the trading day.

The effect of automated trading on clearing and settlement is to compress the amount of time traders and clearing members are exposed to counterparty risk. The clearinghouse assumes this risk for a longer period of time unless steps such as intraday, or intranight, margining are implemented.

The Security and Integrity of Automation Systems

Automation can introduce new security risks to the financial markets. These risks can arise from system failure, from an unauthorized person gaining access to the system, or from the manipulation of trade information or even of the trade algorithm. Automated systems also become dependent, for better or worse, on the systems with which they are linked. We recently witnessed such a dependence with the failure of the linkage between the telephone and trading systems in New York. Trading was halted at the New York futures exchanges for most of a trading day because quotes could not be disseminated to the public over telephone lines.

Market incentives encourage proper management of these risks within the existing legal framework. Potential users have a strong incentive to demand an appropriate mix of security, service, quality, and price from the exchanges. Similarly, the exchange, as the marketer of the service, has an incentive to minimize system flaws or failures. And, the greater the competition in these markets, the more likely it is that exchanges will take action to ensure system integrity.

A good example of such action is AT&T's quick response to the software failure in its long-distance telephone operations. The competition in this market together with user unrest provided a healthy environment for speedy recovery.

Unfortunately, users may have a difficult time assessing the security and integrity of a system, *a priori*. While the user could demand certain assurances regarding performance and security, it may be difficult to determine whether the system design and protection measures are accurately portrayed. That is, does the black box do what its promoters say it does? Disclosure of security arrangements by the exchange would be self-defeating, and disclosure of other system attributes may be limited by the proprietary nature of the system design. This suggests a role for regulation.

International Influences on Settlement

The international integration of financial markets adds another dimension to these security and integrity concerns. Global trading through systems like GLOBEX requires installation of terminals in other countries. This increases the access to these systems, which may also increase the risk of a failure or security breach that may affect trading in a number of countries and financial markets.

Another concern raised by the extension of trading hours across countries is the limited ability to settle and transfer funds when the banks are closed—so-called "out of hours" transactions. The issue is made more complex since the trading individual or firm may borrow from a number of banks in various countries. Thus, the exposure of the individual or trading firm may be difficult to discern.

Furthermore, the clearing and settlement, and particularly the payment processes, differ across countries. This makes the problem of confirmed payment more troublesome than would be the case if the trading hours were simply extended within one country. As a consequence the successful implementation of 24-hour trading may require upgrading the payment and transfer systems in the banking sectors.

The Role of the Regulator

So how does a regulator meet the challenge? As mentioned earlier, the regulator's role is to ensure that the benefits of technology and innovation can be captured without damaging the security and integrity of systems. First, we must recognize potential problem areas. We can start by using a taxonomy based on past CFTC experience, including the questions and concerns we raised during our analysis of GLOBEX and our discussion with other regulators. We have already covered much of the ground in this area and can effectively build on that experience.

Second, any regulatory action in this area must be designed carefully to dovetail with existing market incentives that promote quality service at a reasonable cost. Too often, policy makers ignore market incentives and rely solely on heavy-handed regulation to ensure security and integrity. To be most effective, the policy response of the regulator must be targeted to those issues that cannot be otherwise resolved by existing market and institutional actions.

Third, a regulatory response must be crafted so that we do not inadvertently create new risks or damage the existing market and legal incentives to reduce risks, that is, create a moral hazard problem.

And fourth, we must use our resources wisely and recognize the opportunity costs of our actions. For example, we should focus on upgrading security in areas where the likelihood of damage is high and controls are likely to be most effective, rather than pursue an error-free system at the cost of other equally important regulatory goals.

CFTC Activities

The CFTC will continue to evaluate the regulatory implications of each of these issues to determine where its resources can best be applied.

In recent years, the CFTC has accumulated a great deal of experience in dealing with innovations. In fact, in our experience, one innovation often leads to another. For example, the CFTC addressed concerns attendant to extended hours trading, similar to those raised by GLOBEX, when it approved the CBT's evening trading session. In addition, the Commission considered issues related to internationally linked markets, including issues related to settlement and payment, in its approval of the CME–SIMEX link and the COMEX–Sydney link. The implementation of an inter-market information-sharing system, in which the futures and options exchanges share certain financial data regarding their common members, also provides a model for dealing with automated markets that are linked internationally.

Based upon its ongoing evaluation of GLOBEX, the Commission will take further actions to improve our oversight of automated systems and to clarify further the obligations of the self-regulatory organizations (SROs) and other market participants with regard to the creation, maintenance, operation, and supervision of systems. How can we be sure that all of the possible breaches of system are considered? We can't. Solutions to these problems will evolve along with the skills of those who would violate the security and integrity of these systems.

To aid in its evaluation of issues related to automated systems, the Commission has formed a Task Force to provide it with advice regarding the integrity and security of automated trade and support systems. The Task Force is comprised of experts in a number of other federal agencies, such as the National Institute of Standards and Technology, which has statutory responsibility for security issues in the civilian agencies, and the Information and Technology Office of the Office of Management and Budget. The Task Force will assist the CFTC in offering the latest knowledge as to potential threats to such systems and on the state-of-the-art surveillance and monitoring systems that are available.

On the international front, innovation is again built on past experience. Over the past few years, the CFTC has implemented several arrangements with its foreign counterparts to facilitate cross-border transactions while maintaining our standards of integrity and customer protection. For example, on May 15, 1989, the Commission granted the United Kingdom an exemption under its Part 30 rules, which permit a waiver of CFTC regulations otherwise applicable to firms doing business with U.S. customers under circumstances where compliance with comparable foreign regulators would be sufficient and regulation would be duplication. In this example, the U.K. Securities and Investments Board (SIB) and the relevant U.K. SROs have agreed to provide the Commission with any information that materially and adversely affects the financial or operational viability of any exempted firm domiciled in the United Kingdom and doing business in the United States as well as other information relevant to the exempted firm to conduct a financial services business and the level of compliance in the U.K.

We have also signed a Memorandum of Understanding with the U.K. Department of Trade and Industry and the SIB on exchange of information to assist in enforcing regulations on both sides of the Atlantic and made similar arrangements with the French and Brazilian regulatory authorities. Information can be obtained by either party as necessary to permit the enforcement of rules or requirements, including conducting any investigations and prosecutions of civil, administrative, or criminal proceedings.

The CFTC has several other discussions under way that will further improve our ability to monitor cross-border activities. We will continue to push to eliminate any impediments to effective and efficient regulatory oversight and through these activities promote, wherever possible, competition and innovation in these markets. And most importantly, we will continue to support enhancements to the ability of firms to undertake transactions around the world.

Conclusion

The innovation in the instruments and services in the financial industry has both caused and been affected by the increase in global market transactions. The opportunities and risks presented by international markets have promoted greater coordination and the development of more tailored and efficient risk management and regulatory tools. The futures industry and the CFTC have played premiere roles in these efforts.

Innovation in the futures markets through automation and other process changes and through product development has been impressive over the last five years. The benefits in terms of the efficiencies provided by these innovations and their enhanced surveillance and risk management capabilities will be equally impressive.

All indicators suggest continued growth in the number and variety of products, the number and variety of participants and transactions, and the competitive pressures that all firms in this industry will face. The growth of these markets, however, is sensitive to cost disadvantages and other impediments in product development. Furthermore, with product and process innovation, new issues and potential risks may arise. Therefore, regulatory agencies must be ever more attentive to meeting the challenge of promoting the safety and soundness of our systems without unduly stifling innovation and change. This approach will produce significant benefits for all.

15 TWENTY-FOUR HOUR TRADING, CLEARANCE, AND SETTLEMENT: THE ROLE OF BANKS

Dennis M. Earle and Jane F. Fried

The world's capital markets are entering a very exciting era. Equity and derivative exchanges are extending their trading hours either by keeping their floors open longer and/or by developing electronic trading systems that support trading 24 hours a day. Exchanges are also offering products traded and settled in currencies other than that of their home country. All of these developments are considered to be good news for the trader, who may eventually be able to pass his position book with the sun and trade whatever, whenever, and wherever he wants to. However, demand must be balanced by supply: exchanges will only offer these new products if they have both market depth and a set of back-room processes and procedures that ensure that all buyers and sellers fulfill their obligations. These procedures allow exchanges to transfer market risk to the clearinghouses, which in turn transmit that risk to the banking system, clearing members, and their clearing members' customers (see Figure 15–1).[1]

It is not at all clear how this "system" will deal with the pressures of

The opinions expressed in this chapter are strictly those of the authors and do not necessarily reflect those of Bankers Trust Company, its subsidiaries, or affiliates.

Figure 15–1.   Transferring risk from markets to customers in futures markets.

24-hour clearing and settlement. Central to this discussion are issues of how long a trade remains unsettled; the tolerance of clearinghouses, banks, clearing members, and counterparties to credit exposure; and the degree of multicurrency payments services provided by the banks. These issues may be relatively more or less important depending upon the home country of the market, the home country of the trader, and the type of instrument traded. This chapter will focus on the issues that 24-hour trading brings to the clearinghouses and the banks supporting the derivative markets, since this is where most of the movement toward 24-hour trading has occurred. Of course, many of the concepts are also applicable to extended-hour trading in the cash markets.

The Nature of Clearinghouse Risk

The first step in laying off market risk is the process of matching buyers and sellers and ensuring that both counterparties agree with the terms of the contract. Clearinghouses usually perform this function, and commonly provide trade guarantees for matched trades which reduce overall systemic risk. In a trade guarantee, the clearinghouse interposes itself between the buyer and seller, ensuring each side that the obligations of trade settlement will be met. In this way, traders are only concerned with the profitability of the deal, and not the credit quality of the counterparties. This allows for larger and deeper markets.

Clearinghouses in many countries, but not all, provide trade guarantees. Our survey[2] of 38 clearing entities around the world found that trade guarantees predominate in North America, Europe, and Northeast Asia/ Australia. (In total, of the 38 respondents, 20 offer trade guarantees.)

Once the clearinghouse makes its trade guarantee, it becomes the counterparty to the trade, and must ensure that its members fulfill their obligations. Clearinghouses have several mechanisms for doing this. The first method is a process known as margining. In the futures markets, clearinghouses require their members to pay initial and variation ("settle-

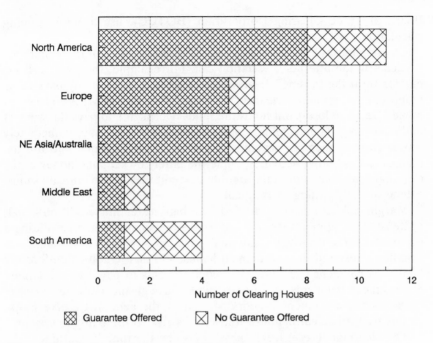

Figure 15–2. Clearinghouses providing trade guarantees.

ment") margin. These are considered, respectively, to be a "good faith deposit" and a mark-to-the-market payment reflecting the change in value of the futures contract over time. In the United States, the initial margin calls are made and satisfied in the early morning on the day after the trade (T + 1), usually by 8a.m. Eastern Standard Time. A variation margin call is also made at this time, and at many U.S. exchanges is made at least once during the trading day, usually in the afternoon, starting on T + 1. (In the options markets, a different, but analogous procedure is used.)

Variation margin may be calculated either on a net or a gross basis. A gross margining system requires a clearing member to pay a certain percentage of the price movement of all contracts on which the price has moved against the member or his customers. A net margining system calculates the margin requirement on the "net," or the addition of the value lost on the contracts against which the price has moved and the value gained on those contracts which have gained value. There is no evidence that either system of margining is safer, from a risk management perspective, during regular trading hours. In the United States, the Chicago Mercantile Exchange (CME) and the New York Mercantile Exchange (NYMEX) use gross margining methods, whereas the rest, including the

Board of Trade Clearing Corporation (BOTCC), use a net margining calculation.

Clearinghouses also differ with regard to the payment of these margins, particularly the afternoon variation call. For example, the CME collects monies from the "losing" clearing members and immediately pays those monies to the "winning" clearing members, while the NYMEX collects the money from the losers but holds the funds overnight and pays the winners in the morning. The two philosophies differ in that the former immediately settles clearing member accounts, allowing clearing members to use the monies to fund other activities, while the latter, by keeping money at the clearinghouse, may reduce the amount of credit that settlement banks must extend at the morning margin call.

Margin calls are usually satisfied by a bank extending credit on behalf of those clearing members that are its customers and then transmitting a payment instruction over a national payment system. These banks are commonly referred to as settlement banks, and their credit extensions are known as payment guarantees or "commitments to pay." In the United States, these payments are usually made through the Fedwire, an electronic money movement system operated by the Federal Reserve Bank. In this way, the clearinghouse transfers its risk to the banking system.

The clearinghouse aggregates risk between the time it guarantees the trade and the time the settlement bank guarantees the payment. Some clearinghouses do this on a real-time basis, which amounts to a guarantee made immediately following trade execution. Others may run periodic batch cycles during the day or a batch cycle following the close of trading. In any case, the time interval between the trade match and the settlement bank commitment varies by clearinghouse, but it can be as long as 20 hours. Throughout this period, the clearinghouse is guaranteeing payment will be made without a settlement bank commitment. When the settlement banks commit to pay the morning margin call, calculated from the prior day's trades, all risk associated with that guarantee is theoretically removed from the clearinghouse. The risk which the clearinghouse incurs by providing the trade guarantee is shown in Figure 15–3.

Once trading begins on day T, the clearinghouse begins to guarantee trades, increasing its risk until the afternoon variation margin call. This risk is the sum of the initial margin due on new contracts opened that day [IM(New)], the variation margin on contracts opened that day [VM(New)], and those opened on days prior [VM(Old)]. At the afternoon margin call, all outstanding contracts issued on days prior to this day are marked to the market, a margin call is made, and the settlement banks make their guarantees. At this point, the clearinghouse has eliminated all

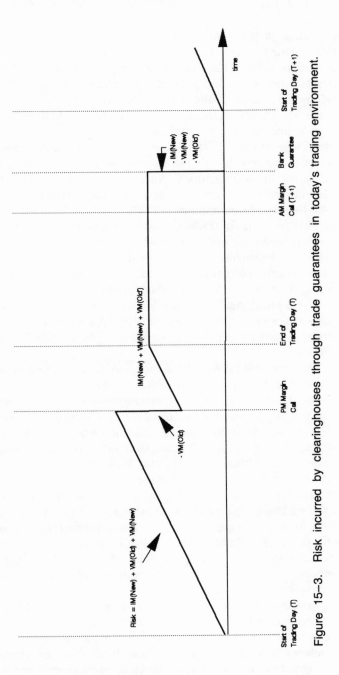

Figure 15–3. Risk incurred by clearinghouses through trade guarantees in today's trading environment.

risk associated with the "old" contracts, but this risk begins to accrue immediately again through the end of the trading day [VM(Old')]. The afternoon margin call does not eliminate the clearinghouse's risk on any new contracts established during this day's trading; this risk [IM(New) + VM(New)] is held through the end of the day. The clearing industry estimates that the afternoon margin call covers 60 percent to 80 percent of the daily price fluctuation of outstanding contracts.

After the close of trading, the dollar value of the clearinghouse's risk remains constant. Even though the clearinghouse has not been paid, it knows the extent of its obligations. And, as noted earlier, the clearinghouse holds this risk until early the next morning when the settlement banks make their credit guarantees.

In extended or 24-hour trading, traders trade, clearinghouses make guarantees, but banks are not open. With no banking system available to transmit risk to, clearinghouses that provide trade guarantees overnight may be aggregating risk because they are not only holding the initial margin risk on new contracts from today's trading [IM(New)], as well as variation margin on all new and old contracts [VM(Old') + VM(New)]; they are also incurring risk by guaranteeing initial and variation margin on new contracts issued during the evening trading hours [IM(Evening) + VM(Evening)].

The extent of this additional risk factor may be a function of how the clearinghouse calculates its margin calls, whether or not the afternoon variation margin call is paid out to the clearinghouse's "winners," and what the margin procedures established for overnight trading are. If "intranight" margin calls to help manage and mitigate risk resulting from overnight price changes are not planned, large intraday credit extensions in the morning by the settlement banks may be a result.

If a U.S. clearinghouse wanted to make intranight margin calls in U.S. dollars, it would need to have its U.S. banks agree to stay open to extend credit in the middle of the night, or enlist foreign banks to extend U.S. dollar credit to its clearing members and their customers. Both solutions increase the costs and risks of settlement for the market and its players, as we will discuss shortly. Of course, the clearinghouse could choose to rely on the other methods it currently uses during the day to ensure the financial integrity of the market.

Most clearinghouses have a multistage contingency plan for the possibility that a clearing member will not meet a margin call. The clearinghouse's recourse can encompass one or all of the following measures: allowing the clearing member to find another settlement bank if its settlement bank refuses to extend credit; liquidating the clearing member's position and

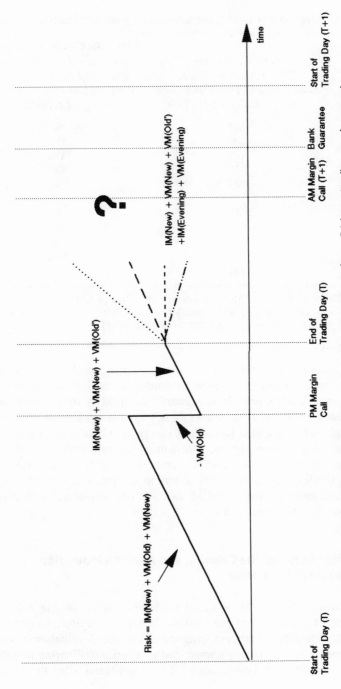

Figure 15–4. Risk incurred by clearinghouses through trade guarantees in a 24-hour trading environment.

Table 15–1.   Overview of U.S. Clearinghouses' Protection Against Default.[3]

	Total Value of the Clearinghouse's Capital, Guarantee and Trust Funds, and Lines of Credit (in $ Millions)	Does the Clearinghouse Have Assessment Powers? (i.e., can they require their clearing members to put up more money after a default?)
BOTCC	184	No
CME	200	Yes
CCA	75	Yes
CCC	25	Yes
CSCCC	25	Yes
ICC	8	Yes
KCBOTCC	11	No
MCC	11	Yes
NSCC	370	Yes
NYMEX	98	Yes
OCC	194	Yes

Source: Extracted from the "Study of International Clearing and Settlement" administered by Bankers Trust Company under contract to the Office of Technology Assessment (OTA), U.S. Congress. Table reprinted with permission of OTA.

collateral already on deposit at the clearinghouse; and dipping into its guarantee fund, comprised of member contributions held in the event of a clearing member failure. If the guarantee fund is insufficient, some clearinghouses may assess their members to make up the difference.

Clearinghouses may also have lines of credit. Of course, it is unclear what influence guarantee funds, assessment powers, and lines of credit have on system stability in a 24-hour market when the banks and custodians safeguarding and moving the assets in the guarantee funds are not open. Clearinghouses may need to extend their credit relationships to ensure coverage 24 hours a day.

The Interface Between the Clearing and Banking Industries and the Nature of Bank Risk

Clearinghouses rely on a network of settlement banks to guarantee and effect payments. The role of the settlement bank is twofold: to guarantee payments for clearing members owing monies to the clearinghouse, and to make payments for the clearinghouse owing monies to clearing members. The latter function is relatively new; it was instituted after the October

1987 market break. The settlement bank must satisfy itself with regard to its credit exposure in two directions: on its payments to the clearinghouse and payments to the clearing member.

Of course, a settlement bank does not have to guarantee a clearing member's payment if it is uncomfortable with extending credit to that member. If it is particularly uncomfortable but still wants to retain the clearing member as a customer, the settlement bank may require that the clearing member provide additional collateral.

Often, the settlement banks extend intraday credit because they are confident that the clearing member has sufficient assets to cover the margin call on deposit with another bank. Or, the settlement bank is confident that if the member does not have the assets on deposit at another bank, the clearing member's credit bank will lend cash, treasuries, or a letter of credit to the clearing member to cover its obligations. It is not uncommon for clearing members of Chicago futures exchanges who are located outside Chicago to use a Chicago bank to settle market calls, but to maintain their main credit and operating relationships with local (i.e., a New York or West Coast) banks. Of course, the customers of the clearing members also have their own credit and banking relationships, and often also require credit to pay the clearing member on time.

The process of converting clearinghouse risk to bank risk, therefore, is only as safe as the banks and the banking system. It is not clear what a payment guarantee means if the settlement bank fails (e.g., the Continental Illinois failure in 1984). The clearinghouse must balance the advantages of diversifying its risk over many institutions, with the operation complexity of managing each of these relationships. Some clearinghouses choose to use as few as six settlement banks, while others use more than 20. Even though all relationships are contractually based, if a settlement bank reneges on a commitment to a clearinghouse, the payment (which is required immediately) may be delayed months or years if a lawsuit is brought. The clearinghouse must therefore be satisfied that each of its settlement banks is financially stable, large enough to incur potentially huge payment guarantees on a daily basis, and willing to honor its commitments.

However, since the credit relationships supporting the payment of the margin call ripple through the banking system, a failure of a nonsettlement bank can affect the integrity of the clearing and settlement process. Therefore, the clearing industry and the banking industry are concerned with the same types of issues in supporting trading activities. Both extend credit and make guarantees, and both work to ensure that payments are made on time. Therefore, their financial integrity is essential for clearing and settlement to be performed safely and efficiently.

Figure 15–5.   The interdependence of clearing and settlement and banking.

The Global Payments Environment and 24-Hour Clearing and Settlement

How will clearinghouses settle margin calls when the banking system and central banks supporting this currency are not open?

If the clearinghouse chooses to require its U.S. settlement banks to provide payment guarantees in the middle of the U.S. night, this impacts not only these bank's operating hours but their risk profiles and tolerances as well. Even if they are open, the other credit banks and the wire system used to make payments between the banks are closed. Settlement banks would essentially be making credit decisions in a vacuum. Conversely, if the clearinghouse invokes new dollar settlement banking relationships with overseas banks operating during U.S. evening hours, its clearing members must maintain relationships with these overseas banks, probably requiring them to keep excess collateral on deposit. Clearing members have enough trouble moving money around the world to get it where they need it to be today. This solution would impose an added layer of complexity to their already difficult collateral management task.

Consider the clearing and settlement ramifications of trading yen-denominated contracts during U.S. business hours and you've turned the problem on its head. Although the U.S. settlement banks can hold yen, there is not wire system available to make yen payments during the U.S. business day. Conversely, if Japanese banks are used during Tokyo business hours, risk is retained for a longer period of time. This is because the clearing member trades on T, but has not necessarily funded his account by the time Tokyo opens just a few hours after the close of the U.S. trading day. To fund his account adequately, the clearing member would need to estimate his trading activity fully the day *before* he traded, or else require very flexible credit terms with his Japanese banks. However, even if the banks provide this credit, risk is only removed from the system once the clearing member actually pays for his trades.

The crux of the problem is that there is no way to make payments in a currency when that country's central bank does not issue that currency. Promises to pay are not as good as an actual payment. For example, in settling a yen variation margin call in the United States during U.S. business hours, one settlement bank invariably would owe another settlement bank some yen. In addition, both banks owe their winning clearing members yen. The best the settlement banks can do is promise each other and their customers that the yen payments will be made in Tokyo during Tokyo business hours. These guarantees are neither final nor irrevocable until the Bank of Japan guarantees them as final and irrevocable.

The time at which a payment becomes final depends on the country and the wire system being used in that country (see Table 15–2 for a comparison of wire systems operating in major developed countries).

This issue of payment finality actually has implications for the length of time during which risk remains in the market. Risk is completely removed from the system only when the payments cannot be reversed. If a bank or other institution fails before that, problems may arise as to whether the payments must be reversed. Therefore, even if clearinghouses employ identical risk management mechanisms themselves, their risk profile will vary if their payments are transmitted via wire systems with different terms of payment finality.

Payment systems with immediate finality are not available around the clock. This is evident if the operating hours of the main wire systems in the United States, United Kingdom, and Japan are transposed (see Figure 15–6).

Table 15–2.   Finality of Settlement of Selected Electronic Payment Systems of Various Countries.

Country	Payment System (and operator or owner)	Finality of Payment or Settlement	Time Before Settlement When a Payment Is Considered Irrevocable
Belgium	Clearing Center for the Belgium Financial System (CEC, owned by the banking institutions)	By close of business on payment date	Not applicable
Canada	Automated Clearing Settlement System (ACSS, owned by the Canadian payments association)	Chronologically by close of business of payment date plus 1. However, the payment system retroactively books settlement on payment date	Not applicable
France	SAGITTAIRE (managed by the Bank of France)	By close of business on payment date	Irrevocable at settlement
Italy	Interbank Electronic Funds Transfer service (SETIF, managed by the Interbank Society for Automation)	By close of business on payment date	Not applicable
Japan	Gaitame-yen (operated by the Bank of Japan)	By close of business on payment date	Immediate
	Zengin system (operated by the Tokyo Bankers Association)	Next day	Immediate
Netherlands	Nederlandsche Bank circuit (managed by the Nederlandsche Bank)	By close of business on payment date	Not applicable
	Bank Giro Center circuit (owned by the banks)	By close of business on payment date	Not applicable
Sweden	Bank Giro (owned by banks)	By close of business on payment date	Not applicable
Switzerland	Swiss Interbank Clearing System (SIC, managed by Telekurs, AG, on behalf of the Swiss National Bank)	Same day or sometime on following 10 (ten) business days	Immediate
United States	Clearing House Interbank Payments System (CHIPS, managed by the New York Clearing House)	By close of business on payment date	Irrevocable at settlement
West Germany	Bundesbank (manager of payment system— currently still paper-based. Electronic pilot expected Fall 1989)	By close of business on payment date	Irrevocable at settlement

Source: Extracted from the "Study of International Clearing and Settlement" administered by Bankers Trust Company under contract to the Officer of Technology Assessment (OTA), U.S. Congress. Table induced with permission of OTA.

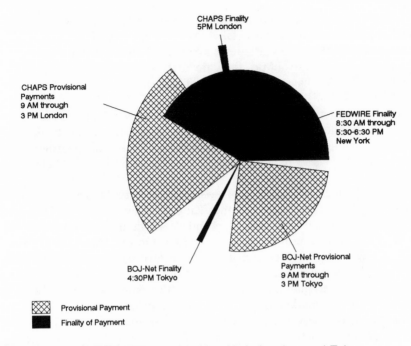

Figure 15–6. Finality of payment in New York, London, and Tokyo.

In the United States, the Federal Reserve's Fedwire system offers immediate finality of payment during its hours of operation. In Japan and the United Kingdom, payments made during normal hours are provisional until cleared by the central bank later in the business day.

Mechanisms for Reducing Risk

The risk profile of a clearinghouse is important to whether a firm decides to trade in a market. If the clearinghouse is sound, the market player will be confident that he will always be paid. Clearinghouse risk profiles may vary according to the level of margin they require, the way that margin is calculated and paid, the size of the guarantee fund in relation to market characteristics, whether the clearinghouse has rights of assessment, the integrity of the settlement banks, and the operating characteristics of the payment wire systems. In addition, regulatory and legislative rules also influence safety and soundness.

Unfortunately, many market players assume that all clearinghouses function identically in all markets. However, even though the differences among the clearing and settlement systems in different markets and in different countries are subtle, they are real.

Clearinghouses have not yet determined the least risky method to handle margin calls resulting from 24-hour trading or from clearing and settling a contract in a nonindigenous currency. However, since the risk to which clearinghouses are exposed includes components from regular and extended trading, it is important to minimize all risks that clearinghouses face. Several ways to reduce clearinghouse risk are discussed below.

1. *Synchronize the holidays of exchanges, clearinghouses, and banks.* There are three days (Martin Luther King, Jr. Day, Columbus Day, and Veterans Day) when U.S. exchanges and clearinghouses are open, but the banking systems supporting them are closed. On these days, banks typically extend credit, but cannot make or receive payments because they (and the wire systems) are closed. Would the settlement banks have been willing, or able, to guarantee the size of settlements that occurred during the October '87 market break if it had occurred one week later, on Columbus Day, when the payment system was not available? To extend this conjecture further, what if margin calls were outstanding from evening trading hours the day prior to the holiday? Perhaps a more basic question is: How dependent are the world's clearing and settlement system on credit, and could the markets have operated if credit was, in general, restricted?

2. *Develop facilities for multicurrency settlement.* Today the United States is behind the world in thinking about the relationship of its currency to the markets. While other countries trade instruments denominated in more than one currency, the United States does not.[4] Although some clearinghouses (such as MATIF in France) will settle margin calls in a currency other than the underlying currency of the contract, they either must accept currency risk or require their members to put up extra collateral to cover this risk. There is no facility to move other currencies with finality when its central bank is closed. This results in more risk and/or more collateral tied up in the system that could instead be used for other purposes.

3. *Allow clearinghouses direct access to payment systems.* In the United States, clearinghouses are not members of the Fedwire system (although some depositories are). The presence of banks as intermediaries introduces another potential point of error in the settlement process, and can only

slow the arrival of critical payment information to the clearinghouse. Some clearing entities have begun to acquire limited purpose trust bank charters in order to become members of the payment system. Some clearinghouses overseas already have access to their country's national payment systems.

4. *Develop a standard for quantifying clearinghouse risk.* As more investors move beyond their traditional markets in search of maximized return consistent with risk, it becomes even more critical that we develop a standard for evaluating clearinghouse risk. At one level most derivative clearing entities are already standardized in terms of process: use of margins, concept of mark to market, and so on. But at the more fundamental level of infrastructure, significant differences remain. How these structural differences (in method of computing margin, payout of variation margin, types of collateral allowed, method of regulation, and so on) impact the risk/return analysis is currently left to the clearing and settlement expertise of the individual firm. There is no industry or regulatory consensus on which differences actually contribute to risk.

Conclusion

Twenty-four-hour trading is coming. In tomorrow's continuous markets, the nature of risk will change. No longer will the natural "circuit breaker" of nightfall allow us time to regroup for the next trading day. Problems will have to be met and dealt with whenever and wherever they occur. The impact of extended-hours trading on clearing and settlement mechanisms must be fully thought out so that appropriate systemic safeguards can be implemented. And the point of much concentration must be the boundary between banking and clearing and settlement. We must ensure that the banking system can handle the clearinghouse requirements so that the markets do not incur additional risk.

The markets are very different now than they once were. Not only are they global but trading strategies have moved from long-term (low turnover; buy and hold) to short-term (high turnover; buy/sell, buy/sell). Money in the financial markets may change instruments, expiration dates, issues, markets, and countries, but, even in times of market volatility, remain committed to the markets. While we may readily accept the fact that the markets are constantly evolving, we also readily accept that the national banking system cannot change at all. It seems clear that the markets will require facilities to settle contracts in different currencies and at different hours than the banking system currently supports.

What is also clear is that even before this "globalization" happens, there is still work to be done at the boundary of clearing and settlement and banking to minimize risk in the world's capital and derivative markets.

Notes

1. Not all exchange members are clearing members. The latter are members of a clearing-house who are certified to clear and settle trades for their own account, for exchange members who are not clearing members, and for customers who are not exchange members.

2. These data were extracted from the "Study of International Clearing and Settlement" administered by Bankers Trust Company under contract to the Office of Technology Assessment (OTA), U.S. Congress. It is published with the permission of OTA. As part of that study Bankers Trust surveyed 38 clearing entities around the world on questions of clearing and settlement in a national and international context.

3. These statistics are for February 1989. The BOTCC, however, notes that its total has significantly increased since then. As of October 1989, $325 million is the correct figure for the BOTCC. The CME and OCC also provide an updated figure: $376 million and $300 million, respectively.

4. Both the Chicago Board of Trade and the Chicago Mercantile Exchange have yen products planned for implementation in the near future.

16 SCREEN-BASED TRADING IN JAPANESE FINANCIAL MARKETS

Iwao Kuroda

Financial trades have several stages. I will classify them into the following three: (1) monitoring and exchanging market information; (2) order matching and contract agreement between counterparties, which may include confirmation of trades; and (3) clearing and settlement. It is important to consider all three stages when discussing any screen-based markets. Advances in computer and communications network technology have changed the ways and means of all these stages from manual or telephone-based to computer-based network processing.

Let us look at screen-based systems in Japan in terms of the three stages. Their features can be summarized as follows; details are shown in Tables 16–1, 16–2, and 16–3:

1. *Monitoring and exchanging market information.* Market information networks have been introduced for foreign exchange, Japanese government bonds, stocks, money market instruments, and the futures derived from them.

2. *Order matching and contract agreement between counterparties (which may include confirmation of trades).* A screen-based trading network on a bilateral basis already exists in the foreign exchange market. In addition, introduction of automatic matching systems is now being discussed in the foreign exchange market by Reuters and other system providers.

Table 16–1. Trading Procedures in Japanese Financial Markets.

Market		Procedures
Foreign exchange		Through brokers: Brokers provide market information to dealers mainly by voice-box systems. Dealers place ask-bid orders with brokers using leased telephone lines and orders are matched manually.
		Direct dealing: Trades are executed bilaterally between counterparties using telephones, telexes, or proprietary terminals such as Reuters. Reuters screens offer market information and matching services to subscribers. Reuters plans to introduce a screen-based multilateral trading system.
Japanese Government Bonds (JGBs)	Spot	TSE member firms obtain market information through TSE screens. Orders are placed by telephone and manual input into the TSE inhouse system by TSE staff to be matched automatically.
		Through broker's broker (BB): BB provides information to dealers through BB terminals. Dealers place orders by telephone, and orders are matched manually.
	Futures	TSE provides member firms with trade information through TSE futures screens. Members input orders from registered terminals and orders are automatically matched within the TSE system.
Stocks	Spot	TSE member firms obtain market information through TSE screens. Members input orders from registered terminals and orders are matched automatically.
	Futures (TOPIX)	TSE provides member firms with trade information through TSE futures screens. Members input orders from registered terminals and orders are automatically matched within the TSE system.
Money market instruments	Call money, bills, CDs, and CP	Through brokers: Trade information is provided to market participants by voice-box systems or screen information systems such as those provided by Reuters and Telerate. Participants place orders by calling brokers and orders are matched manually. In the collateralized call money market, brokers can take positions and act as dealers.
		Direct Dealing: Trades are executed bilaterally between counterparties.
Financial futures		TIFFE provides members with trade information through TIFFE screens. Members place orders by telephone. Orders are manually input into the TIFFE inhouse system by TIFFE staff and are matched automatically. A new system is scheduled to be introduced in spring 1991, which will enable firms to place orders directly from registered TIFFE terminals.

TSE = Tokyo Stock Exchange.
TIFFE = Tokyo Financial Futures Exchange.

These are screen broker systems that gather information from participants and intermediate multilaterally by automated trade matching.

There are fairly large screen-based trading systems for the instruments listed on the Tokyo Stock Exchange (TSE). These include stocks (spot markets); Japanese government bond (JGB) futures; and an index future, the Tokyo Stock Exchange Stock Price Index (TOPIX).

For these transactions, member financial institutions input orders from their registered terminals, and the orders are automatically matched within the TSE system, while a semi-automated system, similar to the TIFFE system described below, exists for JGB spots on the TSE. In addition, major members have linked their own systems with customer terminals or systems. Both corporate and individual customers are provided with these services.

TIFFE (Tokyo International Financial Futures Exchange), established in 1989, has a semiautomated screen-based trading system. It works as follows: the Exchange staff take member orders by telephone, input them from keyboards, and the system automatically matches trades. By February 1991, the system was further upgraded to a fully automated screen-trading system in which members will be able to input orders into the system directly from registered terminals.

No screen-based trading systems exist at present for over-the-counter JGB spots, nor for money market instruments such as call money, bills, commercial paper (CPs), certificates of deposit (CDs), and others.

3. *Clearing and settlement.* Examples of these systems are the Bank of Japan Funds Transfer System (a major part of which is known as BOJ-NET Funds Transfer Service), *gaitame-yen* system, *zengin* system, and the check and bill clearing system.

Implemented in October 1988, the BOJ-NET Funds Transfer Service is a computerized central bank settlement system: the Japanese counterpart of Fedwire in the United States.

The *gaitame-yen* system, equivalent to CHIPS in the United States, mainly settles foreign exchange transactions. This started as a paper-based system in 1980, and shifted to the new electronic system as a part of BOJ-NET in March 1989. Payment instructions are exchanged, netted out, and then settled through BOJ-NET.

These two systems offer same-day funds settlement in which settlements are finalized through BOJ reserve accounts.

The *zengin* system and the check and bill clearing system are, on the other hand, next-day funds systems, with settlements finalized through the BOJ reserve accounts.

The *zengin* system is a private interbank funds clearing system similar to the U.S. ACH (Automated Clearing House). It started computer process-

Table 16–2. Settlements of Financial Transactions in Japan.

Market		Payment system used				Lag between trade day (T) and settlement day (T+n)
		Next-day funds		Same-day funds		
		Check and bill clearing	Zengin system	Gaitame-yen system	BOJ funds transfer	
Foreign exchange (Yen/dollar)		F		M	F	T + 2 (spot value)
Government bonds	Spot	M	F		F	T+10 maximum. Every fifth calendar day (5, 10, 15, 20, 25, and end of month)
	Futures (margin settlement)	M				T + 3
Stocks	Spot	M				T + 3
	Futures (margin settlement)	M				T + 3
Money market instruments	Call and bills				M	T
	CDs and CPs	F	F		M	mainly T or T + 1
Financial futures					M	T + 1

Note: 1. The sample is major participants (banks, securities houses, money market brokers, and others) in each financial market.
   2. M = most frequently in use; F = frequently in use; Blanks = rarely used.

Table 16–3.   Central Securities Depositories in Japan.

Japanese Government bonds (JGBs)	The Bank of Japan (BOJ) is the central depository. The system consists of registration and book-entry transfer services. BOJ has developed a computer-based transfer system for both registered and book-entry JGBs, which started in May 1990 as a part of BOJ-Net.
Stocks	The Japan Securities Clearing Corporation (JSCC, a subsidiary of the Tokyo Stock Exchange [TSE], functions as the quasi-central depository for TSE transactions. The Japan Securities Depository Center was established to upgrade and further computerize the JSCC system to offer a nationwide computer-based book-entry system for stocks. Part of the system will start operating in October 1991.
Money market instruments	None at present except for short-term JGBs. Physical delivery of paper-based bills and certificates.

ing in 1973. The check and bill clearing system is a traditional paper-based system.

How do customers make use of these systems? There seems to be no particular rule for their choice of systems, except for a few cases of established practices. These include the check and bill clearing system for market transactions and BOJ-NET for TIFFE and money market transactions.

Existing securities delivery systems in Japan are listed in Table 16–3. The BOJ is the central depository for JGBs. BOJ-NET was enlarged to add the JGB delivery system (the Securities Transfer Service) starting in May 1990 to computerize its deliveries.

As for stocks, the JSCC (Japan Securities Clearing Corporation, a subsidiary of the TSE) acts as a quasi-central depository, providing member firms with a kind of book-entry service. The system is planned to be upgraded and further computerized in the near future.

As for money market instruments, there are no central depository systems for bills, CDs, and CPs, while short-term JGBs are deposited at BOJ.

Any form of delivery-versus-payment (DVP) mechanism that systematically guarantees simultaneous settlement of both funds and securities is not yet available in Japan. However, we are aware that it is desirable that such mechanisms be implemented for all settlements of large-value transactions, as was clearly stated in the G-30 recommendations in 1989. With this in mind, we have been discussing the possibility of introducing the DVP mechanism for JGB transactions.

The time lag between contract and settlement is relatively shorter in the Japanese stock market than the international standard. However, the lag runs up to ten business days for JGB spots, which is one of the longest among major markets. Margin settlements are conducted four days after trade for TSE JGB futures and TOPIX, and next day for TIFFE.

Implications of the Development of Screen-Based Trading

Screen-based trading has progressed in the financial industry because it is an information industry, as has been proved in many markets including Japan. Accuracy, speed, and diversity of information are the keys to advancement in the financial community. It has naturally become an irreversible worldwide trend to apply fully the sophistication of computer and communication technology into financial activities. What are the implications?

I think there are two significant aspects to this question: one is more efficiency in trades, the other is the encouragement of truly global transactions. Let me elaborate on these points.

Older methods of manual or paper-based exchanges of information are replaced by screen-based systems when the same information is available with less costs in less time. Hence, the introduction of screen-based trading systems causes transaction volume to expand. We have actually experienced this, with recent growth in financial transactions far exceeding the growth of the real economy (Table 16–4). Faster and cheaper availability of information also provides incentives for financial transactions on a global basis. Market participants and instruments will then diversify.

Financial transactions have to be supported by infrastructure adequate to finalize settlements of both instruments and funds. In this regard, the rapid increase in transaction volume heavily burdens the underlying settlement systems. We can never overemphasize the importance of these systems' safety and soundness, since a failure of any participant will contagiously affect others significantly. However, we should not be overly pessimistic on this point, because the same technology that induced the expansion of trade could this time be applied to cope with the risks. The only concern left is whether we can fully identify the problems and have the strong will to overcome them.

Development of screen-based trading can diminish such restraints on

Table 16–4. Transaction Volume in Japanese and U.S. Financial Markets.

Foreign Exchange ($ billion per day)		Mar. 1986	Apr. 1989	Annual Growth Rate (%)
Japan		48.0	115.2	33.8
United States		58.5	128.9	30.1

Government Bonds		1985	1989	Annual Growth Rate (%)
Japan	Spot[1] (¥ trillion)	874.0	1,304.3	10.5
	Futures[2] (¥ trillion)	started in Oct.	1,897.1	—
United States	Spot[3] ($ trillion)	19.1	28.4	10.4
	Futures[4] (million contracts)	45.7	79.7	14.9

Stocks		1985	1989	Annual Growth Rate (%)
Japan	Spot[5] (billion shares)	118.2	218.4	16.6
	Futures[6] (thousand contracts)	—	9,170.0	—
United States	Spot[7] (billion shares)	27.5	41.7	11.0
	Futures[8] (thousand contracts)	15,056	10,560	−9.3

Interest Rate Futures	1985	1989	Annual Growth Rate (%)
Japan[9] (thousand contracts)	—	4,598	—
United States[10] (thousand contracts)	8,901	40,886	46.4

Money Market Instruments (¥ trillion per day)	Dec. 1987	Dec. 1989	Annual Growth Rate (%)
Collateralized call money	n.a.	13.1	—
Non-collateralized call money	2.2	6.5	171.9

Table 16–4. (Continued)

Commercial bills	0.3	1.5	223.6
CP	0.1	5.2	721.1
CDs	1.3	2.4	35.9
Total	3.9	28.7	—

Notes:
   1. Total traded on TSE and OTC market (fiscal year).
   2. Total of 10-year and 20-year JGB futures.
   3. Reported by primary dealers to the Fed, New York. Figures exclude transactions under repurchase agreements, reverse repurchases, new U.S. Treasury securities, and so on.
   4. Total of T-Bond futures, 5-year T-Note futures on Chicago Board of Trade (CBOT) and T-Bill futures on Chicago Merchantile Exchange (CME).
   5. TSE first section.
   6. TOPIX.
   7. New York Stock Exchange.
   8. S&P 500 on CME.
   9. 3-month Euroyen futures and 3-month Eurodollar futures on Tokyo International Financial Futures Exchange.
   10. 30-day dollar interest rate futures on CBOT and 3-month Eurodollar futures on CME.
   Source: "Survey of Foreign Exchange Market Activity" published by BIS in February 1990. Original figures were reported by the BOJ for Japan, and the Federal Reserve Bank of New York for the United States.

markets as geographical and time differences. Market participants can choose from a broader range of alternatives in markets worldwide and look for the products best suited for their purposes. As a result, trades flow out of relatively restrained and closed markets and from markets without efficient and safe settlement systems. For every country and market, various reforms have become indispensable in order to attract more global customers.

At the same time, we must not forget that globalization involves risks. The lack of appropriate infrastructures in one market could cause serious damage to the participants and also to other markets worldwide. In other words, infrastructures in the age of globalization should not be domestic-oriented; each system has to be feasible for global trading.

Public Policy Perspective

These observations have implications for the conduct of public policy. I would like to list some of the fundamental issues from a rather long-term perspective, which I personally consider important.

1. *Diminishing asymmetry of information and the necessity for deregulation.* Screen-based trading offers efficiency in trades by providing easier access to necessary information. Asymmetry of information among market participants diminishes substantially, so that conventional protective regulations established in the paper-based technology era might become redundant or even harmful. Decisions on trades should be the responsibility of each participant, and administrative restraints may need to be removed to achieve this.

2. *Diminishing entry barriers and change in the concept of marketplace.* Screen-based trading systems seem to be substitutes for conventional marketplaces. Indeed, if we think of their potential for global 24-hour trading, they can even replace existing exchanges, since there are fewer time and geographical restraints. The definition and concept of a marketplace, especially as the physical existence of a trading place, will have to be reconsidered.

3. *Global competition and its policy concerns.* Certain domestic rules should also be subject to review in promoting screen-based trading in view of global competition. In other words, we must assure a level playing field from a global viewpoint, and hence review existing antimonopoly policies that focus mainly on domestic competition.

4. *Necessity for strengthening settlement systems.* The establishment of efficient and safe settlement systems is the key to sustaining the steady expansion of a screen-based market. In this context, the following three points are most important. First is the encouragement of efficient computerized settlements. The second is expediting settlements by shortening the time lag between contracts and settlements, and promoting real-time settlements thereby avoiding the accumulation of unsettled balances, to increase the degree of finality. Assuring delivery-versus-payment for each financial transaction is the third point.

I might sound as though I already have some fixed ideas on the precise image of the future world financial market, but that is not true. It is difficult to tell, and nobody as yet knows the exact picture, since we are still in a period of major transformation.

In this regard, I believe institutional frameworks should be open and liberal, at least in major financial markets, to let financial systems fully accommodate these substantial technological innovations. Both the risks and benefits of the innovations should be shared among the involved parties.

I know central banks are fully concerned with such changes in financial systems brought about by these developments, especially from the standpoint of the stability of payment systems. The Bank of Japan, for our part, will continue to cooperate with market participants around the world and also with fellow central banks and other authorities, to contribute to the establishment of better global financial systems.

17 COOPERATIVE APPROACHES TO REDUCING RISKS IN GLOBAL FINANCIAL MARKETS

Wayne D. Angell

Most people with a global perspective are keenly aware of the extent to which economies as well as particular markets have become inter-dependent. They also are aware of the benefits from that integration, such as enhanced growth, greater efficiency in production decisions, improved resource allocation, and an expanded range of choices for consumers and investors.

I first describe what I see as two basic threats to the benefits of an integrated, global trading order, and then I identify cooperative efforts that can address those threats. I conclude by focusing on reduction of credit and liquidity risks in the foreign exchange markets.

Challenges to the Global Trading Order

One obvious threat to the global trading order is protectionism. I see that threat in the United States, where we have protectionist policies with respect to some goods and financial services and where some argue for more widespread and more substantial protection. I fear that threat in other parts of the world as well. World trade has managed to overcome these threats and has expanded strongly, but I would be even more comfortable looking to the future if the current Uruguay Round were to reach a successful conclusion. Prospects for the global economy, including the prospects for those countries seeking to move toward more market-oriented systems, would be enhanced if all countries pursued reductions in all forms of barriers to trade.

A quite different set of challenges relates to the volatility that arises in international trade and in international financial markets. The root causes of volatility are varied. For example, a good deal of volatility in the past has been associated with unsound monetary policies, as well with divergent policies among countries. Uncertainty concerning the priority various governments attach to stable prices permeates the market's determination of exchange rates.

One way to reduce risks in global financial markets is to coordinate international policy so as to achieve greater macroeconomic stability in the global economy. Central banks have a clear role to play here. In particular, their first assignment is to achieve price stability.

The liberalization that has taken place in individual financial markets and in international capital flows fosters greater integration of financial markets around the globe. Holders of wealth, whether individuals or official holders of reserves, can more easily diversify their portfolios across currencies and countries than they could previously. Through new financial instruments in the United States and developing markets abroad, investors now have more alternatives in markets outside their own countries that often require the use of another currency. The opportunity for such diversification is a desirable consequence of the strengthening of the world's financial markets. At the same time, it is an irreversible reality that imposes new discipline on market participants as well as on central banks. Until market participants can rely on central banks to be successful in controlling inflation permanently, nominal exchange rates will not be stable over the longer term. I disagree with the view that, as long as inflation rates are the same in all countries, exchange rates can be stable in a world of high inflation. Steady but high inflation in one country may be something of an aberration; for all countries, it is inconceivable.

Credit and Liquidity Risks in Foreign Exchange Markets

The international diversification of portfolios imposes a second requirement on central banks: the need for coordinated action to address the credit and liquidity risks associated with the explosive growth of foreign exchange transactions. Since 1974, participants in foreign exchange markets have been aware that trading entails significant credit and liquidity risks. That year, the failure of a relatively small German financial institution, Bankhaus I.D. Herstatt, caused substantial, if temporary, disruptions both in the foreign exchange markets and in national payments systems. The failure of a participant in foreign exchange markets can cause such disruptions primarily because no mechanism is available to ensure simultaneous settlement of both legs of a foreign exchange transaction. During the interval between the settlements of the two legs, the party that has made the first payment risks losing the full value of the second payment if its counterparty defaults on its obligation. Herstatt had purchased various European currencies in exchange for U.S. dollars. Its counterparties paid out the European currencies during European business hours. When Herstatt subsequently failed before meeting its obligations to deliver dollars, the counterparties were left with unsecured claims on a bankrupt institution.

Since Herstatt's failure, the foreign exchange markets have expanded enormously. According to a survey conducted by central banks and released recently by the Bank for International Settlements, the average daily volume of foreign exchange trading reached at least $640 billion in April 1989. Moreover, trading had doubled during the previous three years in the four major centers for which comparable data are available—the United Kingdom, the United States, Japan, and Canada. This surge will undoubtedly continue as exchange and capital controls are eliminated in Europe and are generally reduced worldwide.

The credit and liquidity risks associated with foreign exchange activities may have outpaced the growth of trading volume. Given the time difference between the Tokyo and New York business days, settlement risks in foreign exchange trading—now commonly termed Herstatt risks—are undoubtedly greatest for trades of Japanese yen against U.S. dollars. A party that sells yen in exchange for dollars must irrevocably pay out the yen at least eight hours and most often 14 hours before it receives payment in U.S. dollars. With the removal of capital controls in Japan and with that country's emergence as a major economic player, yen-dollar trading activity now accounts for a large share of overall activity in the foreign exchange markets. Indeed, the BIS (Bank for International Settlements) survey revealed that yen-dollar trades account for 75 percent of foreign volume in Tokyo, which is now the third largest center for foreign exchange trading, after London and New York.

Cooperative Efforts by the Private Sector to Reduce Risks

During the past several years, market participants have begun to focus on the credit and liquidity risks they face in bilateral trading relationships.

Along with central banks, they are considering legal arrangements that are designed to reduce these credit and liquidity risks in the foreign exchange markets, as well as to reduce transaction costs. Market participants and central banks now understand their common vulnerability to these risks, which can strain national payment systems.

Dealers in foreign exchange typically enter into successive contracts to pay or receive a particular currency, often for the same delivery date and with the same counterparty. The legal arrangements that are developing are designed to net out the amounts due between counterparties by currency and delivery date. These agreements are designed to ensure that if a market participant defaults, the credit exposure of any of its counterparties on unmatured contracts is the *net* of unrealized gains and losses on those contracts rather than the *gross* value of unrealized gains.

The current arrangements for netting operate bilaterally only, that is, between two counterparties only. They act to reduce risks by pulling together all contracts, whether spot or forward, into a new agreement. For example, FXnet, a London-based partnership formed by several major international banks, has developed an agreement under which trade confirmations for transactions between two banks are matched and netted into a running account maintained between them for each currency and delivery date. Payments are made for the net balances, due to or from each participant, in each currency on each delivery date. Twenty banks from four different countries either currently participate in FXnet or will soon do so. The benefits of participation reportedly have been substantial, with reductions of 50 to 60 percent in payment obligations and associated credit exposures.

Market participants and G-10 central banks currently are studying the feasibility of multilateral netting arrangements for foreign exchange contracts. The proposals under consideration achieve multilateral netting through creation of a central counterparty or clearinghouse, whose legal structure is similar to those of the clearinghouses affiliated with futures and options exchanges. For each contract submitted by a pair of participants, the central party would be substituted as the counterparty to each participant. The central counterparty would maintain a running, legally binding net position vis-a-vis each participant for each currency and delivery date. For a given set of contracts, each participant would have net amounts due to or due from the central counterparty that equaled its multilateral net positions vis-a-vis the other participants in the system as a group.

Proposals for such clearinghouses currently are under development by three groups of bankers in Canada, the United States, and Europe. At the moment, implementation appears at least a year away. Nonetheless, each group of bankers has made important progress during the past year.

Moreover, a dialogue has opened among the groups, and as a result all three proposals now share certain key features. These bankers have recognized that international cooperation in this area is essential. Banks participating in more than one of these systems obviously would prefer to avoid maintaining multiple communications, confirmation, and other back-office systems. Preliminary studies by these groups of banks suggest that multilateral netting could reduce gross payment obligations 80 percent or more.

Cooperative Efforts by Central Banks

The central banks of the G-10 countries have been studying the public policy implications of netting arrangements for foreign exchange obligations, as well as for other types of financial obligations, and for payments. Early last year the BIS released a preliminary report by a working party of payment experts. That report confirmed that netting arrangements could significantly reduce the credit and liquidity risks in foreign exchange markets. However, it cautioned that the legal effectiveness of netting agreements required careful study. Relying on a netting arrangement, participants might allow true gross credit and liquidity exposures that would turn out to be imprudent if the arrangement were not legally valid. Multilateral netting arrangements, in particular, require a risk management system that protects the financial integrity of the clearinghouse. Should the financial condition of a clearinghouse become impaired, the report warned, serious systemic credit and liquidity problems could develop. Finally, the report identified a range of broader issues in financial policy that the implementation of foreign exchange clearinghouses would raise, including the appropriate approach to their oversight by central banks and supervisory authorities.

For the past year another G-10 committee has been thoroughly reviewing the legal and risk management issues that netting arrangements raise. These studies should make possible a cooperative approach to oversight by central banks of multilateral systems for netting foreign exchange obligations. Cooperation in this area clearly is critical, since the host central bank for such a system and each of the central banks whose currencies are accepted for netting would have a vital interest in the system's operations.

I believe that central banks should seriously consider additional steps to facilitate the reduction of risks in the foreign exchange markets. Through well-designed netting systems, the private sector can greatly reduce the risks associated with settlements of foreign exchange obligations. Central banks could help implement such systems by providing accounts through which final, irrevocable settlements could be completed. They also should consider more fundamental changes in central bank operations that would allow simultaneous final settlement of both legs of a foreign exchange transaction and thereby would eliminate Herstatt risks.

Central banks could adopt a variety of measures that would allow creation of such a delivery-against-payment mechanism. For one thing, they could extend their hours of operation in their domestic currency. Participants in the foreign exchange markets could then discharge their payment obligations through synchronized transfers of central bank balances. Or a single central bank could offer accounts in multiple currencies. Both legs of a foreign exchange transaction could then be discharged through simultaneous transfers of credit on that central bank's books.

The offering of such services by central banks raises a number of important issues, including the potential impact on the operation of national money markets and the conduct of monetary policy. In my view, coordination and cooperation among central banks are essential in considering any of these changes. With regard to those options that involve one central bank offering accounts denominated in the currency of another central bank, I believe that due consideration needs to be given to the views of the central bank of issue. Implementation of such options should be considered only after thorough consultations.

I prefer that central banks extend their hours of operation. Indeed, I have already proposed that the Federal Reserve operate its Fedwire system 24 hours a day. Some believe that extended hours would require further extensions of daylight credit by the Federal Reserve. However, I see no reason why an active intraday market in federal funds would not develop that would allow participants to meet their intraday credit needs without resort to the central bank. The pricing of Federal Reserve credit should prompt the development of netting arrangements that privatize the risks currently borne by the Federal Reserve. If netting arrangements incorporated loss-sharing agreements that create appropriate incentives for participants to manage their counterparty risks, a far more efficient allocation of intraday credit should result.

Not only would 24-hour operation of Fedwire eliminate Herstatt risks for foreign exchange transactions involving the dollar but it would also allow timely final and irrevocable settlement of other dollar-denominated obligations. With financial markets moving rapidly toward 'round-the-clock trading, the availability of a mechanism to achieve final settlement promptly is becoming ever more urgent.

VI IS THERE A SYSTEMIC RISK PROBLEM IN INTERNATIONAL FINANCIAL MARKETS?

18 SYSTEMIC RISK IN INTERNATIONAL SECURITIES MARKETS

Michael E. Hewitt

This chapter focuses on the systemic risks that could flow from disturbances in securities markets (i.e., bond, equity, and derivative markets but not foreign exchange or credit markets) to the international financial system. It has two parts. The first part addresses the questions: What do we mean by systemic risks, how could these turn into a systemic crisis, and have such risks accumulated to an extent that raises concern and requires corrective action? The second part looks at possible measures to strengthen the capacity to forestall, manage, or absorb shocks to the system, grouping them under the four headings of market mechanisms, settlement systems, supervisory coverage, and capital requirements.

What do I mean by the phrases *systemic risk* and *systemic crisis*? I start prosaically with a dictionary definition. Any system is a set of interrelated parts that recognizably constitute a connected whole. Thus any organized financial market is a system, the components of which are its participants and its trading and regulatory arrangements. A *systemic crisis* is a disturbance that seriously impairs the working of the system, and *systemic risks* are factors that have the potential to cause or aggravate such a disturbance and, at the extreme, lead to a breakdown in the system. (I recognize that confusion can arise from freely interchanging such terms as *financial difficulty, fragility, disturbance,* and *crisis.* Correct usage is no doubt mainly a matter of degree, but the difficulty is to judge in advance whether one is referring to a moderate adjustment problem or a major crisis—you only find out when it hits you.)

This definition needs to be applied not to one system but to several layers of interconnected systems. To take the most familiar though not the only possible sequence, shocks might be transmitted first from a single national securities market to other national and international securities markets, then to the international financial system of which they are a part, and then, if they were large enough, to the real-world economy.

If such a sequence were to culminate in a full-blown systemic crisis, the critical elements in the process would appear most likely to be the following. First, it would start with a sharp and sudden fall in securities prices either in a major national market such as Wall Street or in international markets such as the Eurobond market. Second, this would spread rapidly to other securities markets, either to bond or to equity markets, and related derivative markets, or conceivably to both. Third, this would lead to the failure of one or more major intermediaries. Fourth, this would generate a crisis in the core banking and payments system. Fifth, if unchecked, this could have harmful effects upon real economic activity.

By taking these stags in turn, we may be able to form a better judgment of the way in which such a crisis could develop, the likelihood of its doing so, and the key operational and regulatory issues that arise.

We do not know enough about the causes of collapses in stock prices to assert with any confidence *why,* or to predict with any precision *when,* an initial price fall of the kind and the scale which would set this sequence in motion would occur. From past experience the conditions most conducive to financial fragility appear to be those where a combination of such factors as the following would apply: a real economic shock, such as the 1973 oil price rise; a major change of regime, such as the shift from fixed to flexible exchange rates; a sharp tightening of monetary policy following earlier relaxation; heavy debt accumulation by major classes of borrowers; or intense competition between financial intermediaries in new instruments leading to underpricing of risk premia and concentrations in high-risk assets. While no doubt some evidence of some of these features could be found at present, just as they could have been at any other time in recent history, there is no special reason to think they are festering at a critical intensity on or underneath the surface. Nevertheless these are the kinds of developments that financial supervisors, and indeed the managements of financial intermediaries themselves, need to monitor vigilantly and continually in order to identify, assess, and deal with the vulnerabilities they may expose.

What may, perhaps, have increased is the sensitivity of securities markets to changes in perceptions about economic and financial developments. At any rate, although there is little evidence that volatility in equity prices has generally increased over the last decade, there is evidence of increased frequency of extreme daily price movements. A Federal Reserve Board staff study (Duffee, Kupiec, and White, 1990) has pointed out that 20 of the 50 largest postwar daily percentage movements in returns to the Standard and Poor composite index occurred in the eighties, and of these 15, of which 10 were price falls, occurred after 1985.

It may be easier to speculate plausibly *where* the initial price fall might occur. As in October 1987 and October 1989 Wall Street would appear the most likely source. Next most likely, perhaps, would be the Euromarkets or a major national market such as London or Tokyo. Admittedly the recent sharp price falls on the Tokyo Stock Exchange were not instantly repeated in America and in Europe. Investors appear to have taken a local view of events. But the size of the Tokyo market and the importance of the Japanese economy make it unwise to assume that they would invariably react in this way.

On this question of the international transmission of stock price falls, some academic studies have found there to be some, though perhaps not conclusive, evidence of an increased correlation between price movements on national equity markets over the past decade. More significantly, however, recent studies have found stronger evidence of correlation during periods of sharp price movements.

The huge changes in capital markets over the last decade point to an intuitive conclusion that markets have become more interdependent. The abolition of exchange and other controls have removed obstacles to cross-border capital flows. Major institutional investors have been looking for investment opportunities for an expanding pool of savings outside as well as inside their domestic markets. Major multinational corporations have looked for opportunities to raise funds at the best terms to suit their own expanding international requirements. New instruments such as swaps and futures have been developed to facilitate this and have acted as integrating forces in international capital markets. The major innovators and intermediaries in this process have been the large American, Japanese, and European banks, and the large American and Japanese nonbank securities houses. These compete and deal with each other internationally across a whole range of securities, derivative, money, and exchange markets. Finally, technological advances in communications have accelerated the flow of information to markets, and so the speed of market response to news. Further advances in electronic trading and settlement on top of those in news and price dissemination seem likely to carry this interdependence further in the nineties.

The increased interdependence among national markets in periods of large price movements and the greater frequency of such movements that have been observed make it sensible, therefore, to allow for the possibility that, however it were triggered, a large price fall in a major market could, as in October 1987, set off a chain reaction which ran rapidly from one national market and one time zone to others.

There would be a danger that in such circumstances one or more individual intermediaries would fail. Given the network of trading and credit interdependencies among the major players across a range of world markets, there could be no guarantee in that event against knock-on effects leading to further failures, or that failures could be confined to small firms. Such a sequence could start with a withdrawal of funding from a firm believed to be least able to absorb losses irrespective of whether its losses had in fact made it insolvent, or counterparties might refuse to deal with such a firm, making it difficult for it to unwind its positions successfully. Forced sales of assets would drive their prices down further.

Such a crisis would also test the efficiency and robustness of settlement systems. Delays between delivery and payment and uncertainties about intraday exposures would increase reluctance to deal. Additional margin calls by clearinghouses could drain liquidity from the market when it was most needed. On the other hand, if, as would have been the case of the Hong Kong Guarantee Corporation in October 1987 without a government-organized rescue, guarantees given by clearinghouses were not backed by sufficient resources to honor them, then this would itself undermine confidence in the market that they cleared. Disorderly conditions thus created in the derivative market could spill over into the cash market.

Banks would inevitably be involved in this process as securities dealers themselves, as creditors and counterparties of other securities dealers, and through their role in payments transmission. Its own difficulties, compounded by those of its customers, could put a bank into a severe liquidity squeeze in these conditions.

It might be reasonably assumed that at this point, if not earlier, central banks would step in to inject liquidity into the system, act as lender of last resort to particular banks short of liquidity, and perhaps, if necessary, even rescue otherwise insolvent banks if their failure would jeopardize the system. Looked at from a central banker's point of view, however, it would seem dangerous to assume that central banks would always be able to limit the damage; too confident a presumption that they will do so may itself create the moral hazard of encouraging imprudent behavior; and in general it would seem better to take preventative measures in advance rather than wait for emergencies to test skills in crisis management.

If we recapitulate the stages by which systemic risks might escalate from securities price falls to a market crisis, then to a crisis for intermediaries and a banking crisis, we can similarly separate the policy and operational issues that arise at each stage.

I take the origin of the initial price collapse to be largely exogenous and unpredictable. But no doubt consistent pursuit of steady, convergent economic policies by major governments would themselves make financial conditions more stable. More specifically, supervisors should anticipate problems to the extent possible by looking for signs of financial fragility of the kind described earlier in this chapter. Exposures to leveraged buyouts provide a ready-made current example.

The transition from the first to second stage—price fall to market crisis—raises questions of market organization, market capacity, interconnections between cash and derivative markets, use of new trading techniques, and settlement and clearing systems. The transition from the second to third stage—from market crisis to a crisis for intermediaries—raises questions for the risk management and for the supervision of such intermediaries. The transition from the third to fourth stage of a banking crisis—and *a fortiori* the transition to the final stage of damage to the real economy—are matters of crisis management if they occur, but more pertinent to this discussion are the outcomes that structural and regulatory improvements identified at the earlier stages are designed to avert.

Market Mechanisms

What can be done to improve market structures or expand capacity? Are there particular trading techniques that need to be controlled or proscribed? Are there faulty connections between cash and derivative markets? A good deal has been written about these subjects, especially since October 1987 and especially in the United States, and I know that a good deal of controversy remains. I will state my understanding of the issues and my views on them very briefly.

There is, first, a variety of opinions on the merits of different market *structures*—that is, whether dealer markets, auction markets, or hybrids like the New York Stock Exchange are the most efficient forms of market. From the point of view of systemic risk, however, the main issue is that markets in which dealers take large positions on their own books produce greater concentrations of risk than do pure auction markets. But since market-makers take these positions to meet the requirements of institutional investors wishing to deal frequently and in large amounts, this is not a case for replacing dealer markets with auction markets but rather for focusing on the risk management of the intermediaries.

Clearly expansions in *market capacity* ought to be helpful in dealing with exceptional order flows. Unforeseen capacity constraints can build up a liquidity illusion that encourages intermediaries and investors to underestimate the risks they will run when the market is overloaded. So such improvements as those that have been made by the New York and other stock exchanges are welcome, and appear to have helped them cope better in October 1989 than in October 1987 with high volumes of transactions. There is no doubt further room for improvement, especially with continued development of automated trading. Nevertheless there are limits to which expanded or automated capacity can be expected to deal with lumpy order flows from institutional investors, especially in a crisis.

The arguments about various types of program trading are particularly contentious. One form, portfolio insurance, was shown to be destabilizing and to have helped create the kind of liquidity illusion just mentioned in 1987; as a consequence it has been discredited. There will always be temptations to devise similar techniques that appear to promise the user the ability to get out first, however, so we should not be too sure that the lesson has been learned. On the other hand, it seems futile to try to ban such techniques. This also applies more strongly to index arbitrage, the other main technique brought into question after 1987. Index arbitrage, if it works properly should be a stabilizing influence. The question is, in abnormal conditions, such as in October 1987, does it become destabilizing, transmitting surges of volatility from the derivative to the cash market, and vice versa? If so, the explanation may be that the opportunity to trade the index is a convenient instrument for active fund managers who wish to deal in large size; and it is their investment decisions, rather than the instrument through which they are conducted, that initiate such movements. At any rate, in Europe, where our financial futures and options markets are much smaller both in absolute terms and relative to the cash markets, we have tended to conclude that we need more, not less, index arbitrage. I am skeptical whether even in the United States it makes much sense to limit or ban particular forms of program trading, except, perhaps, as a means of relieving capacity constraints when market systems are overloaded.

This issue is one contentious aspect of the links between cash and derivative market. Another is whether maintenance *margins in futures markets* are habitually set too low. This raises two questions: do low margins increase volatility and are they too low for prudential purposes? On the first question there are strong differences of opinion. In my view, the case is unproven; it follows that if there is a case for questioning margin levels in futures markets it has to be made on prudential grounds. It is possible that such grounds could exist. The actions of the Chicago exchanges on October 13 and 16, 1989, calling for increased initial and maintenance margin payments, were no doubt sensible in their own terms, but inevitably put an additional squeeze on liquidity at a time it was already likely to be strained; this suggests the previous requirements may have been too low if such action was necessary. There may be a case for national regulators to monitor the margin requirements set by individual clearinghouses more closely to ensure that they allow for a greater possibility of extreme price movements.

Finally, a brief comment on *circuit-breakers*, or more specifically on preplanned trading halts when prices fall below a given point. These are by definition responses to a crisis rather than preventative measures. The intention underlying them is to allow investors, intermediaries, and regulators to pause to recover their poise and assess the situations calmly. This may or may not work. Panic may still revive when markets reopen. Moreover, trading can move from the normal main market. To be fully effective in halting trading, therefore, the closure has to be coordinated with related national markets—for which there is, of course, now an agreed mechanism between the securities and futures markets in the United States. That still leaves a problem of coordination with markets in other countries; how could this be done in the Euromarkets, for instance? It also begs the question of whether trading ought to be halted: it would be perverse, for example, to close a market that was demonstrating its ability to deal with an exceptional order flow because another market could not cope. In short, circuit-breakers may sometimes be helpful in moderating a disorderly market, but it seems unwise to place too much faith in their ability to restore order.

Settlement Systems

Improvements in *settlement* systems are likely to be more helpful in combatting systemic risks than improvements in other market mechanisms. They can be a source or a transmitter of risk. First, they could be a source of risk through a computer breakdown, as in the 1985 Bank of New York episode. In spite of the huge sums involved, however, an isolated mechanical failure of this kind ought not to cause a general financial collapse since the central bank can step in to lend overnight, and market participants will appreciate the nature of the difficulty. This might not be their attitude, however, if such a breakdown coincided—as it might—with a market crisis that already put a heavy load on trading and settlement systems. Second, the interaction of different settlement systems in different markets with different timetables for paying and collecting cash can impose increasing strains on users as turnover rises, and so help to cause or magnify a liquidity crisis. Dispersion of settlement arrangements can also make it more difficult to monitor the exposures taken by intermediaries across the range of markets, and inhibit the use of netting as a means of risk reduction.

There are risks in settlement whatever the arrangements. In that sense settlement systems are most important as transmitters and redistributors of risk. The only secure way of protecting against capital risk—the failure of a counterparty to deliver when paid or to pay for securities delivered—is to have a legally secure system of simultaneous delivery against payment. That, too, is the only fully satisfactory method of dealing with a situation where the positions of a firm in difficulty need to be unwound. Not many securities markets fully achieve this, however. It is more a matter of devising arrangements that come as close as possible to the ideal. To the extent that delivery against payment is achieved through banks taking on exposures for their customers, this transfers risks to the banking system.

In the absence of delivery versus payment there are a number of ways of reducing, redistributing, and protecting against capital risk, and also against market risk (i.e., the risk, not removed by delivery versus payment, of a failure by a counterparty to settle, leaving an intermediary in a position where to meet an order for a customer at the original price he has to take a loss in replacing the deal):

1. Conditions on *membership*, especially the use of tiering with clearing and nonclearing members, clearly represent one basic but limited safeguard.

2. A move to *shorter settlement periods, and to rolling settlement*, as recommended by the Group of Thirty and other recent reports, should not only make markets more efficient and internationally more compatible with each other, but also shorten the period in which counterparty exposures have time to accumulate.

3. If properly constructed, the use of *netting* arrangements can be of considerable help in reducing the number of deals to be settled, thereby

reducing operational strain; the value of deals, thus easing banking decisions; timing differences between cash inflows and outflows; and counterparty exposures. But this proviso is critical: the benefits derived from particular netting schemes depend on the legal conditions which apply in the relevant jurisdiction. If in a crisis the netting has to be unravelled because legal obligations can only be made to stick for the individual underlying deals, netting will only have succeeded in obscuring the situation and complicating its resolution.

4. The use of a *central counterparty* can help deal with some of these and other problems. But if the central counterparty is to meet its commitments to the sellers and the buyers between whom it stands, its own financial integrity becomes paramount. If risks are concentrated in one institution, and that institution then fails to meet its commitments, this is liable to magnify and accelerate the threat to the system presented by the failure of individual members of the clearing system. This reinforces the message about margin requirements already mentioned. More generally it makes it important that the totality of arrangements made by the central counterparty are effective; that proper conditions and controls are applied to members; that the financial resources backing it are adequate, whether they are secured by outside guarantee or by mutual loss-sharing arrangements; and that banking arrangements for the payment and receipt of margin and other moneys are reliable.

Because legal and operating conditions vary so much from country to country, it is difficult to point to an exact path which all should follow in reducing the risks in their settlement and payment systems. A good deal of attention has been given to these issues and continues to be given in various fora, notably the Group of Thirty and the Basle Group of Experts on Payments Systems. The complexities are such that progress will probably be piecemeal and gradual. But there can be little doubt that if it moves in the direction recommended by the Group of Thirty and others, it will greatly contribute to the safety and efficiency of international financial markets.

Even if all defects in the internal workings of settlement systems were eradicated, they would remain the channel through which counterparty risk was transmitted. The failure of a major intermediary would still be the main event in a general price collapse most likely to pose the most serious systemic threat. (The failure of a major intermediary through misjudgments by its management or other special factors in otherwise normal conditions would not be expected to present as great a threat to the system as it would in conditions where confidence was already fragile and widespead losses had already occurred. The orderly unwinding of the Drexel group illustrates this. Even so it could not be ruled out that such a failure, especially if it were by a large bank, might itself provoke a general crisis of confidence.) This makes the risk management and the supervision of those intermediaries—banks or nonbanks—which trade in a variety of instruments, countries, and markets (on and outside exchanges) a critical element in forestalling that threat.

Supervisory Issues

There are three main supervisory issues: Are there gaps in the coverage of risks taken by major international intermediaries? Is the system for supervision of international groups sufficiently coordinated? And, are the capital requirements imposed by supervisors adequate?

The answer to the first question is clearly yes; equally clearly the main gaps are in the supervision of American nonbank securities houses. These place major risk-taking activities—for example, swaps, foreign exchange, bridging loans in leveraged buyouts—in companies within their groups outside the registered broker-dealer, which consequently are not supervised by the Securities and Exchange Commission (SEC) or any other U.S. supervisory authority. I know that a bill is before Congress that would give the SEC powers to obtain information from the holding company, affiliates, or subsidiaries of the registered broker-dealer. If enacted, that will give the SEC the ability to assess the exposure of the registered broker-dealer to related entities, including overseas operations, within the group, and to take any necessary action to protect it against ill effects from such exposures. That would be a big step forward from the present position. Even so it would stop short of giving the SEC direct supervisory powers over the financial operations of the whole group. If you take the view, as I do, that the activities of the world's major nonbank securities houses are internationally so important that the failure of one or more of them could in adverse conditions constitute a grave systemic threat, then this still appears a deficiency.

The answer to the second question is also clear: international coordination between securities supervisors is as yet inadequate. This is hardly surprising given the great diversity of national supervisory regimes in their institutional and functional coverage, legal status, number of different, overlapping supervisors (in some cases within the same countries), and in the activities that different types of institutions such as banks are permitted to perform. Applied to international groupings, this diffusion of national, functional, and institutional responsibilities among supervisors impedes cooperation and fails to deliver a comprehensive oversight of their activities.

What can or should be done about this? First, current efforts to improve exchanges of information between supervisors along the lines of the financial information-sharing memoranda of understanding (FISMOUs) between U.K. and U.S. securities supervisors should be further extended. These raise problems of access to and confidentiality of information, and the conditions under which the recipient supervisor can use them as a basis for supervisory action; but it is important that such legal and practical obstacles be overcome. In operating such exchanges of information, on a regular and ad hoc basis, supervisors will develop better understanding and closer relationships which will stand them in good stead in a crisis.

Beyond that, however, the question arises as to whether a more systematic, coherent international system of coordination ought to be developed for the financial supervision of the most important internationally active financial conglomerates: clarifying the location of responsibilities among the national, functional, and institutional supervisors involved and establishing a system of central oversight over the activities of the whole group. Such a system might logically apply the principle already enshrined in the Basle Concordat for banking supervisors, and in the proposed European Community directives on banking and on investment services, of locating prime responsibility for supervision of solvency with the home country supervisor. Its application could be extended not only to overseas branches but also to overseas affiliates and subsidiaries.

Such a system of centralized oversight need not, and preferably should not, however, take the form of full accounting consolidation but rather aim to achieve a qualitative assessment of the risks taken within a group. Moreover, it would be sensible to confine such a system to financial operations and not to other kinds of commercial operations within a group—although some judgment would need to be made on the extent to which the latter were a source of strength or weakness to the financial companies within the group.

The exact division of responsibilities between the various supervisors might need to vary to allow for the divergences between national regulatory regimes. Where there was difficulty in obtaining recognition of a single prime supervisor or unwillingness by the most obvious candidate to take on this role, it might nevertheless be possible to develop a second-best system of shared responsibilities, such as the lead regulator arrangements operated between different functional regulators in the United Kingdom, with one acting as *primus inter pares*. This might in some ways be easier to bring about because it would not so clearly abrogate the functions of the individual supervisors, and would fit naturally with a more systematic approach to information exchanges.

The development of one form or another of central oversight of the major international players in world financial markets is at least as important a condition for strengthening the ability to forestall systemic crises as is convergence in the capital requirements applied to position and other risks in securities business. Convergence in capital adequacy is required as much for competitive as for prudential reasons. In this context the efforts of the Commission and the member states of the European Community to agree on proposals for a capital directive for investment business are especially notable in tackling the problems of reconciling the very different approaches of banking and securities supervisors in a way that will seek to allow German universal banks and American- and Japanese-owned non-bank securities houses to compete on approximately even terms.

As well as the difference in approach between banking and securities supervisors, there is considerable variation in the regimes applied by national supervisors. A major advance in this respect has occurred with the introduction this year by Japan of a new regime of financial requirements for securities firms which is similar in its approach to those in the United States and the United Kingdom. There remain, however, variations in the actual haircuts applied by the three countries. These again may be more significant for their competitive than their prudential implications. But if progress is made through the International Organization of Securities Commissions (IOSCO) Technical Committee in bringing these requirements and those of other countries more closely in line, it will be important that prudential considerations are given their proper due. In particular, some additional allowance may need to be made for the increased possibility of extreme daily stock price movements noted earlier in this chapter.

The development of a more integrated system of supervising the operations of major international intermediaries in securities markets and the pursuit of convergence on prudentially adequate capital requirements would reinforce the best risk management practices of the intermediaries themselves. The aim would not be to make the requirements so excessive, or the supervision so intrusive, as to penalize all risk taking or prevent any firm from failing. Nor would it entail any explicit or implicit commitment by central banks or by supervisory authorities that they would step in to rescue individual firms from failure. As the President of the Federal Reserve Bank of New York, Gerald Corrigan, has aptly pointed out, central banks should maintain a policy of "constructive ambiguity" about whether and how they would intervene in a crisis, if at all. (Corrigan, 1990)

The objectives would be to make such intervention less likely and less necessary; to increase the chances of resolving a crisis in a manner that caused the least possible disruption to markets; and in general, together with improvements in settlement systems and other measures discussed in this chapter, to reduce systemic risks.

Acknowledgments

Although my views have been informed by work done for my employer, the Bank of England, and especially by work done by my international colleagues and myself for the OECD ad hoc group of experts on securities markets which I have been chairing, the emphasis and conclusions of this chapter are mine and not necessarily those of the Bank or of the OECD group, whose final report will not be completed for several months yet.

References

Corrigan, Gerald E. Federal Reserve Bank of New York, Speech to the New York State Bankers Association, January 1990.

Duffee, Gregory, Kupiec, Paul, and White, Patricia. A Primer on Program Trading and Stock Price Volatility: A Survey of the Issues and the Evidence, Finance and Economic Discussion Series No. 109, Federal Reserve Board, Washington, D.C., January 1990.

19 GOVERNMENT OFFICIALS AS A SOURCE OF SYSTEMIC RISK IN INTERNATIONAL FINANCIAL MARKETS

Edward J. Kane

Systemic risk refers to unspecified dangers in the operation of an unspecified system. To apply the term to international financial markets, we must specify just what we mean by risk and system. In economic affairs, risk refers to chances for loss. System is a trickier word that may be interpreted in at least two ways.

On the one hand, the global financial system may be conceived merely as an assemblage of "financial" things that form some kind of unitary whole. In this usage, the unification of the system's parts is supplied at least proximately by the definition of finance held in the mind of the beholder. Geographers employ this meaning in the phrase *the Rocky Mountain System*.

Alternatively, the global financial system may be conceived after the manner of biology as an organically structured hypersystem: a system of linked subsystems that together accomplish whatever tasks are specified to comprise the realm of finance. In the broadest sense, these are the tasks of *channeling* funds and financial documents between different kinds of transactors whose accounts are usually located in different sites: savers and investors; payers and payees; and traders in diverse financial instruments. Each component subsystem may be depicted as an assemblage of

257

the particular parts of whatever financial institutions include items in their product lines that address the subsystem's specific funds-channeling function. Pursuing the biological analogy, the hypersystem that constitutes an organism such as the human body is, for example, conventionally broken down into subsystems such as the nervous, digestive, or reproductive systems.

Adopting an organic definition makes it clear that in the financial context systemic risk has two complementary meanings. It can mean either the danger that one or more component subsystems may fail the larger system under stress (subsystem-failure risk), or the danger that the coordinating structure that has previously bound the subsystems together may break apart (disintegration risk). These risks are particularly worrisome in finance because the nonroutine nature of systemic disruptions is held to threaten unpredictably nonlinear "chaotic" effects.

In lamenting the dangers posed by the pace of financial innovation and globalization, regulators in major countries seldom see themselves as part of the problem. This chapter's principal theme is that regulators' own carelessly formed opinions and short-sighted behavior make them the most important generators of systemic risk. Suppressing their own riskiness leads them to identify a manifest lessening of their own *autonomy* and *capacity to control* the evolution of both kinds of systemic risk with an increased danger of system or subsystem breakdown. Authorities' root concern may be characterized in the language of epidemiology as a recognition of the increasing exposure of their client institutions to a contagious spread of losses from geographic regions and institutional sectors outside their regulatory span of control. However, an organism's exposure to additional pathogens need not imply an increasing vulnerability to serious disease. The theory of vaccination clarifies that this depends on what is happening simultaneously to associated immune systems. Regulators fail to see that globalization is strengthening the financial system's immune systems in important ways.

No one can dispute that advances in transportation, computer, and communications technology increase opportunities for loss contagion and impose costs of adjustment all around. What needs to be challenged is the assumption that national authorities' loss of autonomy and control constitutes an unambiguous deterioration in the financial immune system, as would be necessary to demonstrate an increased risk of global breakdown.

National and sectoral regulators' loss of autonomy evidences their own increasing exposure to market discipline. To see increased market discipline on regulators as an inherently harmful development that taxpayers should want determinedly offset requires an overly hopeful and unrealistically one-dimensional view of the financial regulatory process and its effectiveness. A particularly naive version of this process is promoted by government officials who portray themselves to the electorate and the press as far-sighted and nearly all-knowing individuals who selflessly and tirelessly pursue the common good in everything they do.

This utopian view of regulation is inconsistent with principal-agent theory and with practical experience. Studies of regulatory behavior in the United States show that in a representative democracy regulators often operate with poor information and typically face important conflicts of interest. Far more often than not, a tradeoff exists between what is good for taxpayers in general and what is perceived to be good for an individual regulatory bureau or the top elected or appointed officials that can influence the bureau's strategy and tactics. Well-informed observers can identify a number of occasions in which politicians and financial authorities have used their discretion to cover up uncomfortable facts, to delay needed action, or to act in short-sighted and discriminatory ways that have worsened rather than lessened losses systemwide.

Two Important Risky Subsystems

Banking

We have defined systemic risk as the possibility of a contagious spread of losses across financial institutions of all kinds. Federal Reserve economist Alton Gilbert (1989, p. 4) defines the concept entirely in terms of the *banking subsystem*, as "the risk that the failure of one bank will cause one or more other banks to fail."

Gilbert and most other Federal Reserve officials conceive of the contagion of losses among banks as likely to be initiated by the sudden failure of what had previously been reputed by informed observers to be a healthy bank. The medium they see for propagating losses to other banks is the distribution of net clearing balances that this failed bank would have with other banks in the banking subsystem at the instant it failed.

Although rooted in individual credit losses, this systemic problem may be described as payments-network risk. This is because the character of the bilateral loss exposures that develop within each day depends vitally on the rules of the institutional network through which specific payments flow. In the case of large-denomination payments that move over the wire-transfer system operated by the Fed (the "Fedwire"), the Fed (i.e., the federal taxpayer) assumes the risk of losses due to a sudden failure of a sending bank as soon as it notifies the receiving bank of a funds transfer. On competing U.S. electronic systems run by private firms, the receiving bank remains at risk until all intraday transfers are finalized at the close of the business day.

Although slow to respond to technologically driven increases in payments-network risk, Fed officials pride themselves on having taken "actions to limit" the Fed's own intraday loss exposure and the systemic risk generated in the principal private payments network (Gilbert, 1989, p. 5). These actions and follow-up proposals for reform have focused either on directly limiting the size of the unfunded debit balances or intraday overdrafts that individual institutions can run or on explicitly or implicitly pricing these balances.

However, the Fed's actions treat symptoms rather than causes, and are less significant than the actions it has chosen not to take. The substantial amounts of both Fed and private-network risk exposures that exist today are rooted in a failure of federal banking officials scrupulously to enforce taxpayer interests in transactions with their regulatory clienteles.

On the one hand, the Fed has failed to conceive of its guarantee of payment finality as a contingent liability for whose value users need to be charged market-mimicking fees. If these services had been supplied in a competitive market by private parties, other avenues of adjustment would have been explored. Frequency of settlement, loss-sharing arrangements such as rights of offset, escrow activity, and the wire network's hours of operation would have tended to expand with the volume of off-hours trading; fees would have come to vary with the financial condition of each sender; and receivers would have developed an option to waive the guarantee whenever it seemed economical to them. As result, the guarantor sector's average exposure to loss would have been importantly reduced.

On the other hand, under existing U.S. regulatory arrangements, the chances of our observing the initiating event assumed in the Fed's analysis is effectively zero. U.S. authorities face overwhelming and well-known incentives not to permit the sudden intraday failure of any previously well-regarded U.S. bank that would be large enough to generate epidemic losses. First, even when a bank insolvency is discovered suddenly (as in a failure triggered by an examination that uncovers substantial hidden losses), uninsured depositors typically receive at least a few days (if not months) of notice, in that the administrative process for closing a bank is inevitably protracted (Kane, 1985). Second, U.S. authorities are particularly reluctant to close very large banks, let alone to liquidate them. Kane (1985, p. 161) notes:

Given the short terms of office that financial regulators enjoy, it makes little sense for them to take an appreciable chance that a spillover of financial pressure will damage other institutions or undermine public confidence in depository institutions as a whole. Why should an agency's leader[ship] risk ruining their own careers when they can reliably truncate further damage with a readily obtained injection of federal funds and federal guarantees that serve to rescue a failing institution and its creditors from the need to sustain uncomfortable losses?

Viewed in this light, the issue concerns the access of *foreign* banks to the U.S. large-payments system and the possibility that one or more foreign regulators may be willing to tolerate a sudden large-bank failure.

Ironically, the root of the systemic risk that Fed officials pride themselves on pressing private networks to control is the failure to price and manage the credit enhancements conveyed by these de facto guarantees of a bank's creditors against sudden loss. The reluctance of the private networks to act on their own is understandable. Official and unofficial guarantees of payments finality eliminate a private network's natural concern for pricing and managing the risk that losses might be transmitted contagiously to its members. Why should the networks incur costs of risk management when government officials offer insurance "for free"?

Of course, government insurance is not truly free. Although its costs may be hidden for long periods, a bill is levied implicitly on the federal Treasury and on the taxpayers that ultimately stand behind the insurance system. However, U.S. authorities can choose when and how taxpayers finance this bill. So far, U.S. officials have chosen to leave the meter running and to speculate on longshot schemes that would discharge the bill with little noticeable pain. This running meter is today the overwhelming source of systemic risk in the world banking system.

Securities and Futures Trading

The depth of worldwide official concern about the structure of securities trading corresponds to regulators' and politicians' need to reassure their publics that regulatory structures are being adapted to forestall a recurrence of the global stock-market "break" of October 1987. The pervasive drying up of trading opportunities during this steep price fall clarifies that problems exist in the structure of market-making in individual markets and in the nature of intermarket trading linkages (U.S. Government Accounting Office, 1990).

However, in the United States, the thrust of federal efforts to address these problems has so far been more cosmetic than real. Rather than determining the extent to which advances in information and communications technology may have outmoded existing trading and regulatory arrangements in securities markets, the Securities and Exchange Commission (SEC) and securities-industry spokespersons have labored principally to pin the blame on other regulators. They have focused on selling the public a self-serving and false theory that portrays futures-industry innovations and futures-market regulation as the root causes of excessive stock-market volatility. In doing this, U.S. securities-market interests are striving to use public demand for action to guard against another stock-market debacle to fuel a power grab. They have refloated proposals that would effect a cartel-like brute-force redistribution to themselves of jurisdiction over domestic trading that has developed in financial futures markets.

Genuine reform must be built on an authentic and complete theory of what needs to be fixed. Whatever role the equity-derivative instruments that are now traded in futures markets may have played in the 1987 or 1989 stock-market breaks, the development of trading in these instruments is a progressive development. It lowers the cost of undertaking a broad class of financial transactions. That this trading developed outside of the traditional securities trading subsystem is the market's way of penalizing longstanding efforts by the SEC and New York Stock Exchange to preserve outmoded patterns of securities trading and regulation against the onslaught of technological change. Giving the SEC and U.S. stock exchanges exclusive jurisdiction over equity derivative instruments in no way guarantees that they can hold it over the long run. U.S. futures exchanges' expanding links with foreign futures exchanges (as in GLOBEX) suggests that, in the absence of more responsive securities regulation, the jurisdictional change would simply relocate the points in the global interinstitutional trading network through which technological forces most quickly express themselves.

To see this, it is helpful to recognize that traditional auction markets are not merely centralized *trading places*. They are more fundamentally mechanisms for routing, clearing, and settling trading orders that are initiated along a farflung *trading network*. The cost efficiency of channeling trades in primary and derivative instruments through a centralized trading floor is bound to fall when and as technological change makes timely and electronically communicated information on price quotations and on order and trading flows accessible cheaply to decentralized "off-exchange" market-makers.

This cost efficiency is undermined further by a federal insurance system that protects investor wealth in the event that an undercapitalized broker or exchange goes bankrupt. The existence of the Securities Investor Protection Corporation guarantees reduces the importance of traditional signals and guarantees of a broker's financial strength and integrity. Customers have less reason to worry about evidence concerning: (1) the reputation and economic capital of individual brokers, and (2) the effectiveness of the regulatory structure by which the SEC and the stock exchanges monitor and police stock-market transactions.

On the exchange floor, trades are effected by specialists and floor brokers. A specialist is a member firm of an exchange that has been assigned the exclusive right of handling transactions on the trading floor in the stocks for which it is registered. In return for this right, the specialist accepts the responsibility to risk its own capital in buying and selling the stock for its own account in ways designed to maintain an "orderly market" in the stock.

The effectiveness of any specialist system is ultimately rooted in the size of the discounted present value of the monopoly rights a specialist's franchise conveys. This franchise value constitutes a source of off-balance-sheet capital whose underlying cash flows and profit opportunities grow with the specialist's average profit margin on trades and with the expected volume of floor trading in the stock. The larger is this hidden capital, the greater is the strength of clearing members' performance guarantees and the greater is each member firm's interest in preserving or winning specialist franchises. In turn, intraexchange competition for valuable franchises is the cutting edge of the exchange's disciplinary powers.

The October 1987 episode provides evidence that the technological change that underlies financial globalization has squeezed specialist profit margins and trading volumes in many stocks to the point where specialists' informational advantages and franchise rights (though far from worthless) are not valuable enough to compel them to risk their wealth to smooth a large price drop. Extending SEC jurisdiction over equity derivatives and introducing a system of volatility-based trading halts or circuit-breakers cannot substitute for the absorptive capacity of willing and strongly financed stabilizing transactors.

The Dangers of International Cooperation in Financial Regulation

Systemic risk concerns the contagion of crisis pressures. To control this risk, it is necessary to recognize that relative to periods longer than congressional and presidential electoral cycles, crisis pressures are being made worse by short-sighted efforts of officials in some individual countries to preserve undercapitalized and technologically outmoded competitors and regulatory systems. In many cases, politicians' and regulators' professional reputations and postgovernment career opportunities are better served by maintaining the misleading appearance of a nonturbulent watch than by conscientiously confronting regulatory problems in timely fashion.

Accounting coverup of the costs of federally insuring large-payment and securities settlement risk is so routine that almost no one even sees it as a coverup. To provide accountability, budget discipline requires that the costs of actuarially reserving for the accumulating bill for these risk-management services be regularly estimated and funded explicitly.

The point is that regulators compete not just in the *quality* of the confidence-building and coordinating services they provide but also in terms of the *efficiency* with which they produce these services and where they lay the burden for financing their costs of production. When the cost burden is laid surreptitiously on taxpayers in general rather than on specific beneficiaries of these services, net regulatory benefits are not subjected to a market-like efficiency test. This makes it possible to lower the quality of regulatory services and to raise their cost at the same time.

Incentive conflict makes it dangerous under current reporting schemes for U.S. taxpayers to trust imperfectly accountable officials to negotiate what amounts to a series of anticompetitive international and domestic agreements that reassign regulatory turf. The problem is to prevent such reassignments from protecting undercapitalized and technologically maladapted institutions and regulatory systems from market pressures.

What is needed is a political and economic environment in which efficient regulatory enterprises routinely receive opportunities to expand and inefficient ones routinely come under pressure to contract. This requires introducing reliable accounting and auditing standards for government regulatory entities. Taxpayers must come to appreciate the wisdom of demanding that regulatory officials be at least as accountable to them for changes in the market value of each regulatory enterprise as the managers of the firms they regulate are to corporate stockholders. At a minimum, this means making authorities analyze honestly and fully the distributional and longer-run market consequences of domestic and international regulatory agreements and exposing this analysis formally to the light of outside criticism.

References

Flannery, Mark. 1988. Payments Risk and Public Policy. In William S. Haraf and Rose Marie Kushmeider, eds., *Restructuring Banking and Financial Services in America*. Washington, DC: American Enterprise Institute for Public Policy Research, pp. 261–287.

Gilbert, R. Alton. 1989. Payments System Risk: What Is It and What Will Happen If We Try to Reduce It? *Review* (Federal Reserve Bank of St. Louis) 71 (Jan./Feb.), 3–17.

Kane, Edward J. 1985. *The Gathering Crisis in Federal Deposit Insurance*. Cambridge, MA: MIT Press.

Saunders, Anthony, 1988. The Eurocurrency Interbank Market: Potential For International Crises? *Business Review* (Federal Reserve Bank of Philadelphia) (Jan./Feb.), 17–27.

U.S. General Accounting Office, General Government Division. 1990. *Securities Trading: SEC Action Needed to Address National Market System Issues*. Report to Congressional Committees B-21979. Washington, DC, March 12.

20 SYSTEMIC RISK AND INTERNATIONAL FINANCIAL MARKETS

Hideki Kanda

Regulatory concerns about systemic risk in international financial markets at a theoretical level are examined in this chapter. First, a description is given about how systemic risk arises in these markets today. Next, systemic risk is unbundled into four components (subrisks), and questions are raised as to whether any form of regulation might reduce such risks efficiently. Third, current and proposed rules for the reduction of systemic risk are discussed. This chapter essentially argues that one of the four subrisks—that associated with interdependence among market participants—should be given more direct and serious attention than the other subrisks.

What and Where Systemic Risk Is

Systemic risk is the expectation or the danger that a financial institution, typically a bank, fails to settle because another financial institution fails to settle. This risk typically exists in large-amount payment transactions among banks. There have been many discussions over the past several years in the United States and elsewhere as to how serious this risk is in the payment area, and many efforts have been made to search for desirable ways to reduce such risk.[1]

It should be noted, however, that payment is not the only area where systemic risk exists. It also exists in money market and securities transfer transactions, and, in theory, in other general financial transactions as well. There are many trade clearing and settlement systems for funds, securities, futures, options, and other financial instruments, all of which give rise to systemic risk (Corrigan, 1989; Hewitt, 1990). Any mechanical breakdown, liquidity problem, or default in one of these systems would affect all direct and indirect participants in the system and could spread rapidly into other systems.

Compared to payment systems such as CHIPS and Fedwire in the United States and BOJ-NET and the *zengin* system in Japan (all described in BIS 1989), clearing and settlement systems for securities, futures and options have complex legal, structural, and operational characteristics. Moreover, a bank engages in many different types of transactions that go beyond various payment transactions to traditional lending activity. And, in countries where banks are permitted to engage in securities business, a bank is involved in the delivery process of a wide range of securities. Thus, if a bank fails because of unwise lending, this failure would directly affect its ability to settle in payment and other transactions, which in turn could have widespread effects elsewhere.

In short, it is important to recognize at the outset that systemic risk exists everywhere. How serious it is depends on the nature and degree of the risk in each relevant context.

Another dimension to consider in this area relates to the international context. Systemic risk is of particular importance in international financial transactions for at least five reasons. First, in modern financial markets the same single bank simultaneously participates in different payment, money market, and securities transfer systems, and these systems have different sets of legal, structural, and operational characteristics. This simple fact aggravates the problem. Second, a local bank with a relatively weak credit standing can still participate in international payment and other transactions through a correspondent money center bank. This structure increases the degree of interdependence among the participants, which in turn makes systemic risk more serious.

One might argue that money center banks are large enough to withstand "shocks" such as the failure of a smaller bank in the chain of payments, and that the existence of these large financial intermediaries thus reduces systemic risk in this respect. The involvement of large banks as "extra" parties, however, may increase interdependence among large institutions in various countries and thus make systemic risk more serious. If domestic transactions are effectively cleared through money center institutions, systemic risk is reduced, and to that extent international transactions do not make systemic risk more serious than domestic ones. But the reality is that this is not always the case.

Third, time-zone differences cause problems. Fourth, differences in central bank policies also matter. Fifth, international transactions often pose a risk of political instability or economic downturn that may not exist in domestic transactions within stable industrial economies.

In summary, systemic risk exists in two dimensions. First, every kind of bank or financial transaction matters; not only payment transactions but also other transactions are important elements of systemic risks. Second, the risk is more serious in international financial markets than in domestic markets.

Unbundling Systemic Risk

To understand the nature and the importance of systemic risk it is important to examine carefully how the risk arises. The traditional understanding of systemic risk as a combination of credit risk and liquidity risk is analytically insufficient and does not prove a case for regulation in this area. Liquidity risk needs a more rigorous analysis.

A useful way to think about systemic risk is to unbundle it into four subrisks: pure credit risk, interdependence risk, time risk, and large-amount risk.[2] Pure credit risk is default risk. Of particular importance are the economic factors producing the other three subrisks, all of which are essential characteristics of modern financial transactions. Interdependence among participants is important because one bank's failure to settle causes another bank's failure to settle and in that way can have endless effects.

Time is important because payment and other transactions are subject to a relatively short time constraint, and some mechanical breakdown or one bank's failure will give rise to a liquidity problem for other banks. It might be extremely costly for those other banks to find sufficient funds to meet their obligations in the time remaining before their settlements are due. A large transaction amount causes a liquidity problem to the extent that it remains unsettled. Thus, time causes problems in two opposing ways. Time constraints for settlement produce a liquidity problem, but if the time remaining before the settlement is long, it results in a large amount unsettled.

The reality in today's financial markets is that the volume of individual payments and other financial transactions tends to be quite large, and each transaction takes place with certain time constraints for settlement. The risk associated with unsettled amounts exists unless settlement occurs immediately upon the transaction.

Also, there are more participants in each transaction. As an illustration consider when Japanese companies obtain funds by issuing U.S. dollar bonds with stock purchase warrants in the Euromarket. Because they ultimately want yen, they need a currency swap arrangement. To accomplish this, a bank becomes involved as an extra party. Thus, an increased number of parties become involved in the normal capital-raising process, and consequently, the degree of interdependence among the parties increases.

In addition, the presence of market demand for an increased number of transactions, each of which has these characteristics, makes systemic risk more serious.

Current and Proposed Solutions to the Problem

There are many rules, both current and proposed, to try to reduce systemic risk. This is hardly the place to explore all of them, but describing some of them in the payment transactions area might help.[3]

Essentially there are two types of rules. The first, "risk control" rules, are aimed at reducing systemic risk by directly confining the component subrisks or by creating among the participants incentives to reduce the component subrisks. This can be done by statute, regulation, or private agreement among the participants. In some payment systems such as Fedwire, the central bank itself serves as the clearing agent for certain interbank payment transactions.

Quantitative rules—such as "caps" and pricing daylight overdrafts— are also in this category.[4] In Japan, for instance, the Bank of Japan does not permit daylight overdrafts, so an interbank intraday credit market emerged. The pricing mechanism in this market is somewhat unclear, however, and therefore it is difficult to evaluate whether such a market sufficiently gives the participants optimal incentives to reduce the component subrisks.

Risk control rules have problems. First, the role of central banks affects the marketplace. If the central bank is ready to help solve the liquidity problem faced by banks as they arise, there would be virtually no systemic risk. But there would be no incentives on the part of the participating banks to reduce the component subrisks. Second, and more fundamental, confining time risk or large-amount risk would discourage transactions that parties want in the marketplace and thus lead to suboptimal financial transactions. Confining pure credit risk is hardly defensible without being judged against the costs associated with such regulation.

The second type of rule relates to "finality of payment." Such rules specify the rights and obligations of the parties to a transaction, with the goal of giving them incentives to control the relevant risk through private agreement or otherwise. Many discussions have been held as to how one can best assign legal entitlement for this purpose, but this type of rule also has problems. First, again, the strategy of these rules does not work if the participants believe the central bank at some point will intervene to help. Second, even if one can successfully establish the legal framework to make finality clear, one bank may not meet its obligations to another bank, and, as a result, that second bank might fail to settle due to its interdependence.

Justifiable Regulation

In today's financial markets, there is a demand among market participants to engage in transactions involving the four component subrisks identified above. The benefits that stem from any type of regulation must be weighed against the associated costs. Confining pure credit risk, time risk, or large-amount risk might harm, rather than benefit, market participants. That systemic risk exists does not itself justify regulation. Moreover, the extent to which regulators should aim to reduce the risk is itself open to question.

Controlling time risk or large-amount risk should probably be delegated to the market, where the participants can best deal with the problem. Whether pure credit risk should be controlled by regulation has been the fundamental issue in bank regulation; this question is beyond the scope of this chapter. Suffice it to say that systemic risk is insufficient to justify stronger regulation of pure credit risk.

Interdependence risk justifies some degree of regulation for two reasons. First, interdependence produces what economists call externalities. Each participant faces risk that can be originated and expanded by a party with which it does not deal directly. It is extremely difficult and therefore costly for each participant to obtain information both as to where in the chain of participants the problem exists and how serious it is. This may justify regulatory intervention.

Second, under current law in most countries, there may be a discrepancy between economic and legal interdependence. Specifically, current laws on setoffs and bankruptcy may not mirror economic interdependence.

For instance, when two banks enter into dozens of foreign exchange executory contracts, economic interdependence is the outstanding or unsettled *net* amount they are obliged to pay to each other. But it is unclear whether current bankruptcy law recognizes this. Even if two parties explicitly agree to net out their obligations, it is unclear in some jurisdictions whether such a private agreement is enforceable when one of the parties goes into bankruptcy.

Reviewing the two types of current and proposed regulation from this perspective leads to the conclusion that neither type deals directly with interdependence among participants. The regulations may have some degree of effect on the reduction of systemic risk, but they also may impede desirable financial transactions.

Finally, a familiar and interesting question is whether there should be uniform rules worldwide or if there are different rules, whether the rules should be transparent. Only if the "right" rules can be known is there reason to have uniform rules. The reality is, however, that it is extremely difficult to agree on the right rules. Thus, one must rely on private incentives for market participants. For this reason, the rules should be as clear and transparent as possible.

Reducing Interdependence Risk

It is impossible to eliminate systemic risk unless one can reduce credit risk and liquidity risk to zero. That would impede the financial transactions demanded in today's financial markets and is thus undesirable. Systemic risk existed two decades ago, but it was not a great concern because there was little interdependence, few time constraints, and few large-amount transactions, and thus the level of systemic risk was probably lower. During recent years, however, these three components have emerged and made systemic risk a serious problem. But they have emerged because there was a demand in the marketplace for transactions having these characteristics. Among them, only interdependence justifies regulation.

Viewed this way, the importance of various netting arrangements should be given more serious attention, and in this connection, the current framework of insolvency law may need to be reconsidered with the idea that private netting arrangements should be given legal standing.

There are many different types and forms of netting arrangements, and this chapter must remain brief.[5] The idea of "netting by novation" is probably the most important. It seeks to net out outstanding obligations among network participants by substituting a single obligation for original obligations as soon as each new transaction is entered into, and netting is done before the settlement date. To what extent and to what scope this arrangement is, and should be, effectively adopted is beyond the scope of this chapter. At first glance, this arrangement seems to reduce only the amount of unsettled obligations. But it has a wider effect than that. It reduces interdependence among the participants, particularly if it is structured multilaterally.

A netting arrangement, even if treated as valid under insolvency law, does not reduce interdependence risk to zero. It does, however, reduce legal interdependence to a level at which it matches economic interdependence. True, the costs of validating such an arrangement are borne by someone, normally the creditors of the insolvent party who are not network participants. But this result would mirror economic reality better. Note also that parties have incentives for netting arrangements to reduce transaction costs, but this benefit must be judged against the cost associated with the operating system, and such a system usually requires computer-aided facilities.

There is a tendency to give at least bilateral netting arrangements validity under bankruptcy law. The United States moved in that direction when the Financial Institutions Reform, Recovery and Enforcement Act of 1989 was enacted.[6] The United Kingdom took a more comprehensive approach by enacting the Companies Act of 1989, but curiously this does not cover off-exchange transactions such as foreign exchange transactions. The trend toward validating netting arrangements is desirable, and we should keep moving in that direction in the future.

Conclusion

Even after heated discussions on systemic risk during recent years, the problem still seems chaotic. Some overreact to the issue, while others even fail to recognize that a problem exists. This confusion stems partly from a failure to consider the "right" level of risk we should want to face, and partly from a failure to consider the "right" way of controlling that risk. In theory systemic risk has always been with us. What makes the risk a serious problem in today's financial markets are interdependence among market participants, required time constraints for settlement, and unsettled large-amount transactions. The benefits of regulation should be weighed against the costs. Of the four components of risk, interdependence is the one that most justifies some form of regulation. Consequently, more direct and serious attention should be given to interdependence among network participants.

Acknowledgments

The author thanks Geoffrey Miller, Yoshiharu Oritani, and Yoshio Suzuki for their comments and suggestions.

Notes

1. An excellent theoretical analysis is found in Mengle (1989) and Scott (1989).
2. The last three are the components of liquidity risk; see Mengle (1989, p. 151).
3. The following discussion is based on Mengle (1989) and Scott (1989).
4. See Board of Governors of the Federal Reserve System, 1990.
5. For details on netting arrangements, see Group of Experts on Payment Systems of the Central Banks of the Group of Ten Countries (1989) and Wood (1990, pp. 170–92).
6. See 12 U.S. Code 1821(e).

References

Bank for International Settlements (BIS). 1989. *Large-Value Funds Transfer Systems in the Group of Ten Countries.*

Bank of Japan. 1989. *Japanese Transfer Systems in the Era of Financial Deregulation and Globalization.* The Bank of Japan Report No. 1.

Board of Governors of the Federal Reserve System. 1990. Modifications to the Payments System Risk Reduction Program: Caps and Measures of Capital for U.S. Chartered Depository Institutions. *Federal Register* 55, 22092–22095.

Corrigan, E. Gerald. 1989. Perspectives on Payment System Risk Reduction. In David B. Humphrey, ed., *The U.S. Payment System: Efficiency, Risk and the Role of the Federal Reserve.* Boston: Klumer Academic Publishers, pp. 129–139.

Group of Experts on Payment Systems of the Central Banks of the Group of Ten Countries. 1989. *Report on Netting Schemes.*

Hewitt, Michael E. 1990. Systemic Risk in International Securities Markets. In this volume.

Humphrey, David B. 1989. *The U.S. Payment System: Efficiency, Risk and the Role of the Federal Reserve.* Boston: Kluwer Academic Publishers.

Mengle, David L. 1989. Legal and Regulatory Reform in Electronic Payments: An Evaluation of Payment Finality Rules. In David B. Humphrey, ed., *The U.S. Payment System: Efficiency, Risk and the Role of the Federal Reserve.* Boston: Kluwer Academic Publishers, pp. 145–180.

Scott, Hal S. 1989. Commentary. In David B. Humphrey, ed., *The U.S. Payment System: Efficiency, Risk and the Role of the Federal Reserve.* Boston: Kluwer Academic Publishers, pp. 181–195.

Wood, Philip R. 1990. *English and International Set-Off.* London: Sweet & Maxwell.

VII NATIONAL AUTONOMY VERSUS INTERNATIONAL COOPERATION

21 COMPETITION VERSUS COMPETITIVE EQUALITY IN INTERNATIONAL FINANCIAL MARKETS

George J. Benston

Competition and the Public Interest

Competitive markets generally benefit consumers and usually benefit society in general. When markets are competitive, consumers tend to get the kinds and qualities of goods and services they want. These things are produced by firms and people according to their comparative advantages in production and distribution. Competitive markets are said to be "fair" to consumers because they, rather than some "higher" authority, determine what is produced—subject to the consumers' ability to pay, competing demands by other consumers, and the costs of production and distribution. Such markets are considered "fair" to producers because those who succeed are better at meeting consumers' demands than those who fail. Competitive markets tend to increase a nation's wealth because they are efficient allocatively and productively. That is, resources are used such that they result in the greatest output that can be achieved with existing technology. This occurs because competitive producers gain from shifting purchasing, selling, and using resources to the point where all advantages from changes are achieved (returns are equated at the margin).

Competitive equality that benefits the public would permit any firm—

domestic or foreign, commercial bank or investment company, specialized or universal, financial or industrial, or any combination thereof—to offer people any product and service, subject only to three considerations. The first is that externalities are not important. That is, the decisions made by the firms are internalized—they obtain the benefits and absorb the costs of their decisions. Furthermore, if there are externalities, the costs of dealing with them exceed the benefits, at the margin and in total. For example, manufacturers would not dump their waste into rivers or spew smoke into the air unless they either compensated those who are disadvantaged or people agreed that the loss in output was more costly than the loss of good water and good air.

A second consideration is that some people may not like the way the market freely allocates goods. In particular, a concern may be that people who are less able or less well endowed than others will get less. This can occur because competitive markets produce goods according to consumers' demand and producers' abilities, which depend on the distribution of wealth and talent among people. Not all such differences are disparaged, however. For example, although a very talented or lucky person may earn much more than others, this disparity usually is accepted as being fair. But the situation may not be acceptable when rich people's demands for a product in limited supply that is vital to health, such as heart transplants, leaves nothing for the poor.

The third consideration is that only the government, or some other collective coercive agency, can achieve a desired outcome. For example, standardization of weights and sizes might be imposed on a market when competing firms cannot agree on common measures. Or government certification of doctors' competence might be considered beneficial if many patients are unable to make effective judgments.

Applying the three considerations to financial markets leads me to the conclusion that some constraints on competition might be desirable. First, financial firms produce few of the usual types of negative externalities, such as pollution. But if unconstrained competition among some firms results in financial instability, causing the collapse or distress of other firms and the loss of wealth and work by "innocent" parties, restraints on competition might be justified.

Second, concern that the distribution of wealth and talent among persons in financial markets is "unfair" might justify restraints on competition. Generally, few people seem seriously upset when some players in financial markets become much wealthier than others. (Income taxes also are justified as being in accord with equity based on ability to pay.) True, there is evidence of jealousy that appears responsible for some restrictions and taxes being imposed on firms and individuals. But the greatest opprobrium appears reserved for people who are seen as playing the game unfairly. Such "unfair" acts include misinforming (cheating) people who seem unable to fend for themselves, such as the old and gullible, and trading on inside information.

Third, standardization of information disclosed in prospectuses and financial statements and government-provided deposit insurance may be justified as being more efficient than having each firm decide which information will be produced or each depositor determining which bank is prudently managed.

To summarize, restraints on competition imposed to serve the public good might be justified to reduce the probability and severity of financial instability, to make markets more fair for people who cannot protect themselves well, and to reduce the cost of information.

However, competition also may be restrained for reasons that serve the interests of some producers at the expense of consumers and other producers. In particular, some laws and regulations are designed to allow producers to form cartels that benefit them at the expense of consumers. Other restraints may help domestic producers at the expense of foreign producers and consumers. In the analysis that follows, the limitations on competition delineated are identified as serving the public or private interest.

Does Competitive Equality Exist in the United States?

At least two aspects of competitive equality are usefully distinguished. One is competition among similar types of institutions: commercial banks with commercial banks, investment banks with investment banks, thrifts with thrifts, and so forth. The other is competition among different types of institutions: commercial banks with investment banks and thrifts, banks with insurance companies, and so on. In the United States the first type of competition is practiced, at least within individual states. But competition among different types of institutions is restricted. In both regards, domestically and foreign-chartered institutions are treated equally well and equally badly.

Foreign and Domestic Firms

U.S. laws and regulations restrain domestic and foreign-chartered financial institutions equally. Securities firms are subject to the Securities Acts of 1933 and 1934, which govern the contents of securities prospectuses and the ways in which trading can proceed. The Banking Act of 1933 prohibits investment banks and securities firms from offering depository transactions accounts and banks from offering underwriting and some securities services (particularly corporate securities underwriting) to the public.

The Banking Act of 1933, the MacFadden Act, and the Douglas Amendment (Section 3d) to the Bank Holding Company Act of 1956 subject all banks to the restrictions imposed by individual states on branching and holding company acquisitions. The International Banking Act of 1978, which gives the Comptroller of the Currency the authority to license the branches and agencies of foreign banks, subjects them to the same restrictions that are imposed on national banks. (Prior to July 27, 1978, a foreign-chartered bank could open branches in several states, except those that expressly forbade their establishment.) U.S. branches of foreign-chartered banks must have federal deposit insurance unless they have no deposit accounts below $100,000, and are subject to the Federal Reserve's reserve requirements if they have worldwide assets in excess of $1 billion.

Alternative Producers of Financial Services

The United States does not treat producers of similar financial services equally. Depository institutions must purchase federal deposit insurance. They also must keep non-interest-bearing reserves with the Federal Reserve. Securities firms that transfer claims over funds by check, but with accounts not necessarily redeemable at par, cannot purchase federal deposit insurance and can invest fully all the funds they receive.

Depository institutions also are subject to field examinations and to restraints on the assets in which they can invest and activities they can conduct. However, these restraints are not consistent among depositories. In particular, commercial banks cannot invest directly in such assets as real estate and equities. Bank holding companies cannot have direct or indirect ownership or control of more than 5 percent of the voting securities or assets of any company that is not a bank or a bank holding company. Such nonbanking activities include real estate syndication, management, brokerage and development, management consulting, and underwriting life insurance not sold in connection with a credit transaction of the holding company or a subsidiary. Savings and loan associations and savings banks can hold direct investments, subject to severe limitations, and can be involved in many types of real-estate-related activities. Depositories cannot underwrite corporate securities and other than general-revenue state and municipal securities. Nor can depositories chartered in all but a few states sell insurance. Insurance firms can make loans but cannot offer transactions accounts directly.

Depository institutions cannot branch except within states. While bank holding companies now can own subsidiaries within regions (by mid-1992, most states will permit nationwide acquisitions), this form of organization is not as efficient as branching is. Branching within many states is additionally restricted. Other suppliers of financial services, however, are not geographically limited.

Furthermore, only banks can own banks, although any firm can own a savings and loan. As a result of this restriction, together with geographical limitations, it is very difficult to displace the managers of poorly run banks. Economies of scope and scale also are limited by constraints on mergers between banks in different states and with nonbank firms.

Public Interest Reasons for Restricting Depository Institutions

As discussed above, the public-interest rationale for these restrictions on depository institutions can be justified by reference to avoiding externalities, fairness to disadvantaged persons, and superior government efficiency. The externality of financial instability has been asserted as an important reason for restricting assets and activities, particularly securities-related services and equity investments. However, both economic reasoning and a large body of empirical findings do not support these restrictions. Relatively few failures in the United States prior to or during the Great Depression or elsewhere at any time have been due to banks' securities holdings or activities. Indeed, a number of empirical studies support the view that securities operations allow banks to diversify more effectively, thereby reducing the variance of their cash flows and the risk of failure.[1] It also is well established that restraints on geographical diversification imposed by prohibitions against nationwide branching and limitations on intrastate branching have been responsible for a very large number of U.S. bank failures in the 1920s, 1930s, and 1980s.[2] Restraints on the portfolios of savings and loan associations are responsible for the insolvency of thousands of these specialized institutions in the early 1980s as a result of the sharp rise in interest rates in 1979–1981. The cost of this disaster is likely to exceed $150 billion (in present value terms).

Furthermore, should one or more banks fail or should there be a run on solvent banks, the Federal Reserve can prevent a systemic collapse by providing reserves through open market operations or directly to banks through the discount window. The necessity for the Federal Reserve to act has been sharply reduced by the presence of federal deposit insurance, which removes most depositors' incentives to withdraw protected funds from any insured depository, regardless of its solvency.

Concern that disadvantaged persons might be treated unfairly because of conflicts of interest has been raised in support of prohibiting depository institutions from offering such products as securities and insurance. The Glass-Steagall Act's separation of commercial and investment banking is based, in part, on the belief that when the two functions were commonly provided, unwary depositors were misled into buying bad securities, banks underwrote securities of borrowers so that they could repay unprofitable loans to those banks, banks made loans to securities purchasers to support their purchase of securities the bank underwrote, and bankers used inside information to the disadvantage of their customers. I examined these and all other conflict of interest claims raised in the literature, in great detail, and found none of them supported by the evidence (Benston, 1990, ch. 4). Prohibiting banks from offering insurance and other products is based, in part, on concerns about tie-in sales where, presumably, bank borrowers would have to buy these products at higher-than-market prices to get loans. Aside from the lack of empirical evidence supporting this concern, it makes no economic sense, because a bank that has the power to force borrowers to pay higher prices for collateral products can more readily use that power to get borrowers simply to pay more for their bank loans. Furthermore, conflicts of interest possibilities are present in most dealings among people, including securities sales by brokers who also are dealers, loans offered by insurance companies, and credit offered by retailers and manufacturers. Considering the relative simplicity of bank products and the clarity with which they are priced, and the general sophistication of consumers of financial products, there would seem to be less reason for public concern about conflicts of interest and fairness to disadvantaged people who deal with banks than for the customers of other suppliers.

Superior government efficiency might justify requiring depository institutions to have federally supplied deposit insurance. Such insurance saves individual depositors from having to learn about and monitor the activities of their banks. Furthermore, since only the federal government can prevent or cause a systemic collapse, only the government can be the ultimate insurer of deposits. A consequence of federal deposit insurance, though, is that the deposit insurance agencies must do the monitoring that depositors otherwise would do. As is noted above, restrictions on the assets and activities of depository institutions have been justified as necessary to protect the deposit insurance funds. However, as applied, these restrictions have had the opposite effect. As I and many others have argued, the legitimate concerns of the deposit insurance agency can be met better with capital requirements that are sufficiently high to absorb expected losses and give capital owners incentives to avoid excessive risks, together with predetermined rules that require restraints and recapitalization as capital is depleted, and reorganization and closure before capital is used up.[3]

Private Interest Reasons for Restricting Depository Institutions

I believe that the principal reason for restricting depository institutions is protection of suppliers of financial services and other products. Restrictions on branching can be explained, in part, by public fears of centralized financial power. While these fears may be used politically to support geographic restrictions, they are empirically and logically baseless. Technological changes have made it possible for banking services to be offered to consumers almost anywhere, thereby making it virtually impossible for any supplier to monopolize a market area. Furthermore, geographic entry restrictions apply only to deposits. Any firm can offer loans anywhere. In addition, the increasing internationalization of financial services and the U.S. policy of allowing foreign firms to compete equally with domestic firms provides an important source of alternative suppliers. And, both formal empirical studies and casual observation indicate that depository institutions do not enjoy economies of scale such that a few giant-sized institutions would dominate the market if there were no legal restraints on growth.

Restrictions on the products that depository institutions can offer the public similarly are due, I believe, to efforts by other suppliers to restrain competition and by organized consumer groups to obtain funds at favorable terms. Restricted products and activities include securities underwriting and trading, insurance underwriting and sales, real estate operations, and travel services. The continued governmental insistence (as expressed in the Financial Institutions Reform, Recovery and Enforcement Act of 1989) that savings and loan associations make and hold residential mortgages or mortgage-backed securities and that depository institutions pay particular attention to their local markets (as required by the Community Reinvestment Act) similarly represent the successful efforts of some people to obtain favorable treatment. Considering that mortgages now are available from a very large number of suppliers, almost on a nationwide basis, the reasons for these laws do not appear to be otherwise explained.

Comparative Advantages and Disadvantages of Domestic and Foreign Firms

As noted above, domestic and foreign producers of financial services are subject to the same laws and regulations in the United States. In this important regard, they enjoy competitive equality. But both types of firms have comparative advantages with respect to the customers they serve, production and distribution costs, and possibly subsidies provided and taxes imposed by their governments.

Customers Served

Banks and other financial services firms usually have comparative advantages in serving their own countrymen. This advantage comes from their knowledge of customs, laws and regulations, and from prior and continuing business and sometimes personal relationships. Consequently, it is not surprising that the major variable associated with the extent of foreign banking in the United States is the presence of companies from the foreign banks' countries. Foreign securities and insurance firms, on the other hand, are not likely to have comparative advantages of this sort, except in serving expatriates from their home country who feel more comfortable dealing with them than with U.S. firms.

Production and Distribution Advantages

One lesser cost of production that foreign banks might have is lower cost of capital. This advantage is said to accrue to Japanese banks because of the much higher rate of domestic saving and fewer investment opportunities in Japan than in the United States. In addition, explicit government liability insurance and cooperative practices among institutions may allow Japanese (and other foreign) banks to hold relatively less capital than U.S. banks must hold. Consequently, Japanese banks might find loans profitable that U.S. banks find unprofitable.

Some foreign banks may be able to employ production and distribution innovations that U.S. consumers find desirable. For example, being polite to customers seems to be an innovation that Japanese banks employ. However, U.S. banks seem to have a comparative advantage in creating innovative financial instruments, takeover and merger financing, and consumer services. European bankers who have experience in providing total financial services to customers (including securities underwriting) may have comparative advantages over their U.S. counterparts. Alternatively, European bankers may not be able to operate as well in the United States because of their lack of experience with restrictive U.S. laws.

In any event, consumers in the United States benefit from any comparative advantages held by foreign bankers, whether these are due to lower costs of capital, superior technologies, or the application of innovations and knowledge developed in other markets. While domestic bankers may find competing with foreigners difficult, they also are likely to benefit from adopting these bankers' innovations. Indeed, they may be able to profit from being followers who, having more knowledge about their markets, can adapt foreigners' innovations more effectively than can the innovators.

Government Subsidies and Taxes

It is very difficult, if not impossible, to determine whether foreign governments subsidize their banks, thus giving them a comparative advantage over U.S. banks. A study by a committee of the American Bankers Association (ABA) reports the tax rates paid by banks in 11 major industrial countries (Economic Advisory Committee, ABA, 1990, exhibit IV.5). The lowest average tax rates are paid by banks in Belgium (27 percent), Switzerland (21 percent to 26 percent), and the United States (28 percent). The highest average rates are levied by West Germany (49 percent to 60 percent), Japan (44 percent to 56 percent), and Italy (48 percent). However, these rates do not reflect the cost to banks of avoiding taxes. For example, U.S. banks can avoid taxes by investing in state and municipal bonds, but they must accept a lower yield. Thus, the tax rate they report is understated. U.S. banks also must keep non-interest-bearing accounts with the Federal Reserve, which is another form of tax.

A bank can be subsidized with government deposits on which interest at market rates is not paid, and with below-market-rate borrowings from the central bank. The ABA study (1990, pp. 78, 85) shows that only banks in Japan had such borrowings in more than very small amounts; the Japanese banks' percentage is 1.2 percent of assets. Federal funds are held in banks at below-market interest rates in Belgium, Canada, France, Italy, and Japan (ABA, 1990, p. 85).

But, even if it were clear that some country subsidized its banks, the effect is a transfer of wealth from one group of taxpayers to another in that country. If that country's banks used their subsidy to reduce the cost of their products to consumers in the United States, some of the subsidy would be transferred to U.S. consumers.

To summarize, if foreign banks can offer less expensive or better products to U.S. consumers, those consumers benefit. There is no public interest in protecting domestic suppliers of these products from such foreign competition.

International Financial Supervision

The analysis presented thus far indicates that restrictive legislation in the United States primarily disadvantages U.S. consumers and some U.S. producers, particularly chartered depositories. It sometimes is alleged that less onerous restrictions in other countries give foreign banks an advantage over their U.S. competitors. This allegation gives rise to demands for a "level playing field," where all similar producers are similarly restrained.

I should state that there is no public-interest advantage from international regulation. If a country regulates its financial institutions badly (that is, in a manner that harms its consumers), the cost is borne by people in that country. For example, should a badly supervised or undercapitalized bank in a foreign country fail, depositors whose funds are not insured may lose some or all of their investments. The cost of inadequate supervision, therefore, is born either by depositors or taxpayers in that country. This should not be a concern to citizens of another country.

However, domestic suppliers of financial services might complain that their poorly supervised or capitalized foreign competitors enjoy lower costs, and hence have a competitive advantage. But, as I discuss above, this "subsidy" is paid by the taxpayers of the foreign bank's country and is enjoyed, in part, by consumers in other countries. While this disadvantages suppliers in those countries, their losses are more than offset by consumers' gains.

Two possible externalities, though, should be considered. The first is disruption of the international payments system and losses imposed on banks to which failed banks are indebted. This risk, however, is no different than the risks faced by a bank in lending to any customer. Indeed, the risk is lower because most countries tend implicitly to guarantee their banks' deposits. Furthermore, the risk of loss can be reduced by requiring banks that use the international payments system to hold sufficient levels of capital to render failure very unlikely.

The second externality is disruption to international financial markets as a result of a "loss of confidence." This possibility, though, should be of even lesser concern. Indeed, banks perceived to be sound benefit when depositors run from banks thought to be insolvent. Furthermore, unlike a domestic situation, there cannot be a multiple contraction of world money as a result of people taking funds out of a fractional reserve banking system by hoarding specie or currency, for the simple reason that there is no world money.

Therefore, I conclude that lax supervision and insufficient regulation of foreign banks, should that occur, might be of concern to taxpayers in their countries, but not to U.S. taxpayers. It also is doubtful that U.S. banks would lose customers with whom they want to do business to failure-prone foreign banks.[4]

What, then, is the function of the international capital standards recently promulgated by the Bank for International Settlements (BIS) and adopted by most of the major financial countries? The BIS capital standard is said to be "risk-based." But, as the following brief summary of the standard shows, risks are very poorly measured. Four very broad asset "risk" classes are specified. No capital is required for government debt, even though considerable losses can be incurred from fixed-interest-rate obligations when interest rates unexpectedly increase. A 50 percent weight is applied to home mortgage loans, despite the fact that large losses were incurred on such obligations in the United States and elsewhere during periods of deflation and local real estate collapses. Full weight is applied to all commercial loans, whether they are made to large or small firms, to thinly or well-capitalized companies, or to any country. No consideration is given to the fact that the total risk of a bank is a function of the interrelationships among the cash flows from its assets *and* its liabilities. Subordinated debt is not fully counted as capital despite the fact that it protects depositors as much as does equity capital. Furthermore, banks' assets and liabilities are measured in terms of traditional accounting historical costs rather than economic market values. Thus, it cannot be said that the BIS capital standard puts banks on an equal footing or is of much value in reducing the risk of bank failure.

The principal function of the BIS standard, I believe, is to give banking regulators a means by which they can affect the capital held by banks in their own countries. U.S. taxpayers and well-run banks would benefit from this situation if, as a result, incentives toward excessive risk taking engendered by deposit insurance were mitigated. Unfortunately, the BIS standard is seriously flawed in two regards. First, as is just discussed, risk is measured very poorly. Second, not allowing banks to fully count subordinated debentures as capital imposes a tax burden on them without compensating benefits. Consequently, U.S. banks and banks in countries with a similar tax structure are likely to be disadvantaged by the BIS capital standard.

Conclusions

Competition is beneficial to consumers of financial services. Few externalities are present in financial markets, and considerations of fairness and the distribution of wealth play small roles. Most consumers of financial products are sophisticated, and the benefits from these products are roughly proportional to one's wealth. Hence, there should be few concerns that unrestrained competition would not result in social benefit.

However, suppliers of financial services can benefit from constraints on their competitors. Such constraints pervade U.S. financial markets. Commercial and investment banks are not permitted to compete for underwritings and demand deposits, banks cannot open deposit-taking offices in any state or sell insurance, and different regulations and restraints apply to institutions supplying essentially the same product. The effect of these constraints is reduced benefits to consumers.

But foreign and domestic suppliers of financial services are treated approximately equally in the United States (and most other developed countries). To the extent that one group or the other has a competitive advantage, the benefits are attained by domestic consumers. This is the case whether the advantages stem from production or marketing efficiencies and innovations or from subsidies paid by taxpayers in foreign countries.

Moves toward international regulatory standardization may be costly to U.S. consumers of financial services if the result is the imposition of higher costs on either domestic or foreign producers. The BIS capital standard, in particular, will be either ineffective (because it does not provide a meaningful measure of risk) or costly (to the extent that banks must hold equity rather than debt capital). If the BIS standard actually requires foreign banks to hold more capital, the taxpayers and well-capitalized banks in those countries may benefit. But U.S. consumers will lose the subsidy formerly paid by taxpayers in those countries.

Notes

1. See Benston (1990, chs. 3 and 7) for reviews of this evidence.
2. See White (1983). Evidence on the Great Depression is reviewed in Benston (1990, ch. 3).
3. See Benston and Kaufman (1988) and the Shadow Financial Regulatory Committee's Statement 41, February 13, 1989. This proposal and an alternative of having deposits either invested only in marketable securities or collateralized by such securities in amounts sufficient to secure the deposits (a form of the "narrow bank" proposal) is described and discussed in Benston et al. (1989).

4. I am not aware of any evidence supporting the allegation that financial institutions relocate to escape prudential supervision. This claim is made by Richard Dale in his book *The Regulation of International Banking* (Cambridge, UK: Woodhead-Faulkner, (1984). However, the only examples he provides are of banks attempting to avoid taxes and government restrictions on capital movements.

References

Benston, George J. 1990. *The Separation of Commercial and Investment Banking: The Glass-Steagall Act Revisited and Reconsidered.* New York: Oxford University Press.

Benston, George J., and Kaufman, George G. 1988. *Risk and Solvency Regulation of Depository Institutions: Past Policies and Current Options.* New York: Salomon Brothers Center for the Study of Financial Institutions, Graduate School of Business Administration, New York University, monograph 1988–1.

Benston, George J., Brumbaugh, R. Dan Jr., Guttentag, Jack M., Herring, Richard J., Kaufman, George G., Litan, Robert E., and Scott, Kenneth E. 1989. *Blueprint for Restructuring America's Financial Institutions.* Washington, DC: The Brookings Institution.

White, Eugene N. 1983. *The Regulation and Reform of the American Banking System, 1900–1929.* Princeton, NJ: Princeton University Press.

22 REGULATORY HARMONIZATION TO ACHIEVE EFFECTIVE INTERNATIONAL COMPETITION

Paul Guy

International regulation of financial markets is becoming more and more of a pressing question. *Regulation* may actually not be the correct word, since we are really speaking of improving cooperation and coordinating and harmonizing securities and futures regulations on the international level.

The International Organization of Securities Commissions (IOSCO), an international, private, not-for-profit organization, was created in 1984 to address these issues. Its predecessor organization, the Interamerican Association of Securities Commissions and Similar Agencies, was created in 1974 to assist in the development of securities markets in Latin America. At its annual meeting in 1984, the members approved new bylaws designed to transform the organization into an international body. In 1986, at its annual meeting in Paris, the members decided to set up a permanent secretariat in Montreal. I was then designated its Secretary General.

Securities administrators of 50 countries are now members of IOSCO and have resolved, through its permanent structures: (1) to cooperate to ensure better regulation, on the domestic and the international level, in order to maintain fair and efficient markets; (2) to exchange information on their respective experiences in order to promote the development of domestic markets; (3) to unite efforts to establish standards and an effective surveillance of international securities transactions; (4) to provide mutual assistance to ensure the integrity of markets by a rigorous application and enforcement of standards.

The Structure of IOSCO

The General Secretariat coordinates the diversified year-long activities of the specialized committees of the organization. IOSCO's Presidents Committee meets once a year during the organization's annual conferences. It is made up of all the presidents of member agencies (regular and associate members) and is vested with the powers necessary to achieve the purpose of the organization.

IOSCO's Executive Committee meets periodically during the year and makes all decisions necessary to achieve the purpose of the organization in accordance with the guidelines established by the Presidents Committee. The Executive Committee is made up of eight elected members, from which are chosen a chairman and a vice chairman, and a representative of each of the three permanent regional standing committees. The elected members are elected by the Presidents Committee for a term of two years.

The eight elected members of the Executive Committee are from the following organizations: the National Companies and Securities Commission of Australia, the Commission des operations de bourse of France, the Commissione Nazionale per le Societa e la Borsa of Italy, the Securities Bureau of the Ministry of Finance of Japan, the Comision Nacional de Valores of Mexico, the Ontario Securities Commission, the Securities and Investments Board of the United Kingdom, and the Securities and Exchange Commission of the United States. Currently, the representative of the U.S. Securities and Exchange Commission is acting as Chairman, and the French Commission's representative is acting as Vice-Chairman of the Executive Committee.

The other three members of the Executive Committee are the securities administrators designated by the regional standing committees, currently those from Chile, New Zealand, and Sweden.

IOSCO has three regional standing committees that meet to discuss the specific regional problems of member organizations: the Interamerican Regional Committee, the European Regional Committee, and the Asia-Pacific Regional Committee. As noted, these representatives sit on the Executive Committee.

The Executive Committee of the organization has also created two specialized working committees. The first, the Technical Committee on

International Transactions, was created in May 1987 and is composed of representatives of the securities agencies that regulate the most developed markets. Its aim is to review regulatory problems related to international securities transactions and to find expedient and practical solutions. The second body, the Development Committee, is composed of representatives of regulators of emerging markets; it seeks to promote the development of these markets and to find solutions to the problems they face.

In addition, two Consultative Committees have been established to allow affiliate members to participate in the work undertaken by IOSCO. These committees meet at the discretion of the Secretary-General. Affiliate members who are not members of the Presidents Committee and who do not have a right to vote use the Consultative Committees as vehicles for input concerning the work of the Technical or the Development Committee, and for first-hand information on the different activities, of IOSCO.

There are three categories of members: regular, associate, and affiliate. Each regular member has one vote. The associate members have no vote and are not eligible to serve on the Executive Committee. The affiliate members have no vote and are not eligible for the Executive or Presidents Committees, but are members of a Consultative Committee that meets to discuss specific issues.

A securities commission, or a similar government agency, may apply to become a member of the organization. The same applies to a self-regulatory organization, such as a stock exchange responsible for securities regulations. IOSCO is financed by the annual contributions of its members.

Competitive Equality and the Role of IOSCO

Competitive equality can only be achieved if there is equality of regulation or, at least, compatible regulation. *Regulation* is used here in a very broad sense and includes access, capital requirements, clearing and settlement, and securities and futures regulations and other regulatory questions.

The question of access is very important because barriers can be so great as to effectively limit or impede foreign competition. Such limitations would seriously affect or prevent competition in international transactions. Markets must therefore be open to allow competitive equality. As defined by the OECD, an open market is one where securities-related services have full access to the market and full freedom to operate in any subsector of the securities sector, either as an established presence in the country or on a cross-border basis. An open market can also be viewed as a market where the treatment of foreign participants is no less favorable than that of domestic participants.

Some of the barriers to access are political—erected by governments to limit entry of foreign participants. Others are regulatory; some countries, for example, create barriers to prevent the entry of foreign banks, while others insist on strict reciprocity.

IOSCO cannot do much about political barriers except to pressure governments to relax restrictions. These barriers are disappearing in developed markets, but IOSCO must continue to actively support their removal and press for open markets.

IOSCO is most effective in the area of regulatory barriers. It created the Technical Committee on International Transactions in 1987 to examine impediments to international transactions and to propose ways of eliminating these impediments. To achieve this objective, the Technical Committee set up a number of working parties.

The Technical Committee, which is composed of senior-level representatives of the securities agencies of the more developed of world markets, met for the first time in London in July 1987 for a review of the problems facing securities regulators in international transactions. Important issues were prioritized, and corresponding specialized working groups were created to identify and implement acceptable solutions. These working groups periodically report to the Technical Committee, which reviews progress, provides guidance, and has the authority to make final decisions. The working parties are examining the following questions:

1. The first working party is studying the problems related to equity offerings of securities on an international basis (including "euro-equity offerings") and the problems of multiple listings.

2. The second works with the International Accounting Standards Committee and the International Federation of Accountants with a view toward establishing accounting and auditing standards that securities regulators might accept in the event of international offerings and multiple listings.

3. The third examines problems of definition and maintenance of capital requirements for multinational securities firms (and also for banks doing securities business) and the exchange of financial information.

4. The fourth has the mandate to identify problems with existing Memorandum of Understanding (MOUs) between securities and futures regulators through practical case analysis, along with problems experienced in negotiating MOUs.

5. The fifth is responsible for identifying regulatory problems created by the growth of international off-market trading.

6. The sixth works to find solutions to international clearing and settlement problems.

7. The seventh has the mandate to draw up proposals which ensure coordination among futures regulators, including the establishment of criteria that could be used by regulators to recognize futures markets and futures intermediaries.

A new working party on rules of ethics for financial intermediaries was set up in January 1990. It seeks to develop an internationally acceptable code of conduct for intermediaries.

For each of these questions, major work never before undertaken has been accomplished in a great spirit of international cooperation. The results were first made public during the Venice Conference in September 1989. Two major reports were published: one on international equity offers and the other on capital adequacy standards for securities firms. These are the first concrete steps taken toward harmonization in these areas of regulation. Of course, substantial work remains to be done. It is important that the international financial community give wide and effective support to the initiatives of IOSCO.

In the matter of clearing and settlement, IOSCO has followed with great interest the proposals of the Group of Thirty, the International Federation of Stock Exchanges (FIBV), and the European Economic Community. The importance of this question for the stability of the international financial system is undeniable and the Technical Committee has, as a first step, given its unequivocal support to the private initiatives undertaken. During the next year the question of clearing and settlement of international transactions will be the focus of close attention by IOSCO. The objective is, first, to examine the basic attributes of national clearing and settlement systems, including their relationship with derivative markets and their interface with national payment systems; and to evaluate these attributes from the perspective of systemic vulnerability, risk management, and ultimately risk elimination, which is a prime responsibility of regulators. A second objective is to propose and set up common minimum regulatory standards for the approval of cross-border linkages.

Accounting and auditing standards are also an important area where significant steps have been taken. The working party, in cooperation with the International Accounting Standards Committee (IASC), concentrated its efforts on proposals designed to reduce the number of options in international standards. This effort culminated in the publication, by IASC, of *Exposure Draft 32 on Comparability of Financial Statements*. After a worldwide consultation, the IASC Board has taken a final position on E-32 and issued after its June 1991 meeting a formal statement of intent concerning changes to be made in international standards. At the request of IOSCO, IASC has also created another Steering Committee to deal with questions of completeness of standards, disclosure, and the amount of detail required. IOSCO will be an active participant in the work of this committee. In terms of auditing, an analysis of international guidelines has been completed and an agreement has been reached with the International Federation of Accountants on the changes to be made to these guidelines. The issue of independence was also examined, and proposals should be forthcoming.

IOSCO provides a high-profile forum where the securities regulations of all the largest and most sophisticated markets of the world meet to: find practical solutions to the most important problems affecting international securities markets; and generate the necessary consensus to legally implement the above-mentioned solutions through major "national" markets.

It is important to stress that practical solutions are not elaborated in a regulators' vacuum; the international financial community meets for consultation during the Annual Conferences of IOSCO and the Consultative Committees provide specific feedback from self-regulatory organizations (SROs) and international organizations. Stock exchanges and other SROs can now become affiliate members of IOSCO and participate in the activities of the Consultative Committee. These committees allow the affiliate members to contribute directly to the work being carried out by the Technical Committee.

Since IOSCO also regroups the regulatory authorities of several emerging securities markets, the implementation of innovative solutions becomes all the easier.

Given that the present world regulatory structure is based on a mosaic of state regulations, it is illusory to think of a supranational regulator to deal with the pressing problems affecting international securities markets. As a consequence, the only practical and effective alternative is the consensus approach with national regulators meeting in the neutral international forum that is IOSCO.

If the consensus approach is to be successful (i.e., lead to the eventual voluntary decision of participants to adopt consensus solutions) experience has shown that a basic rule of thumb must be respected: solutions are more likely to be realized if they have been detailed by those who will actually implement changes. The member securities regulators of IOSCO must, through their own efforts, staff commitment, and resources, together hammer out the solutions to be proposed for implementation. The adoption of a proposal by a majority of the Technical Committee brings significant pressure on the other regulators to go forward with the recommendations. IOSCO must not become a huge international bureaucratic machine only capable of producing theoretical reports adopted in principle but likely to be forgotten in the archives of good intentions.

A frequent and very unfair criticism is that IOSCO has not matched the results of the Bank of International Settlement (BIS) Committee in the regulation of securities markets. This fails to recognize it took the BIS Committee 12 years to reach agreement on capital adequacy. IOSCO has been working on the above issues for less than three years, and it will not take IOSCO 12 years to get results. Also, the question of capital adequacy for IOSCO members is much more complicated than for BIS members. We must arrive at capital adequacy standards for multinational securities firms and for banks doing securities business and we must find solutions where the notion of equivalence or convergence will be used.

In conclusion, I am very pleased by the work accomplished, but we must not rest on our laurels. Competitive equality will not be achieved until we resolve some of the problems I have described. IOSCO must continue to press for open markets and to work toward harmonization of regulations that create major barriers to full competition. Harmonization does not necessarily mean that regulations must be identical. In some cases—in the area of international offers, for example—it may mean that we will recommend a reciprocal approach with mutual recognition of disclosure documents. In other cases—such as capital adequacy—it may mean that world regulators will have to agree on minimum standards. Application of the solution recommended will vary depending on the issue in question, but it is important to ensure some uniformity of the level of standards; low standards create a serious impediment to competition if they are not put in place by all the major markets.

If competitive equality is to be achieved, the regulators of major markets will have to work together and agree to compromise. Harmonization will not come about unless most regulators are willing to devote major effort to the work in progress. It must be done; there is no other choice. Members of the Technical Committee of IOSCO realize this and have committed significant resources to this end.

When we have solved some of these problems—and we must do so quickly—we will have made important steps toward competitive equality.

23 REGULATING GLOBAL FINANCIAL MARKETS: PROBLEMS AND SOLUTIONS

Brian Quinn

I will begin with some general observations and look ahead at the factors that may affect national and international markets. I will then go on to discuss the resulting pressures on institutions and financial systems, and finally discuss the challenges these pose for regulators and supervisors.

Outlook

First, there seems no reason to think that substantial imbalances between the supply of and demand for funds will not continue in the period ahead, and perhaps even grow. At the level of national economies, this has been a feature of the system in the United Kingdom in the last 15 years or so, where the savings ratio of the personal and corporate sectors has varied considerably in defiance of forecasters' expectations. Mr. Yamada described flows in the corporate and personal sectors in the Japanese economy, offering a useful insight into the forces at work there. The same situation may well occur in other countries, perhaps even the United States. Significant imbalances may well persist at an international level as well. That is not necessarily to say we will have something on the scale of

299

the oil shock, but the relative behavior and attitudes of investors toward, for instance, the United States and Southeast Asia may well evolve and undergo very substantial change. The United States has been fortunate to have its twin deficits financed by flows of funds coming from Japan and other surplus countries, but this is perhaps unlikely to endure in quite the form and within the price range that has characterized the last few years. Developments in Eastern Europe are also likely to have a profound, if at this stage unpredictable, effect on the future movements of available funds.

Second, the liberalization and internationalization of finance will continue. The genie is out of the bottle. Suppliers and users of funds will not be content to shop at home and, while the pace of liberalization may flag in North America or Western Europe, there is still enormous scope in other parts of the world. It is interesting and encouraging to see the change of emphasis that has occurred in the European Community itself. In 1989, when I visited the United States, I was repeatedly met with worries that Europe was turning inward and denying access to participants from other markets. That feeling now seems much less prominent and less prevalent than it did then. However, while internationalization may grow, I am not sure that globalization will grow in the same way. The word has, of course, different meanings according to the person using it, but a study carried out by Price Waterhouse about a year ago suggests that the number of participants on both supply and demand sides who engage in globalization of financial services and products—that is to say, 24-hour, 'round-the-clock business—is actually very limited. The main contenders for that role are probably already in place.

Third, there can be little doubt that technology will continue to create the ability to do new things and to do old things better, or at the very least quicker.

Fourth, competition both nationally and internationally is unlikely to abate. It goes hand in hand with both liberalization and the internationalization of finance, and I see no signs that participants in the marketplace are likely to withdraw from competition for the available customers. In that connection it is striking that capital markets have in some sectors substantially overtaken banking markets. This has happened already in the United States, and it is happening in the United Kingdom. Indeed, many banks who come to London from Europe and from other countries are interested not in doing conventional banking business but in trading operations and capital market transactions. Significantly, both Germany and France are seeking to develop their own capital markets, and it is very likely that this type of business will continue to evolve.

Pressures

If the trends outlined above are broadly right, or at least not significantly wrong, financial institutions, and particularly banks, will be pressed to do more and to take more risks. Capital and managerial skills, increasingly mobile, will seek out the most profitable outlets, both nationally and internationally. This will prompt banks in particular, but also securities houses, to move into, or perhaps to stray into, new areas of risk. At the same time, they will also seek to economize on capital as well as liquidity. It is not surprising that netting has become such a prominent theme of discussion: it is a very good example of a technique which, at least in principle, reduces the number of transactions and therefore the transaction costs. It reduces also the need to hold liquidity, again by reducing the number and size of transactions; and it reduces the amount of capital needed to support the credit risks involved in the transactions. Netting is therefore being examined and advocated by banks, who are interested in it both on a bilateral and multilateral basis. As a supervisor, I am concerned that the risks in some of these efforts to economize are not fully understood; I will come back to this point later.

Market volatility will add further pressure. It may continue to increase in a straight line; it may accelerate. Turnover in certain markets, particularly the principal securities markets, will probably increase, and I do not believe the explosion of activity in derivative products is finished yet. Nor has the rediscovery of trading in foreign exchange among banks yet fully run its course. If there is expansion in these kinds of activities, then it may be that contagion, the communication of risk between those markets (which are becoming more closely interlinked), will become a stronger possibility.

In the face of these pressures—and perhaps as a pressure in itself—there will be further rationalization, particularly among banks. Traditional retail banks with large branch networks and associated expenses are often competing with others who do not have to support these burdens. The investment in computerization and in capacity is a huge one if they are to compete in the new markets, and some will not make it. When rationalization comes, the principal question for the supervisor or central banker is whether it will be orderly and well managed or whether it will be disorderly.

Finally, there is the possibility that financial crime may increase. Someone whose views I respect argues that there is a given quantum of crime in the world, distributed between the financial sector and the other sectors; it will manifest itself most obviously and most notably in a bull market. But certainly, as competition increases and with it the temptation to take risks, and as the association between risk-taking, performance, and remuneration grows ever greater, the specter of a further increase in financial crime must at least be raised.

Implications for Regulators and Supervisors

If the picture painted above is broadly true, that markets will become even more competitive, that international markets will become increasingly capable of affecting one another in terms of performance, and that the financial pressures on institutions, whether banks or securities companies, are unlikely to abate, then it follows that there are a number of issues that supervisors must address. First, preventative action by supervisors and regulators is crucial. Second, there needs to be a framework and arrangements for crisis management, which may need reconsideration or development. And third, international cooperation and coordination should be pursued.

Preventative Action

Perhaps most important, supervisors and regulators must understand the risks that banks and securities companies are running, and must satisfy themselves that those companies also understand the risks. Nor, as markets become increasingly integrated, should insurance companies be forgotten. That may sound an obvious, even a modest, objective; but I believe it is crucial. It is not the regulator's job to tell the banks how to run their business and control their risk. But, as financial institutions get further toward the edges of the marketplace, involved in ever more complex financial transactions, there are reasonable grounds for suspecting that there may be deficiences in their understanding of the risks they are running.

For instance, there is quite strong pressure in the United Kingdom and more generally for regulators to reduce their capital and liquidity requirements on the basis of netting systems that have been set up by the banks. Even relatively straightforward bilateral netting, of the same kind of transactions in the same currency in the same jurisdiction, has hardly been tested in law; and the risks involved in this form of netting are simple and easily identified when compared with those involved in multilateral netting systems that cross borders and may involve institutions netting in a third country's currency and jurisdiction. Such schemes may not be as robust in a liquidation as the participants suppose.

The publication of the Cross Report on the risks of derivative products and the generality of off-balance-sheet activity revealed something of an information gap. Senior bankers responded to that report by saying that they hadn't quite realized the nature of what they were doing, nor were they fully informed by their own traders or staff of the magnitude of the risks involved. I suspect something of the same kind may be true in respect to netting schemes.

More recently, the Bank of England and other central banks have readdressed and drawn attention to the risks associated with payments systems generally. The Governor of the Bank of England spoke at a 1989 Sykes Memorial Lecture about the risks in wholesale payments systems, where the volume of transactions, the speed of activity, and the nature of the risks have changed quite considerably in recent years. Similarly, the Federal Reserve Board in Washington, D.C., held a symposium in 1989 in which they set out, in a rather frightening but nonetheless thoroughly worthy way, the risks attending the operations of the principal payments systems in the United States.

Second, supervisors and regulators have to keep in view the "extracurricular" operations of the institutions which they regulate. It is vital that new products and off-shore and unconsolidated activities should not escape the supervisor's attention. This is not just a case of preventing gaps in supervision from developing and enduring; supervisors must also look at the whole package. There is a general tendency in today's financial world to specialize, to segment the various risks that an institution runs—credit, liquidity, operational, market risks. While it is valuable to analyze these risks separately, a supervisor must also put them all together. There may be one supervisor or many looking at individual risks, but someone has to stand back and look at the totality of risk in the whole balance sheet.

In addition to these measurable risks, the supervisor needs also to look at the quality of a bank's management, at risks that are inherent in a bank or financial institution's systems and controls. He must also be certain that deposit protection arrangements are both adequate and appropriate. In the European Community, progress toward a single market has begun to address standards of deposit protection and whether those arrangements need to be harmonized.

Third, supervisors should be seeking to establish a reasonable equivalence of regulation between the various financial institutions and across financial markets. I say "equivalence" and not "equality" or "harmonization," because I believe that those objectives are a chimera, unachievable in anything like the time we have to decide the policy issues. Furthermore, too many of the critical variables have their origins in areas beyond the supervisor's influence. Financial institutions are, first of all, companies (for the most part) and therefore subject to company law, to the fiscal regime, and to the accounting framework as well as the regulatory requirements in each country. It is not realistic to expect that legal, fiscal, and accounting frameworks will be harmonized along with the regulatory framework, just for banks or financial institutions. Broad equivalence of regulatory frameworks is therefore an appropriate target, and one for which the BIS (Bank for International Settlements) Capital Convergence Standards aimed. While some may criticize these standards for their failure to produce a truly equal competitive environment, I nonetheless believe that the result was a significant move forward. There has been a material enhancement of the strength of banks worldwide, and a good deal of the erosion of capital standards and of prudent behavior has been stopped. These are, of course, early impressions, but I believe they are already being vindicated.

Crisis Management

A similar theme characterizes my view of crisis management. Since each crisis has its own characteristics, it will never be easy to draw up blueprints for handling them. It may well be that it is not appropriate to try. There is, however, a framework already in place for dealing with a crisis, and the experience of 1987 suggests that it works effectively. When the equity market underwent an unprecedented drop in a very short time, central bankers and supervisors talked with one another by telephone, and the crisis was managed. Although the Federal Reserve has been criticized a great deal, in this conference, it provided liquidity to the system at just the time it was needed. Although this may have brought other problems, I do not doubt that the repercussions of their failure to act would have been much more serious. The Fed is to be thanked and congratulated, not chastized.

Second, for a crisis to be managed effectively, people need to know who is in charge. They have to know whose responsibility it is to pick up the telephone; to begin assessing the availability of information, the understanding of risk, the position of individual companies; and to judge what effort should be expended to prevent a worse-than-necessary outcome. That is to say, in the jargon, the lead supervisor or regulator must be clearly established and identified.

Cooperation and Coordination

As I have suggested above, it is important that progress in cooperation and coordination between supervisors should not set too ambitious a target. If one takes the European Community as an example, it is interesting to see how the ambitions have changed. Initially, attempts were made to harmonize all aspects of the operation of a single market—legal, accounting, fiscal, regulatory frameworks, and so on. The attempt was eventually abandoned because it simply proved too difficult. Ambitions then changed, with the welcome realization that an element of the market dynamic could be brought to play. Attention focused instead on the establishment of minimum prudential standards, in the form of capital requirements and clear authorization procedures, answering to objective criteria. On this basis, the single market program could go ahead, while one regulatory authority might still be inclined to be more lax or more firm than another. It is possible that, as a result, there may be transmigration of business from tougher to laxer regimes; but this is not inherently a bad thing. If London, for example, finds itself under threat for that reason, it is up to London to decide whether there is an acceptable answer. It may well be that firmer regulatory regimes will find their firmness a strength that has the capacity to attract as well as to repel.

One should not, in any case, underestimate the difficulties of establishing even minimum standards. The often protracted discussions in both Basle and Brussels should have taught us that. And, as indicated above, the agreement of these minimum standards is helpful in avoiding unfair competition and erosion of prudential standards, although it may not place all banks or financial institutions on a completely level footing.

It is also important, as markets become more interrelated, that supervisory gaps be closed internationally. The Drexel case is an example; there was a possibility, at one stage, of the risk crystallizing in an unregulated entity in the United States which had operating subsidiaries in the United Kingdom. Fortunately the potential difficulty was solved. Although Drexel was relatively easily dealt with, however, partly because the signs were seen well in advance, it would be foolish to think that the difficulties of dealing with conglomerates in today's international markets have been solved.

If it does not seem too presumptuous, supervisors should also be seeking to educate, offer analysis, and publish results since they at least have the benefit of seeing and listening to the full range of views. I am a firm believer in the consultation process, and if regulators and supervisors can publish the results of their analysis at an early stage, and invite the comments of market participants, then both sides can more easily learn from one another. The cross-fertilization of ideas is an important dynamic. It offers a greater likelihood of developing solutions to which all parties have made a contribution, and is thus less likely to alienate or to lead to evasion of supervisory requirements. Nor is it fair to describe the exchange of information as trite or "nursery school." It is terribly important that supervisors listen to one another's experience. I am a great supporter of the United States and its way of doing things: I was educated in part in this country and lived here for a number of years. But I hope that Americans will forgive me for saying that they concentrate and draw general conclusions from their own affairs, perhaps to an excessive degree. There are great benefits to be had from talking and listening to others; perhaps no more so than today when Europeans are endeavoring to put together a new structure for financial markets.

Finally, I hope the supervisors and regulators can avoid disorderly closures. There is a little prayer that I say to myself every evening: "Please God, give me a small, orderly collapse."

Index

307